MW01153166

My Carrier War

— THE LIFE AND TIMES OF A WWII AVIATOR —

Norman E. Berg

To Dorothy
with warm regard
to a fellow student
in writing ones memoirs
Norm
Nov 01

Hellgate PRESS

CENTRAL POINT, OREGON

My Carrier War: The Life and Times of a WWII Aviator
© 2001 Norman E. Berg
Published by Hellgate Press

HELLGATE PRESS
P.O. Box 3727
Central Point, Oregon 97502-0032

(541) 245-6502
(541) 245-6505 fax
info@psi-research.com e-mail

Editor: Vickie Reierson
Editorial and compositing assistance: Jan O. Olsson
Book designer and compositor: Constance C. Dickinson
Cover and map designer: J. C. Young
Managing editor: Constance C. Dickinson

Library of Congress Cataloging-in-Publication Data

Berg, Norman E., 1920–
    My carrier war : the life and times of a WWII aviator / Norman E. Berg.
        p. cm. — (Hellgate memories World War II)
    Includes index.
    ISBN 1-55571-619-9
    1. Berg, Norman E., 1920– 2. Bomber pilots—United States—Biography. 3. United
States. Navy—Aviation—Biography. 4. Torpedo bombers—United States. 5. World War,
1939–1945—Personal narratives, American. 6. World War, 1939–1945—Aerial operations,
American. 7. World War, 1939–1945—Naval operations, American. 8. World War,
1939–1945—Campaigns—Pacific Ocean. I. Title. II. Hellgate memories series
D811.B455 A3 2001
940.54'4973—dc21   2001024973

Hellgate Press is an imprint of Publishing Services, Inc., an Oregon corporation
doing business as PSI Research.

Printed and bound in the United States of America
First Edition 10 9 8 7 6 5 4 3 2 1

 Printed on recycled paper when available.

To my wife, Diane Borst Manning
and
Marion Landew, my writing instructor

Contents

Maps

Foreword

If you have ever wondered what it was like to be a carrier pilot during 1941 to 1945, I recommend the book, *My Carrier War*, by Norman Berg. I was the author's CO (commanding officer). We were both flying torpedo planes off the carrier USS *Monterey* in 1944.

I first met the author, Norman "Doc" Berg, in the fall of 1943 during the reforming of Torpedo Squadron 28 at the Naval Air Station in Alameda, California. We served together from October 1943 to January 1945.

Norm has done a wonderful job in relating the life of a naval aviator in wartime. As my executive officer, he and I were only in our mid-twenties when we were leading a carrier-based torpedo squadron into action. Fortunately for me, I was not married and had only three married pilots in the squadron. Norm's family responsibilities understandably caused him much additional stress. The two other married officers had no children. In this regard, my overall responsibilities as commanding officer were much simplified. In wartime one has to condition oneself to the necessity of killing other human beings or being killed by them. As aviators, we could accept bombing airfields to deny their use to the enemy. When anti-aircraft gun emplacements were attacked, it was the guns we were hitting. When ships were attacked, it was the ships that were being hit. The fact that humans might be killed as a result of these attacks had to be incidental in our minds.

I think Doc's memories in his book will stir the memories of many readers of that era as well as intrigue those readers who did not experience World War II first hand. I heartily recommend *My Carrier War*.

Captain Ronald "Rip" Gift, U.S.N. (Ret.)

Acknowledgments

It is with gratitude that I recognize The Tailhook Association, publishers of the magazine *The Hook: Journal of Carrier Aviation*, for allowing me to use pictures from their Winter 2000 issue. Also, grateful recognition is extended to the U.S. Navy for allowing people to access the wealth of information and photographs collected in its archives. Another source of descriptive photographs for which I am most grateful is my 1941 yearbook, *The Slipstream*, published by the aviation cadets of the USNAS located at Corpus Christi, Texas.

When one is fortunate enough to come under the wing of a dedicated teacher, very special things can happen. The inspiration and unending help of Marion Landew, my writing instructor at New York University, was instrumental in my developing my thoughts into publishable manuscripts, which also includes *Regret to Inform You: Experiences of Families Who Lost a Family Member in Vietnam* published by Hellgate Press.

There is no end to my appreciation for my wife, Diane Borst Manning, whose consistent encouragement and writing assistance helped nudge into existence this personal history of a most important part of my life.

In addition, I want to thank Emmett Ramey for publishing my writings, and his remarkable editorial and production team for their excellent work in bringing my story to life on these pages, especially Vickie Reierson for her guidance and keen editorial eye, Jan Olsson for his invaluable editorial assistance, and C. C. Dickinson for her easy-to-read design and skilled composition.

Chapter 1

Coming of Age in Washington State

The watersheds of life—those events that occur, sometimes planned, but often seemingly by chance—invariably tend to transform one's life. The planned events, such as graduations, marriages, and the births of one's children, are easy. The other happenings—the unplanned ones—suggest that chance plays a significant part in life.

I was born on February 17, 1920 to Clarence and Lucille Berg. My father owned a gas station and my mother taught kindergarten in our home in the small town of Chehalis, Washington. My father did not finish high school; however, he was a highly intelligent man who firmly believed in learning from others. I still remember him telling me, "Norm, always listen to others, especially to those whom you admire and you'll always learn."

For a woman of the 1920s, my mother was well-educated. She had finished high school and had a teaching degree from Perdu Normal School in Nebraska. She was an ambitious woman, wanting a successful and happy life for her family. She was a strong influence on my father, my younger brother, and me.

Ours was an average middle class family. My life centered around my parents and home. Since Mother's kindergarten classes were in our home, she was always there when my brother and I returned from school. My father was always there after work. Mother played the piano and Dad had a fine tenor voice; there were many evenings when we boys listened to our parents, enjoying the music they made together. We did not have a radio, although early in my life, Dad did build us a crystal set. It wasn't much of a radio, but it was fun for us boys to try and find a station. We played a lot of card games, Old Maid and Fish to name a few. Then there were the books. My mother would take my brother and me to the library for books, and Mother would help us explore the pleasures of reading. As I remember, I was reading the funny papers to my younger brother by the time I was six. My life as a young boy was typical for the 1920s and 1930s.

Then in 1927, my father changed jobs and became a very successful salesman selling cookware for a large East Coast company. Mother and Dad did this by putting on dinners in private homes, and doing the cooking in the cookware they were tying to sell. Dad would then make appointments with the dinner guests to go the their homes and sell the cookware. As a result of his job, our family began to move on almost an annual basis. From the time I was seven until I was fourteen, I went to five different schools in three states—Oregon, Washington, and California. I remember it was kind of fun always meeting new kids and new teachers. I got along all right, although I don't think I learned much. When the Depression of the 1930s hit, the company my father worked for went bankrupt. My father lost his position in 1933, and our family settled in the community of Bremerton, Washington, where my mother and father opened a highly successful restaurant. Chicken dinners were 35 cents and hamburgers 10 cents.

I started my freshman year at Bremerton High School in 1934. As the new kid on the block, I discovered that most of my classmates had started the first grade together and had been together ever since. I made some friends, but my friends, Rex, Ralph, and Chuck, were not, in my mother's eyes, the kind of boys she wanted me to associate with. When two of them lit up cigarettes in front of her, she suggested I make some new friends.

Then there was my school work. My record of changing schools had affected my ability to do the classwork expected of me. Mathematics, algebra and geometry were complete mysteries. English was even worse, especially spelling. I found I could not write an assigned paper without the use of a dictionary. If I had to write in class, I was lost. The result? My grades were barely passing. One positive attribute I had going for me was that I had an outgoing personality and dealt well with my peers and teachers. I spoke well on my feet, and I was an avid reader. Consequently, I did well in the history and literature courses—that is, if I didn't have to write.

I found a summer job after my freshman year. I had no close friends, although I still saw Chuck and Ralph when I wasn't working. I didn't tell my mother, but I had to have someone to pal around with. In September 1935, I started my sophomore year, which I finished, still on probation, with grades that were barely passing. I was 16 and had no idea what I was going to do with my life. My father dropped out of school when he was 16 to work on his uncle's farm. I knew I didn't have that option. My mother had already made plans for my brother and me, and that was college.

It seemed to me that more than half the kids in school knew exactly what they were going to do after graduation. Those with good grades were headed for college. Others were planning to go to work in the Bremerton Navy Yard as apprentices. They were going to learn a trade and spend their lives in Bremerton. Then a chance happening entered my life. Her name was Jean Devaney.

A Bremerton Love Story

It was a Saturday. My mother told me that all of us, including my brother and me, had been invited to have evening dinner with Mr. and Mrs. Devaney, friends of my parents, at their beach cabin. I can still hear my mother saying, "You know, Norman, the Devaney's have a daughter, Jean. I think she's about your age. Do you know her?" I nodded that I did to my mother. Sure, I knew who she was. She was one of the most popular freshmen girls in school. I'd seen her on the tennis courts too. Boy, was she good-looking. Great legs. Tall, with reddish-brown hair. I tried to beg off going but mother insisted. I worried all the way to the Devaney's beach cabin. Jean Devaney! What was I doing meeting Jean Devaney?

We left the Devaney's beach party about ten o'clock that night. I sat in the back of Dad's car thinking about the evening. Jean had been wonderful—so friendly—so easy to talk to. We had played badminton, eaten a home-cooked chicken dinner, and after dinner, we had a beach fire. Jean turned to me and asked, "Norm, did you bring a swim suit?" When I replied I had, she said, "Good. Let's change, and we'll go swimming. It's a nice, warm night and the moon is so pretty. Wait until you see the phosphorus in the salt water. It will look like it's covering your whole body as you swim through the water."

We quickly went up to the cabin and changed into our suits. Jean came out of her room in a white bathing suit that outlined her figure. I remember how beautiful she looked as we ran down to the water's edge and walked into the small waves washing against the sandy shore. Jean struck out swimming ahead of me. The sparkle of the phosphorus was streaming off her body as she swam, bathing her legs and arms in bits of light. As she slowed down, we began swimming side by side, looking into each other's face, so aware of each other. Jean's smile was warm and friendly and I was tempted to kiss her. She turned away, saying, "I'll beat you to the beach!" We changed into dry clothing and finished the evening in front of the fire roasting marshmallows.

The memory of that long ago evening is as bright as if it happened yesterday. Sitting in Dad's car on the way home, I wondered if I'd ever be with Jean again. Oh, in front of the fire she was nice to me—really friendly, but she was so popular. Hell, I figured I didn't have a chance.

I started my junior year in 1936, and every day at school I'd see Jean in the halls. She was usually with her girlfriends, but she would always say hello to me. The sight of her would trigger the image of the night we went swimming when the phosphorus clung to her body. I thought to myself, "Ask her out. Ask her to go to a movie. Do something!" I couldn't; she was too popular. I'd wait—maybe someday. Then in October 1936, chance once again presented an opportunity that would affect my life.

Bremerton High School had a championship football team that year. All we had to do was beat a team from Everett, and Bremerton would be the Washington State football champions. The school P.T.A. arranged to charter a ferryboat to take all the students and some parents as chaperones from Bremerton across Puget Sound to Everett for the game. The end result? We won the game by a field goal in the last minute, and the trip back to Bremerton was very exciting. Everyone was thrilled with the win over Everett. Our high school dance band was on board the ferry. It wasn't long before the dancing started.

I had asked a girl, Pat Douglas, to go to the game with me, but she ended up with her girlfriends and was still with them watching the dancers. I asked her if she wanted to dance, but she replied, "No thanks," and stayed with her friends. "Some date," I thought, as I stood listening to the music and watching the dancers. Then I saw Jean standing with a couple of her girlfriends. She turned and saw me, smiled and said, "Hi, Norm. You're not dancing?" I mumbled something; I don't remember what it was, but I do remember what happened next. Jean moved towards me and asked, "How about dancing with me?"

After a few dances, we wandered out on the upper deck of the ferryboat. The stars were out, and a brisk wind was blowing. We stood in the shelter of the warm stacks from the engine room. We talked about school and the game. Then I asked her if she remembered the evening when we went swimming at the beach cabin. I saw a wisp of a smile as she said, "Yes, I remember, and I wonder why you didn't kiss me that night while we were swimming." Right then and there, on the upper deck of the ferryboat, *Kalakla*, I kissed her for the first time. That kiss started a romance that lasted more than 50 years.

The rest of my junior and senior years in high school were certainly a happy time for me. Jean Devaney was my steady girlfriend, and I soon became part of Jean's group of friends. Strangely enough, my grades even improved. I was in the senior class play; I was on the staff of the school paper; I had friends; and I was in love.

Graduation came all too soon, and in the fall of 1938, I began my first year at the University of Washington in Seattle. I was admitted on probation because of my high school grades. At that time, there was no such requirement as an SAT score for entrance to a university. If you had the money for tuition, the school accepted you. Jean was a high school senior then, and I found it difficult, if not impossible, to separate myself from the many high school events she wanted to attend. As a result, I was returning to Bremerton every weekend to be with Jean. I had turned down the opportunity of pledging a fraternity and was living in a boarding house. I was the only student living in the house. I was constantly lonely. I knew no one, and I was miserable. I was also afraid of losing Jean. She had become my anchor—my safety net to keep me from returning to that boy who was just another unknown individual—a boy who didn't have the slightest idea of who he was or where he was going.

At last, Jean graduated. I had managed to save enough from my monthly allowance to buy her an engagement ring, and the night she graduated, I gave it to her. The very next day, there was a family conference with Jean's parents and mine. The outcome of the conference was that my father put the ring in our family's safe deposit box, and Jean got a cedar chest for her graduation gift. Jean and I had no choice. Both families felt we were too young to consider an engagement. Jean and I didn't think so. She was 17 and I was 19. But the families wanted us to wait, and we reluctantly agreed.

The summer after graduation, Jean found a job as a secretary in Bremerton and I worked in a fruit and vegetable market. We had a wonderful summer, but in the fall, I went back for my second year at the university. I moved into an apartment with three other young men I knew from high school. I wasn't dating anyone, nor was Jean, but we weren't seeing each other every weekend. I remained on academic probation throughout my sophomore year. I just couldn't write or spell. All my exams were essay type and I would lose points because of my writing problems.

Eventually, my sophomore year ended in June 1940, and happily, I found a summer job in Bremerton. Jean and I were together again. It was another wonderful summer, full of dances on the weekends with old high school friends, beach parties, and even weekend trips to the ocean, provided we stayed with family. It was during this summer our relationship took on another dimension. Although we tried to resist our feelings, we began to engage in active lovemaking. It was a mutual decision on our part. We knew the risk we were taking, but we were in love, and we were going to be married as soon as I finished college. Our lovemaking was truly an act of love. When summer ended, I went back to the university for my junior year. Now, however, my responsibility to Jean became all important. She had given me her most important gift—herself. She had done it willing, trusting me with her future. And there I was back in school, still on probation. It all seemed so useless.

Then another of those unplanned, life-changing events happened.

I was home in Bremerton for the Christmas break when our family had a visit from my cousin, Preston Anglin. Pep, as he was called, was a few years older than me and was already an officer in the Army. He arrived for his visit in uniform, an olive-colored green jacket with light tan pants. "Army Pinks," he called them. The silver bars of his officer rank were fastened to the shoulders of his jacket and glistened in the sunlight. "Boy," I thought, "he looks great!" That uniform was something.

During an evening visit, Pep, my folks and I got into a discussion on world politics. We were all aware of what was happening in Europe and Asia, through the newspapers and the radio. I told everyone I thought America would probably have to enter the war in Europe. After all, I explained, nearly all of Europe had fallen to Nazi aggression. German troops controlled Paris, and England was isolated and fighting Germany alone. In Russia, Stalin was rapidly building up a huge army to defend his country. In addition, Japan had signed a ten-year military pact with Germany and Italy.

Pep reminded all of us that, in his opinion, President Roosevelt was preparing the United States for a possible future conflict. He was rebuilding the military. The Lend-Lease Program with England had started. Turning to me, Pep said, "Norm, you know that when you turn 21, the draft will be waiting for you. You know, don't you, that Roosevelt has activated the draft?" He continued, right in front of my folks, and suggested, "Norm, I wouldn't wait for the draft. Won't you be 21 next year? With your college education, you'd qualify right now for an officers' program."

Throughout the remainder of my vacation, I urged my parents to let me at least explore the possibility of volunteering for an officers' program. What if the university dropped me because I was on continued probation? I would lose my college exemption. I pointed out that most of the young men my age in Bremerton were working in the Navy Yard, and they would be exempt from the draft. It would be guys like me who would be called. I didn't mention Jean, but in my mind, she was certainly part of my future. We had made a commitment. Once I became a commissioned officer, we could get married.

Wanting me to finish college, my mother urged me to wait. Finally, though, she and my father agreed to support my plans. That week, I met with the naval recruiter, and within a ten-day period, I had passed the physical exam for the Naval Aviation Cadet Program, a program designed to train me as a pilot. Successful completion of the year-long course would result in my being commissioned an ensign in the U.S. Navy.

On 1 March 1941, I reported to the Naval Air Station, Seattle, Washington, to commence my training. I was 21 years old. Chance had intervened again in my life. I was on my way.

My First Solo in Seattle

The first three weeks in Seattle were both enlightening and hectic. Everything was a new experience. Reveille was at 0530, off to calisthenics, and then breakfast. I'd never had baked beans for breakfast, let alone for three mornings in a row! Then there was ground school with classes in navigation, Morse code, theory of flight, and meteorology. But even worse, we weren't even flying airplanes; we were spending the afternoons washing airplanes. Every new class was required to perform this task. It was part of our indoctrination in Naval Aviation. Actually, it wasn't wasted time since we did learn the nomenclature of the aircraft.

The most severe shock, however, came when we learned that we would not be classified as Naval Aviation Cadets until we had completed the training program at the Naval Air Station in Seattle. Until then, we were sailors—Seamen 2d Class. We had to pass all the ground school classes with at least a 3.0 grade point average. Then came the toughest task of all: we had to be able to fly a naval aircraft alone, a solo flight, after no more than ten hours of flying with an instructor. Suddenly, I realized I was in a highly competitive program. You met the standards, or you were out.

On 21 March 1941, the U.S. Navy issued me a small brown book. It was called an *Aviator's Flight Log Book*. My flight training was about to begin. Every flight I would make would be recorded in this little brown book. Looking back, I remember sitting on my bunk that night holding the new log book. I opened it, flipping through all the blank pages. The first three weeks of my training were over, and I had really surprised myself. I had completed the ground school with exactly a 3.0 average. I sure hadn't done that well in college. Maybe it was because all the tests were true or false; I didn't have to write. Now the flight training phase would begin. I still remember the feeling of fear as I looked at all those blank pages. I had never faced such a challenge. My thoughts had gone from, "What in the hell am I doing here?" to "Come on, Norm, you can do it."

My log book's first entry is dated 22 March 1941; the day I met my flight instructor and made my first flight in a Navy aircraft. It was a bi-plane, an N2S-3 with two cockpits. The Stearman Aircraft Company had built those planes specifically for training new pilots. The wings and fuselage were fabric-covered and the plane had a fixed landing gear. Because of its bright yellow color, I soon learned the N2S-3 was always called a "Yellow Peril."

Before climbing into the aircraft, my instructor, Lieutenant Barrett, had me walk around the plane while he showed me how to inspect the plane prior to flight. After we both got into the plane's cockpit, he started the engine and we taxied out onto the grass landing strip at the Naval Air Station, Seattle,

Washington. I sat very quietly in the front cockpit as the instructor, who was in the rear cockpit, advanced the throttle and we took off. Because there was no radio in the plane, the instructor spoke to me through a flexible rubber tube called a gosport, which was attached to my helmet. He spoke into a face mask that covered his mouth. Actually, he didn't speak—he yelled. The memory of that flight, which lasted only about 35 minutes, still remains fresh in my mind.

"Cadet Berg, here's your first lesson. Get your head out of the cockpit. Look around. The only way you'll stay alive as a pilot is to be aware of what's happening outside of the cockpit."

Suddenly, I felt something hit me along side my head. I had wondered why my instructor held what looked like a riding crop in his hand when he climbed into the rear cockpit. Now I knew. Then I heard his voice through the gosport.

"Damn it, Cadet! I told you to keep your head on a swivel!" Again I felt that riding crop hit the side of my head. I was really looking around now. For the next 26 years of my flying career, I could always sense that sharp blow to the side of my head whenever I strapped myself into the cockpit of a Navy air-craft. I never forgot that part of my first lesson.

For the next few weeks, I was flying almost every day with the lieutenant. I had learned to start the aircraft's engine and to taxi it. I was also practicing takeoffs and landings. There were dual controls in the rear cockpit, and I could sense the instructor's hands and feet were always touching the flight controls as he monitored my movements in the front cockpit. He was also yelling at me through the gosport if I did something wrong. My worst problem was leveling off too high as I approached the landing. When this would happen, he would yell, "You're too damn high!" and take over the controls, add power and we would climb back to 1,000 feet over the field. I would hear, "OK, Cadet Berg. Take over and let's try again and this time (I swear I can still remember his sigh of frustration) do it right!"

Of all the many entries in my log book, the one I remember most vividly was the entry on April 24, 1941. It read, "Pilot, Berg: Aircraft N2S-3: Type of Flight: Solo." I met my instructor at 0800 on a beautiful, clear spring day. I walked around the plane inspecting it and got into the front cockpit and waited until my instructor climbed into the rear cockpit. I started the aircraft's engine and care-fully taxied out onto the grass runway at the field at the Naval Air Station. I knew that if I didn't solo after ten hours of instruction, I would be dropped from the Naval Aviation Program. I already had over eight hours of dual instruction before that morning. This might be my last chance to convince my instructor I was ready to solo. I knew I had to fly a perfect flight. I heard my instructor telling me to fly north to an airfield where I had been practicing land-ings. He made no comments during the ten-minute flight. His silence didn't bother me because I was too busy trying to fly the airplane without making any mistakes.

As I approached the grass landing field at 1,200 feet, I heard the lieutenant shout through the gosport, "Cadet Berg, go ahead and shoot a landing for me."

Very carefully, and always looking around, I reduced power. I could see the wind sock on the ground so I knew the wind direction. I wanted to be sure that I landed into the wind. As I crossed over the end of the grass runway, I was careful not to level off at too high an altitude. I slowly closed the throttle and felt the wheels contact the ground. The tail of the plane settled onto the ground and we rolled to a stop. My instructor didn't say a word, but I was aware that he was climbing out of the rear cockpit. Suddenly he appeared on the lower wing alongside my cockpit. He leaned towards me, his face close to mine. Over the noise of the idling aircraft engine, he said, "OK, Cadet Berg, take it around. Make two circles of the field and then land and pick me up." He stepped off the wing and moved away from the plane.

At the time, I felt no sense of joy or elation. All I was thinking about was trying to remember all the procedures I had been taught and hopefully learned. I had to fly the Yellow Peril alone. I added power, turned the plane around and taxied back to the head of the grass runway. I lined up with the runway and went over the check-off list. Mentally, I noted, "Trim tabs set; fuel pressure steady; engine rpms checked; controls free." Slowly, I moved the throttle to a full power position and after a few bumps, as the wheels moved over the ground, I felt the upward surge of the plane leaving the ground. I reduced power, gently moving the control stick back and let the plane climb to 1,200 feet where I leveled off and started to circle the field.

Looking down, I could see the lieutenant sitting on the ground. At that point, a wave of excitement washed over me. I did it! I was flying by myself! All I had to do now was make a good landing. After my second circle around the field, I prepared for the landing, lining up with the grass runway, and making my approach. The landing was so smooth, I hardly realized I was on the ground. I taxied up to where the lieutenant was standing and waited as he climbed into the rear cockpit. Then I heard his voice through the gosport. "Take me home, Cadet Berg. Congratulations. You're on your way."

That evening, some of my classmates gathered for the "tie cutting" ceremony. As a new solo pilot, I was required, by custom, to appear in uniform, which was a pair of khaki pants, khaki shirt, and a black tie. After appropriate comments suggesting that I didn't have the brains or the physical attributes to become a Navy pilot, the senior cadet ceremonially took a pair of scissors and cut off the bottom half of my tie and presented it to me in honor of my solo flight. I then had the pleasure of pinning the remains of my tie under my name on a wall plaque, as a newly soloed pilot. I was on my way to becoming part of an elite group—naval aviators.

Saying Good-bye to Jean

I had completed my initial naval aviation training. I had soloed and now had my first Navy travel orders. I read them over and over.

> "When detached on 1 May 1941, from the Naval Air Station, Seattle, Washington, you are directed to proceed to the Naval Air Station, Jacksonville, Florida, for future assignment to Naval Air Station, Corpus Christi, Texas, for duty as a Naval Aviation Cadet."

There was a lot of other information that followed, but most importantly, was the last sentence: "Ten days leave is authorized before reporting."

I knew why I was going to Jacksonville first. The Naval Air Station at Corpus was still being built. It had been commissioned in March 1941, when the first class of cadets arrived and we were told that until additional barracks space became available, we would be in a "pool" awaiting transfer to Corpus.

The delay really didn't bother me. For me, the most important news was the ten days of authorized leave. This gave me time to be with Jean and my family. It was going to be great. I had especially missed seeing Jean. My schedule as an aviation cadet had not allowed me any time away from the Naval Air Station; consequently, I had not been back to Bremerton since reporting for duty back in March.

Looking back now, I recall vividly Jean's lack of interest in my plans to go into the Navy flight program. When I would talk with her about the opportunity the program offered us—a commission as an officer and marriage when I graduated—she would only say, "It's your choice, Norm." I was, of course, somewhat disappointed with her lack of interest. She didn't even congratulate me when I completed my training at Naval Air Station, Seattle. In fact, I just didn't understand it. She seemed so resigned, and it worried me. I knew she didn't want me to go into the apprentice program in the Navy Yard. Her father worked in the Navy Yard and Jean often told me how he hated his work. I wondered too, could it be that she thought I was making this decision, so I could break my promise of marriage to her? Then, too, there were some of her girlfriends. I felt sure they were asking, "What's Norm doing? Why doesn't he just stay in college? He wouldn't be drafted." Or, "What's wrong with working in the Navy Yard? That's what my boyfriend is doing. He's not leaving me." I knew that I was facing a crisis in my relationship with Jean. I was especially confused over her resistance to my desire to make love with her. After all, we had been separated for almost two months, and now I was leaving for at least a year.

I decided to ask my dad to give me the engagement ring that was in the family's safe deposit box. I reminded him that I had bought it for Jean two years before. I felt that if I could give her the ring, we would seal our commitment to each other. I remember Dad urging me to consider how Jean might feel if I insisted she wear my ring while I was away. I dismissed any concerns about Jean not wanting the ring—after all, we were in love and were going to be married as soon as I finished my training.

My last day at home, May 10, 1941, arrived. My train to Jacksonville, Florida left Seattle at noon. My mother and father were driving me from Bremerton to the Seattle train station. I knew Jean wasn't coming with us. She had told me the night before that she didn't want to go with me to the train. As we drove to the Seattle train station, my mother asked if there was something wrong—why hadn't Jean come with us? I assured her that things were fine. Thinking about that moment now, I know I was trying to hide the anxiety I felt about Jean and my decision to join the Navy. Years later, my mother told me that I looked like a lost little boy as I got on that train.

The evening before, I had made reservations for dinner for Jean and me at one of our favorite restaurants overlooking Puget Sound. I found myself doing most of the talking. Jean was quiet and withdrawn. Sensing her mood, I avoided any talk about the Navy and the flight training program. Most of our talk was about the old high school days and our friends. I remember too, that there were long stretches of silence—just the sound of the two of us eating. I felt reassured though; I had our engagement ring in my pocket. I knew that ring would keep Jean in my life. She would know that I loved her. She would understand that my only reason for leaving her was to return as a naval officer so we could be married.

After dinner, we walked out on a long pier extending over the water. It was a warm May evening, a half moon in a clear sky. I picked up a rock laying on the pier and tossed it into the water. The phosphorus was sparkling, bits of light flashing in the dark water. I turned to Jean, wondering if she remembered that beach party long ago.

I took the ring box out of my pocket. I had seen the slight smile on Jean's face as she watched the rock, phosphorus streaming from it, disappearing into the quiet water. Very gently I took the ring box and placed it in Jean's hand. She looked at it and then at me. I could see the questioning look on her face. I still remember my words, "Jean darling, it's our engagement ring. I thought you might want to wear it while I'm gone."

Her response is still vivid in my memory. She took the ring out of the box, tossed it up and down in her hand, and then, clenching it in her fist, she said, "I think I'll just throw the damn thing away!"

I reached out, taking her arm, holding it, preventing her from throwing the ring into the water. As I held her arm, I recall her voice as she expressed her feelings. She accused me of no longer loving her, of leaving her alone to accept the pity of her friends and, worst of all, asking her to wear my ring as if she was a piece of property while I was away. Then came her final charge—she questioned my faith in her as a person. Did I think that she would be unfaithful with other men while I was gone?

I released her arm and she seemed to wilt as her anger disappeared. She stood, her shoulders slumped, her head bowed. I could see she was trembling. I took her in my arms and with my voice almost a whisper, I told her how sorry I was. I asked her to please just put the ring in her dresser drawer and keep it there until I came home. Then I stepped back until I could look into her eyes. I could see her tears and I knew what I had to say. I told her to have fun while I was gone—go out on dates—enjoy life, but please, sometime during the next year, put our ring back on and announce our wedding date. She did not respond. She just asked me to please take her home.

I took her home and we kissed each other goodbye. It was one of the most difficult moments of my young life. Jean had been my life net, my helper, my friend and my lover. I had to trust her—I just had to if I wanted to keep her love.

Next Stop: Jacksonville

The trip to Jacksonville was long, almost three days. During the first few hours of the trip, my thoughts were centered on Jean. I was sure I had done the right thing by giving her freedom and trusting her. I finally decided that worrying about our relationship was useless. There was nothing I could do about it now. I could only write to her, telling her what I was doing, and telling her that I loved her.

I settled back in the club car of the train and began to enjoy the excitement of the trip. The only traveling I'd ever done was in the back seat of my folk's car. I was assigned to a pullman car, so a berth would be made up for me. I must admit that I enjoyed the porter making up my bed each night. And then there was the dining car with its linen table cloths and napkins, lovely glassware and the food. I enjoyed every moment of the dining. I was even offered wine with my dinners, although I didn't have the courage to try any. The only wine I knew was either red or white and I didn't see any of that on the wine list.

After dinner on the first day out, I looked again at my ticket. I saw I had a layover of nearly six hours in Chicago. We would arrive at eleven in the morning and depart at five o'clock the same day. Time to maybe see the city, I thought. I decided to put on my "cadet whites," have breakfast and then see a little of Chicago. The whites were a summer uniform and looked really sharp— white trousers and a white, long-sleeved, snug-fitting jacket with five, shiny brass buttons in front. The jacket had a high collar that fit tightly around my neck. I had epaulets on each shoulder with the two slim gold strips signifying my rank as a Navy cadet. My shoes were white. The hat had a short black visor with an insignia of an anchor on the hat band. As I looked in a mirror, I thought I looked great.

I sauntered into the dining car and waited until one of the waiters saw me. His face broke into a fabulous smile as he greeted me and escorted me the full length of the dining car. He seated me at a table for two and gave me a menu. My back was to the front of the dining car, so I was taken by surprise when I was joined by a woman. We greeted one another with the usual, "Good morning." As she studied the menu, I took a peek at her. She was stunning, beautifully dressed in a rather severe-looking suit and wearing a hat that didn't hide her soft blond hair. "She's no teenager," I thought, "Bet she's at least 25." It wasn't long before she began to ask me questions. What kind of uniform was I wearing? Where was I going? What kind of a program was I assigned to?

It was almost eleven o'clock before I realized it. We were still sitting in the dining car. Then she asked me what I was going to do until my train left at five o'clock. When I told her of my plan, she took a long look at me. I returned her look, our eyes locking on one another's. She smiled at me and asked if I'd like to have lunch with her at the Drake Hotel in downtown Chicago. She explained that she was in the city on business and was staying at the Drake.

Hot damn! The Drake! I'd heard of it, of course. It was world famous and she wanted to have lunch with me. She must have had a room at the hotel. God, I'd hoped I wouldn't get flustered. She wasn't trying to pick me up. She was just asking me to lunch. "Come on," I thought, "just say, 'Sure, I'd love to lunch with you and see a bit of Chicago.'" I thought about how I'd just said goodbye to Jean, and to forget about a beautiful blond woman with a hotel room.

Hours later, I boarded the train for Jacksonville and settled into my pullman seat. I was very relaxed. It had been a wonderful lunch. It might have been the wine; we had a bottle with our meal. She explained the wine list to me in a gracious way. She never suggested we go to her room, and to this day, I'm still relieved that she didn't.

My trip ended the next day, and I reported to the duty officer at the Naval Air Station, Jacksonville, Florida. The next few weeks were a blend of surprise and hard work. One surprise for me was the hundreds of young men from all over America, such as those from Texas cattle ranches, cities like Chicago, and little towns. We all spoke (and sounded) a little different. I particularly thought the guys from Texas had a language all their own. Half the time, I couldn't understand them. It was the same with those from the deep South. One common trait, though, was very noticeable to me. Everyone there was white. Coming from the Northwest, I was used to being in school with Orientals, Mexicans, and Negroes. Even then, I realized the Naval Aviation Cadet Program didn't fairly reflect the diverse population of America in 1941. I adjusted to these surprises and quickly developed a relationship with three cadets who were assigned as my roommates. Two of them, Archie and Harry, were from Texas and the third, Jack, was from Idaho.

Our days in Jacksonville, like those in Seattle, started early, 0530, with calisthenics. To this day, I hate doing jumping jacks. Breakfast was followed by two hours of close order marching drills with rifles. Why we had to learn to march soon became evident. A great many politicians from Washington D.C. were visiting the Naval Air Station. The base commander always ordered a parade in honor of the visitors, and cadets were the parade. We also spent a great deal of time on the flight line, where cadets who were already in the program were flying. We washed airplanes; we re-fueled airplanes; we turned the cranks that started the airplanes; but we didn't fly any airplanes.

Fortunately, it wasn't all work. We enjoyed playing lots of sports, such as basketball, flag football, tennis, and swimming. There were even some afternoon dance parties at the cadet club. Our dance partners were young women from Jacksonville, which was a delightful change from our all-male environment.

In late June 1941, I received my orders to report to Naval Air Station, Corpus Christi, Texas. My reporting date was the Fourth of July. Luckily, my roommates received the same orders and Harry had a car, a convertible. We departed Jacksonville on July 1 with a stopover in New Orleans. We didn't stay very long in New Orleans—we all wanted to get to Corpus. We were ready. We wanted to fly with the Navy.

Chapter 2

Training at Corpus Christi

On Independence Day in 1941, my cadet roommates and I spied the gate of the Naval Air Station, Corpus Christi, Texas. It wouldn't be long before I would be flying again. Three other Naval Aviation Cadets and I had driven from Jacksonville, Florida, after having spent more than a month at the Naval Air Station there waiting for our assignment to begin flight training at Corpus Christi. The Fourth of July, however, was no holiday for me. The Navy began processing me into the program with physical exams, uniform issues, and a room assignment in the barracks. All I could think about was getting back into an airplane. The memory of my solo flight in April at Seattle was so vivid. I felt the joy at that moment when I was flying alone, proving myself. I could hardly wait to experience that marvelous feeling of confidence again. I knew I could do it.

It took nearly a week to complete the check-in until I, along with some 75 other cadets in Naval Aviation Cadet Class 6B, finally received our first training schedule. For the next two weeks, we were bombarded with information about Navy customs and traditions. We were actually learning a whole new language. We were also back doing close order drills with rifles, calisthenics at 0500, and worst of all, "getting the word" from the senior classmen. I was assigned to a particularly aggressive senior cadet.

There was always something that I didn't know about the Navy. I found myself marching off demerits that I had earned because I didn't have the correct answers to some pretty dumb questions, like, "How do you get a rat out of a leeward scupper?" My reaction was "Who gives a damn? I joined up to fly." A senior cadet counseled me on my poor attitude and assigned ten more demerits, which gave me a total of 15. Fifty demerits, and I would be washed out of the program.

Thankfully, the two weeks of indoctrination finally ended. Those demerits had worried me. The confidence I had felt when I arrived at Corpus was suddenly missing. I was scared of failure—of washing out. I just couldn't let that happen. I had to make it. On top of it all, we were all scheduled for four weeks of intensive ground school.

I looked over the ground school program. Nearly all of the classes were two hours long. Most of the subjects didn't look too tough: aircraft engines, radio procedures, Morse code, and then I saw celestial navigation. That meant math. Damn, it was just like back in high school. My roommates were all enthused and anxious to complete the ground school phase of training and start flying. How I envied them—so confident—and here I was fearful, knowing that I would have problems with ground school, especially the navigation course.

Thoughts of my failures in high school began to overwhelm me. Was this going to be the same? All that time trying to learn math in high school was just a waste of time, right? Damn, to be so stupid. Now, a stupid navigation training course.

God, I need help. What in the hell are you praying for? You had Jean to help you back then. There's no help now. Shit, Norm, why did you ever think you could succeed? You've always been a nobody. Forget it, Norm. Quit feeling sorry for yourself. You've got to make it through this damn ground school.

The first two weeks of ground school went well, despite my fears. We had exams every Friday and I was passing every test. Then our schedule changed. Ground school the first half of the day; flying the second half. On August 12, 1941, my log book entry reads, "Type of aircraft: N2S-3. Duration of flight: 1.5 hrs. Inst.: Ensign Wilder." I was back in the air, but with an instructor. I was having problems. My instructor didn't like my air work, my landings, or my takeoffs.

Aircraft engines explained by instructor

Practicing Morse code in study period

In celestial navigation class cadets take readings of the sun with bubble octants

Same old troubles—you'll never make it. Why did you ever think you could be a pilot? Hell, you couldn't even make the high school track team. A Navy pilot! Quit kidding yourself. You're just facing another failure.

After three more dual flights, I was qualified to solo, but on August 16, I failed my final exam in navigation. I was taken off the flight schedule and was ordered to appear before a board of officers to explain my failure to pass the navigation course.

Shooting clay pigeons on the gunnery range tests abilities in deflection gunnery

I knew it. It's just too much. Why do you keep on fucking up? Maybe someone should check your IQ. You must be stupid. No one else is flunking navigation. Just dumb, old Norm. Now what?

When in front of the board, I successfully explained that my flying problems had reduced my ability to concentrate on the navigation course. I didn't mention Jean. The board authorized extra instruction in navigation for me. A senior cadet was assigned as a tutor. On August 24, I passed the navigation course. On the 25th, I was back in an airplane, again with an instructor, for another dual flight. I flew a good flight and the instructor qualified me as "safe for solo" on August 26.

I began flying again on September 2, and by the end of the month, I had 20 hours solo time and 17 hours of dual time. The flight program was designed to build confidence in pilot control of the aircraft in all types of flight conditions. To do this, the instructor would demonstrate a flight maneuver like a small field landing, or a slip to a circle or a loop or wing over, and then I would practice it solo. I felt very confident. Every time I flew with my instructor, he would tell me I was doing OK.

Clarifying problems at the instruction board

I had, of course, been writing Jean on almost a weekly basis. She was responding about once a month. I attributed this lack of contact with her to her job change. She wrote me in September that she had passed the civil service exam and had taken a job as a secretary at the Torpedo School in Bangor, a Navy base just outside of Bremerton. I did wish she'd write more often. In early October, I received an unsigned letter from someone in Bremerton. I have always suspected that it was one of her girlfriends who must have been jealous of her. The letter claimed that Jean was deeply involved with a student at the Torpedo School. I didn't know what was meant by "deeply involved." In fact, I was afraid to even think about it. That, of course, was impossible. It was all I could think about, but I was afraid to ask.

I tried my best to concentrate on my flying and learn all I could from my instructor, who told me that I was about ready for my final check flight. The first 40 hours of the primary phase of the flight program had been divided into four phases: small field landings, aerobatics, landings and takeoffs, and landings without power. At the end of each phase, I would fly with an instructor other than my own on a "check ride." I had passed each one of these check rides. I was then scheduled for the final check before moving on in the training program. I had to fly with three different instructors and pass two of the three check rides. On October 10, I passed my first check ride. Poor weather developed and I had to wait until October 22 to fly my second check ride. I failed it.

Just before takeoff, sign the yellow sheet

How could this have happened to me? Damn, why me? It's over. You just don't have it, dumb Norm from Bremerton. That's it, bury your face in the pillow so no one will hear your sobs of frustration. It's over—you're not going to make it.

That night, I did not sleep. The next day, I was scheduled for the third check ride. If I failed again, I was faced with being washed out of the program, of being sent home. Maybe the weather would be bad and the flight would be postponed. I was still awake at 0500. It was a beautiful sunny morning, and there was no doubt I would have to fly the check ride. So I met the check pilot at the assigned aircraft. The takeoff was smooth, and when we returned, I felt I had flown a good flight.

I don't remember what the check pilot said, but I do remember the concerned look on his face. That was all I needed to see. I had failed the check ride. I arrived back at my room in the barracks. My roommates had all passed their final check in the primary phase, but I had failed.

Essential weather information is gathered to aid in flight decisions

Who can I turn to? There's no one. You're to blame for this. You never should have tried. Working in the Navy Yard is where you belong. Jean will never marry you. Your wonderful plans are dead forever. Sure, my roommates will feel sorry for me. That's what I deserve—their pity. To hell with the whole program!

I knew what I had to do. I would not go back to Bremerton as a failure. I put on my civilian clothes, went to the officer of the day (OOD) and picked up a pass authorizing me an overnight liberty. I was going into the city of Corpus Christi. I knew the Canadian Air Force had a recruiting office at the Neuces Hotel. They were interviewing cadets who were failing the Navy program. I'd go talk with them, and then I would get drunk. As I started out of the barracks, however, the OOD called to me saying I had a phone call. Once more, chance entered my life. I went back to the OOD's desk and took the call. It was my regular instructor. He told me that he had asked the Review Board of Officers to review my status. Then he said, "Cadet Berg, you are to appear on 24 October before the board." I didn't go into Corpus that night.

The next morning, I appeared at the scheduled time, hopeful, but fearful too. With the exception of the 15 demerits on my record and the failed navigation test, my record was exemplary. The board was sympathetic, and they granted me twelve additional hours of dual instruction.

A chance! Please God, help me! This is so important, so necessary, please make it happen. No more failures. I've tried so hard to make it—to have people like me, to have friends who are proud to know me. I'm trying, really, I'm trying.

Between my meetings with the review board on October 24 and November 26, I received twelve hours of instruction. Terrible flying weather during November cancelled many of my flights, but on November 27, I passed my final check ride. The extra instruction had paid off.

That night, I called Jean. I told her about passing my final check ride. Then I asked when she was going to announce our engage-

An N2S-3, Yellow Peril, takes off after a rainstorm

ment. She wouldn't give me a date, but the sound of her laughter was the only answer I needed. I knew she would make the announcement, and I knew I was going to be a naval aviator. No one ever "washed out" after finishing the primary phase of the flight program.

That evening, lying in my bunk, all I could remember was Jean's laughter over the phone. I knew she was pleased that I had called and was obviously happy that I had completed the first phase of my training. In fact, she told me how proud she was of me. Her reaction certainly eased my concerns about that "serious relationship" she was supposed to be involved in. Her laughing response to my question about our engagement and her statement that "she was thinking about it" was a hopeful sign. I really felt that she had accepted my decision to go into the Naval Aviation Cadet Program and was now willing to seriously consider our engagement. I fell asleep thinking about her, hearing her laughter.

Refueling after each flight was the responsibility of every cadet

The next day, Friday, December 5, my log book shows three flights, one with an instructor and two solos. A total of 4.5 hours of flying. The Naval Aviation Cadet Program was keeping me busy. I got back to my room at the barracks about 1630 and discovered that my group of cadets was authorized liberty commencing the next day, Saturday, December 6, 1941. With all my troubles—failing the navigation phase of ground school and then my flying—I had been restricted to the base right after I failed my flight checks. No liberty. Nothing but worry. I was really looking forward to some free time. I felt as if it was party time.

So on that Saturday, I packed my gear, shaving stuff, an extra shirt and socks, underwear, and swim trunks. The OOD was a classmate and I remember him telling me, as I picked up my liberty pass, to have some fun. I was ready. I earned it. I knew exactly where I was going. I headed for the base's bus stop station and a half an hour later, I was standing in front of the Neuces Hotel in downtown Corpus. I knew I'd find some friends there. The hotel was a popular hangout for the cadets. "Boy," I recalled to myself, "was I ever close to coming down here after I failed those final check rides just a couple of weeks ago." I'd been ready to talk to the Canadian recruiters about joining their Air Force. Thank God that was all behind me.

I checked into a room, dropped my gear and headed for the hotel bar. I wasn't disappointed. The place was filled with cadets, some of whom were classmates of mine. Four or five of us had a few drinks and dinner at the hotel, and then we headed for a club with a dance band. We'd heard that a few of the local girls might show up. I knew some of the guys were looking for more than a dance. A couple of them knew I had a girlfriend back in Bremerton, so I took some razzing about being faithful. I didn't mind; I was still remembering Jean's laughter. I had a couple of dances and then decided to go back to the hotel bar where I ran into some more cadet friends. I don't remember much more about that evening. I know I closed the bar somewhere around two o'clock in the morning. I think the elevator man helped me to my room.

A Day of Infamy

I woke up the next day, Sunday, December 7, 1941, lying on the bed still dressed, shoes and all. I looked at my watch; it was afternoon already. At least I remembered that it was Sunday. God, maybe a shower would help that head of mine. I must have really celebrated. I took a long shower, finishing with cold water. I dressed, packed up my gear and headed for the coffee shop. It was crowded with cadets and a few civilians. It was very noisy. Everyone was talking at once and trying to listen to a small radio to what sounded like a news broadcast. I couldn't hear the radio from where I sat. I remember turning to the cadet sitting next to me and asking, "What's going on?" His response hit me hard. "The Japs have bombed Pearl Harbor! A bus is coming to pick us up. We've been ordered back to the base."

The rest of that day and night was a blur. We had a radio in our room, and we all listened until well after taps, hoping for more information. We did get some good news, however; none of our carriers were in the harbor at Hawaii when the Japanese attacked. I remember too, that I experienced some very mixed feelings as I listened to the news.

When I joined the Navy flight program, the idea of fighting a war wasn't in my plans. I joined because I wanted to marry Jean. Now here I am training to be a Navy pilot. If I make it through the program, I'm going to fight the Japs. I have no doubts about that, but I'm not so sure that is what I want to do. Sure, the whole idea is exciting and challenging, but I'll be fighting an enemy who will be trying to kill me. It will give me a real chance to prove myself, though. I will no longer be just an unknown kid from Bremerton. I'm not afraid of the challenge.

The day following Pearl Harbor, the base commander ordered all cadets to prepare to "pass in review." We assembled in formation, by class, with our

Cadets pass in review during an indoctrination period at Corpus Christi

rifles. As we stood in formation, the base commander spoke, giving us the official details of the Japanese attack. We were told that the president was going to declare a state of war between the United States and Japan. The commander closed his remarks by reminding us that we would soon be facing a well-prepared and vicious enemy. He closed, wishing us God's speed in our future as naval aviators.

I still remember the thrill I felt as the station band began to play, "Anchors Away" and I heard the ringing orders of our cadet officers: "Cadet battalion, pass in review." Eight hundred cadets marched to the music, passed the reviewing stand, and each battalion honored our commander and our Navy. Our country was at war. I remember how proud I was to be a Naval Aviation Cadet.

Advanced Training Decisions

That evening, my roommates and I spent the time before taps talking about our future as we continued our training. Each cadet could request the type of advanced flight training he wanted. Archie knew exactly what he wanted to do. Of the four of us, his flight grades were the best, especially in aerobatics. He had already requested fighters for his advanced training. His position was that, after going through all this training, he wanted to fight the Japs. Harry wanted multi-engine training in the PBYs, the big twin-engine seaplanes. (The *P* stood for patrol plane; the *B* for bombing; and the *Y* for the aircraft company that built the plane. See the Appendix, also.) He wanted experience in heavy aircraft. I remember him explaining that his goal after the war was to fly with the commercial airlines. My third roommate, Jack, claimed he didn't care. He'd go wherever the Navy sent him.

As for me, I just sat and listened. I wanted to be a carrier pilot. I knew my flight grades were not good enough for fighter training, but I felt I had a good chance to be assigned to advanced training in dive-bombers. I knew what I wanted to do after graduation. I wanted to fly off carriers. But then there was Jean to consider. I just didn't know what to do.

After taps, I lay on my bunk hearing only the sounds of my roommates settling into sleep. I could hear the tick of our alarm clock. Laying there in the dark, my mind felt like a ferris wheel going around and around. What should I do? I really wanted to be part of the excitement of going to war and to defend my country. That's what I was being trained for. I wanted the excitement of flying against an enemy and to come home a hero, maybe even with some medals. But then there was Jean. Should I go ahead with our marriage and then leave her when I left for sea duty as a pilot aboard an aircraft carrier and the danger of combat? I could ask the Navy to keep me at Corpus as a flight instructor. We could get married and be together. Hell. That wouldn't work, not with my flight grades. The Navy probably wouldn't assign me as an instructor.

My thoughts shifted to Jean. I wondered if she was planning our wedding yet. Probably not, since she hadn't even announced our engagement. Should I suggest that we delay any marriage plans until after graduation when I would receive my orders? That wouldn't work. I knew Jean would want a nice wedding, bridesmaids, reception and that would take time to plan.

I lay there in the dark, twisting and turning. What should I do? I guessed the best thing to do was to write Jean suggesting that she announce our engagement and then offer her options depending on the kind of orders I received. If I were to be ordered to duty as a pilot aboard a carrier, should we delay our marriage until I returned? If I were assigned sea duty, but have some time in the States before I left, we could get married and have some time together. "Ah, to hell with it." I concluded to myself, "Go to sleep, Norm. You're going to start flying a new plane tomorrow. No more Yellow Perils. Your only goal will be to get those gold Navy wings. Get that done, and the rest of your life will work out."

This Kind of Flying Can Kill You

I had flown three flights on December 5, 1941, but following the Japanese attack on Pearl Harbor, my next flight wasn't until December 16. The problem was that the base was on a high alert, and we weren't flying. The newspapers and the radio were all warning that the Japanese might attack the West Coast. After all, with the exception of our carriers, the U.S. Pacific Fleet had been badly damaged at Pearl Harbor. The battleship, *Arizona,* had been sunk with over one thousand lives lost.

I remember receiving a letter from Jean very soon after Pearl Harbor. She had been in Seattle with some girlfriends for a concert during that weekend. She wrote that she had been awakened on Sunday morning, December 7, hearing some kind of announcement from the street below the hotel. From her hotel room window, she saw a police car moving slowly down the street. The police were making announcements through bull horns telling all military personnel to return to their commands.

Her letter explained that it was only then, when she turned on the radio in the hotel room, that she had learned of the Japanese attack. She and her friends quickly packed and went down to the hotel's lobby entrance. While trying to find a taxi, a police car stopped in front of the hotel and took them to the Bremerton ferry dock. I remember Jean's letter telling me how frightened she was. The ferryboat was filled with sailors, Navy officers and civilians like Jean who were working for the Navy. A Navy vessel, with fully manned guns, escorted the ferryboat across Puget Sound to Bremerton. That was the scary part—did the Navy expect an attack by Japanese planes? Then, of course, the fact that no one knew what was going on made it even scarier.

Funny, Jean didn't say a word about us and our future. We are at war. Does she wonder about us, about me? She says she was scared, but says nothing about what I might be facing, a Navy pilot fighting in the war. Maybe she hasn't really thought about it. No sense in saying anything. I'll just wait.

I later learned that within a few days after the Japanese attack on Pearl Harbor, the Army arrived in Bremerton with "barrage balloons." These were large (over 100 feet in length) helium-filled unmanned balloons. They were anchored by long steel cables to large Army trucks and sent into the sky to altitudes of about 1,000 to 1,500 feet. They had been designed to prevent enemy planes from diving on targets in the Navy Yard. One of them was stationed in a cemetery just behind Jean's parents' home. The military also issued orders to all civilians, setting up "black-out rules." Windows had to be covered so no lights could be seen. No night driving was allowed without special headlights. In the case of some civilians who normally drove home from work after dark, the military arranged to house them on the base. Jean was one of those civilians. Others were issued special covers for their car headlights. In a later letter, Jean wrote that, "After about two weeks, I guess our government became convinced that the Japs weren't going to attack Bremerton. We were allowed to return home and to drive again after dark. Once we realized we were safe, it wasn't so bad. It fact, it was sort of exciting."

Before my flight on December 16, I had been involved for two full days in ground school. I had spent the time reading aircraft handbooks, taking written tests, and sitting in the cockpit of three different aircraft. We were required to pass a written exam on each aircraft we were going to fly and to pass a blindfold cockpit checkout. That meant that we had to be able to touch and identify all the controls in the cockpit while we were blindfolded. Those aircraft were much more complicated than the Yellow Peril. Not counting the new instrument panels, they had radios, wing flaps, propeller controls, different throttle controls and one of them had a retractable landing gear. It was an entirely different kind of flying. The aircraft were much closer to the type I would be flying when and if I received orders to a carrier squadron after graduation.

Jesus, I hope the Navy knows what it's doing. I only have 39.5 hours of solo time, and they're expecting me to fly three different kinds of aircraft. They said some of the flying will be in formation. Damn, it's hard enough to fly alone. Now they want us to fly with six other planes— even with eight other planes! I hope I can do it. Don't get nervous up there. Shit, this program gets more dangerous all the time.

Between December 16 and 24, my log book shows seven flights in an SNV with a total of 9.5 hours of flight time, 4.5 hours of which were solo time. The SNV was a low-wing, all metal monoplane with two cockpits. The cockpits were covered with a sliding canopy. The Vultee Aircraft Company had built it for the Navy as a scouting plane, but it had never been used in the fleet. We called it the "Vultee Vibrator." The nickname came from the fact that at certain rpm settings of the prop, the entire airplane would start vibrating, which was rather unnerving.

On December 28, I had a dual flight with an instructor in an OS-2U. The cadets' nickname for this plane was the "OS screw you." Built by the United Aircraft Company, this aircraft was originally designed as a seaplane to be used off battleships and cruisers and was currently being used in the fleet. The aircraft we were flying had been modified and was equipped with a fixed landing gear like the Vultee. Like the SNV, it was a low-wing, metal monoplane with two cockpits covered by a canopy and with similar cockpit controls. So the transition was quite easy.

A right echelon formation

By mid-January 1942, I had 18.5 hours of solo time in the OS-2U. The flights both in the SNV and OS-2U were designed to teach us to fly larger aircraft in formation. We were learning to fly close together, first in three-plane formations and later in six- and finally, in nine-plane formations. We were also learning how to join up with other planes after takeoff.

Join-ups. Looked easy enough with the little wooden models the instructor used to demonstrate in class. I'm in a big damn plane flying at 150 miles an hour, and they expect me to get within six feet of another plane. You can bet your ass I'm going to be damn careful!

Each cadet was scheduled to be the lead pilot of a three-plane formation and a six-plane formation. By rotating the leader's position, every cadet received training not only in leading the formation, but also in joining the formation. We soon learned we had to trust the other pilot who was flying so close on our wing. A mid-air collision could be deadly.

OS-2Us in an echelon of Vs formation

More than 50 years later, those log book entries can make me vividly recall the thrill, the excitement, even the danger I felt. We were all inexperienced pilots. My total solo flight time was slightly over 50 hours. Some cadets were better than others at joining up and flying in formation. In many cases, we did not even know the pilot flying on our wing. This was completely different from flying the little fabric-covered Yellow Perils. I was learning to live with danger, to realize that at any moment I could be killed. Another plane could fly into mine, or I could hit another plane. I was often afraid, but all I could do was face the continuing challenge of completing the cadet program and receiving my Navy wings.

A flight gets together after completing a formation hop

Flying Blind

On January 20, 1941, I flew my first flight "under the hood." I would learn to fly "blind." I was starting the instrument phase of my training and still flying the SNV aircraft, but it was sure different from the formation flying that I'd been doing.

I first met my instructor, Ensign Barber, at the airplane. I got into the front cockpit and he climbed into the back one. The SNV, unlike the Yellow Peril, was radio-equipped. Using the intercom feature of the radio, Barber briefed me on the flight as I taxied out for takeoff. I was to climb to 4,000 feet, and at that time, he would take control of the plane. I was to then reach behind my head, pull a black cloth canopy shaped like an accordion with stiff ribs and attach it to the top of the instrument panel. As the cloth canopy closed over the cockpit, I felt a sudden sensation of panic. I had no outside reference point, no horizon, no blue sky, and worst of all, I could hardly even see the instrument panel. All outside light had been cut off. Suddenly, I heard the instructor's voice in my headset.

"Cadet Berg, don't forget to turn up your cockpit lights."

Damn, that's why I couldn't see the instruments. I adjusted the cockpit lights and felt a bit stupid, but also somewhat more relaxed.

"Cadet, you've had some instruction in the link trainers, right?"

I responded positively, recalling the time I had spent "flying the link trainer." It was a mockup of an aircraft cockpit and had all the controls of a real aircraft. When I moved the flight controls, the trainer

Talking over the flight after being "under the hood" for an hour

would also move. A cover came over the cockpit of the trainer, so all I had as a reference point was the aircraft instrument panel. Now I understood why the experience of flying the links was so important. It gave me a chance to "fly" using the flight instruments that I would find in an actual aircraft. There was a big difference though—here I was in a real airplane climbing to an altitude of 4,000 feet. This was no link trainer.

Close-up view of the link trainer, showing part of the complicated instrument panel

Again I heard the instructor. "OK, Cadet Berg—you've got it. Just remember the link trainer. Believe those instruments."

I acknowledged taking control of the plane over the radio and concentrated on the flight instruments. My mind automatically began to review the link trainer experience.

Watch the altimeter and air speed indicator—they tell me if I'm flying level and not gaining or losing altitude. Watch the gyrocompass and the turn and bank indicator to be sure the airplane is flying straight. Don't chase the rate of climb indicator or the magnetic compass. They bounce around too much to try and follow. Scan all the instruments and don't stare at just one.

"Cadet Berg, give me a one needle width turn to the right to a heading of 045 degrees."

I remembered what I had to do. My gyrocompass read 275 degrees. I checked it against my magnetic compass. "OK, concentrate," I told myself, "Start to turn." There was a small quarter-of-an-inch-wide vertical bar called a needle in the turn and bank instrument. I started my turn, and I saw the needle in the turn and bank instrument moved one needle width, about a quarter of an inch to the right.

Now, stay in the turn until you get to the compass heading of 275. Damn, my air speed is going up. I'm losing altitude! I have to get the nose up! Too high—now the air speed is dropping! What's my compass heading? Still losing air speed, better add some power. Shit! What the hell is happening? I'm getting in trouble. Better stop the turn. Center the needle. Get the wings level! Get the nose down! There! The air speed is OK. Altitude, OK. Damn, I'm still in a turn; I can feel it! I'm still turning. Vertigo! We were told about this. It has something to do with the inner ear. I check my instruments. I'm flying level, no turns, level. Almost lost it. Still feel like I'm in a turn. It's an awful feeling.

My senses are all mixed up. How long does it last? Just watch those instruments, Norm. Hold on. Don't force the instructor to take over the controls. There, it's better! I've got it now.

Then I heard my instructor. "Had a little vertigo, Cadet? You did just fine. You believed those instruments. Never forget that lesson, Cadet. Trust those instruments. OK, I have it now."

I released the controls and sat back. I could feel my parachute pressing against my back and butt. I felt my muscles begin to relax as I wiped the sweat off my face. This wasn't going to be easy, I thought, as I heard Ensign Barber again.

"Cadet Berg, I'm going to put the plane in some unusual positions. Then, when I tell you, I want you to recover and return to level flight. Ready?"

I was watching the instrument panel, when suddenly I thought I felt the plane roll violently to the right. The altimeter needles indicated that I was losing altitude and the air speed increased. The needle in the turn and bank instrument was all the way to the right, but the little black ball in the turn and bank instrument was clear to the left. Then I heard the instructor say, "Cadet, you have the controls. Make your recovery."

I grabbed the controls, staring at the wildly gyrating instruments.

OK. I am in a skidding and diving turn to the right. The little needle tells me I'm in a right turn. The small ball at the bottom of the instrument has moved way to the left, so the plane is out of balance. It is skidding. I have to get the wings level first. Get the fucking needle and the ball back in the center! Now get the nose up! Stop the descent. Reduce the power till the air speed gets back to normal. Now add some power. Whew! I'm back level again.

"Nice work, Cadet Berg. Nice recovery. You're doing fine. Now let's try some turns. Remember, when you start a turn, the nose of the airplane tends to move down. You must apply some back pressure on the stick to maintain your altitude."

The rest of the flight went well. Again though, I felt stupid. I knew the nose of the plane would drop in a turn. I had to remember to trust the instruments as they can become the pilot's only reference points. They replace the sky, the clouds, the horizon, and the ground that the pilot normally sees when flying. Without those reference points, either visual with the space outside the plane or the instruments in the plane, the pilot is literally blind. The pilot's sense of balance is affected, vertigo results and control of the aircraft is lost.

Reviewing my log book from January 20 to 25, I flew eleven hours of instrument flying. I recovered from a great many unusual positions, did a lot of turns to compass headings and a lot of climbs and descents. Gradually, I found that I was quite comfortable flying blind. I had learned to trust the instruments and my own flying ability.

Then on January 26, I checked the flight schedule. I was scheduled for a cross-country flight on instruments. I knew the procedure from ground school and my training in the link trainer. I went into the operations office and prepared a written flight plan using the proper form and submitted it to a sailor in the operations office for filing with the Civilian Aviation Authority, the CAA. I was going to fly from Corpus Christi, Texas to San Antonio, Texas, and return. The flight would take about two hours. Since I was filing an instrument flight plan, I would have to get clearance from the CAA, the governmental agency that controlled the airways throughout the United States. In 1942, the airports across America were linked together by these airways, which were reserved air space, 20 miles wide, for use by aircraft filing flight plans with the CAA.

After I received a weather report on cloud and wind conditions en route to San Antonio, I worked out the navigation, including compass headings and most important, I reviewed the radio range frequencies I would be using on the flight. I then went out to my assigned aircraft to meet my instructor.

"Morning, Cadet. Nice morning for our flight. Would you brief me please on your flight plan?"

"Sir, I've requested a cruising flight altitude of 4,000 feet. I've requested 4,000 feet because we're flying west, and must be at even altitudes. Estimated flight time is two hours. We will fly the outbound west leg of the Corpus radio range until we contact San Antonio radio and pick up the inbound leg of the San Antonio radio range heading 284 degrees. I will reverse the flight plan on return. The weather is projected to be excellent—CAVU, Sir."

The instructor laughed. "Ceiling and visibility unlimited. Well, you won't see it under that hood will you? Let's get going."

We both climbed into the airplane cockpits and using the radio, I called the CAA flight controller in the airport control tower and received my clearance for the flight. "Navy 03095, you are cleared to San Antonio via airway Green One. Maintain 4,000 feet. Contact San Antonio control prior to the return flight. You're cleared for takeoff." I acknowledged the clearance, made the takeoff and quickly pulled the canopy over the cockpit. I was on instruments by the time we reached 500 feet.

OK, Norm, just settle down and fly this bird. It's just like the link trainer. You can do it. You know how. Stay loose and watch those instruments. Get onto that beam and fly it right to San Antonio.

I began a left-hand turn from my takeoff heading of 190 degrees and continued the turn until I intercepted the outbound compass heading of 284 degrees. I was now on the proper heading for San Antonio. I tuned in the frequency for the Corpus radio range. This would be the first time, except for the link trainers, that I had actually flown using the radio range system.

In 1941, this system was the primary method for aircraft to fly under instrument conditions. Instrument conditions existed when the pilot did not have visual contact with the ground or the horizon because of weather conditions. The system consisted of a radio transmitter located either at airports across America or between airports, but on the airways depending on the distance between airports. The transmitter would broadcast a continuous sound on predetermined compass headings. These headings were called "radio range legs." There were usually four legs at each range station. The compass heading for one of the legs from the transmitter at Corpus was 284 degrees. This was the heading I was to fly to San Antonio and the range leg was aligned with the Green airway.

I rolled out of my turn onto a heading of 284 degrees. I could hear the steady sound of the radio range leg in my radio headset. I was "on the beam," heading for San Antonio. I was constantly scanning my instruments to ensure I was on course and on the assigned altitude. I began to hear a signal other than the steady sound of the beam. It was in Morse code—a "dit-da"—the code for A. I was drifting off the beam.

I knew from my link training what was happening. The radio transmitter also sent out signals other than the steady sound of the beam. If I flew in the air space between the radio range legs, I would hear the Morse code signals. In this case, hearing the A, I knew I was drifting to the right of the beam. If I had heard an N, a "da-dit," I would have been drifting to the left of the beam. I only had to look at the picture on the chart of the Corpus range I had on my knee pad to know where I was in relation to the beam. That wind from the south was stronger than predicted, I thought, as I turned a few degrees to my left. Quickly, I heard the steady sound of the beam. I was now on a compass heading of 280 degrees. After 30 minutes of flying time, I tuned in the San Antonio radio range station. The heading of 280 and a flight time of 30 minutes took me over the station on my ETA (estimated time of arrival).

I heard my instructor say, "Nice work, Cadet. You hit the range cone right on time."

Just before my instructor called me, I had lost the sound of the beam. This was the "cone," the signal that I was over the range station. I now reversed course to the return compass heading of 100 degrees and started my return flight to Corpus. I was on the beam all the way.

When I was about 20 minutes from my ETA at Corpus, my instructor called me. "Cadet Berg, please request a clearance to make an instrument approach to the Corpus airport."

He wants an instrument approach to the field! God, I've got to get down to 500 feet from my altitude of 4,000 feet and all I have are the damn instruments! Just do it. Fly this bird nice and smooth. Don't panic. Come on, stay loose on the controls. Easy does it.

I acknowledged his message, called Approach Control at the airport, and received a clearance for an instrument approach. The radio range system not only provided a method for aircraft to fly in poor weather conditions from point to point, it was also used to make an approach to the field under instrument conditions. Radar had not yet been invented so all we had was the low frequency radio range.

I was right on the beam, getting a solid signal. I checked the time. I would be over the range station in two minutes. Then I lost the sound of the beam in my radio headset. I knew I was over the cone because there was no signal over the station. Next, I heard the solid sound of the radio beam again. OK. I checked the time. I had to fly out bound on the beam for three minutes, then reduce altitude from 4,000 feet to 1,500 feet. I began to hear a slight sound—a da-dit—a Morse code *N*. I checked my radio chart. I was drifting off the beam. I made a slight turn to my left and quickly heard the solid sound of the radio beam again. I checked my watch. Time to reverse course. I checked my gyrocompass, my heading was 100 degrees. I started my turn to the left.

Watch the altitude and air speed. Keep on turning to a heading of 280 degrees. Intercept the radio beam. OK, hold it.

I began to hear the solid sound of the radio beam. I had to stop the turn at 280 degrees. I was inbound to the airport. I could hear the solid sound of the radio beam. I reduced power and began my descent, leveling off at 500 feet. I checked the time. I was one minute out from the field when I heard my instructor remark, "Pop your hood, Cadet Berg. Nice work." I reached up and released the cloth hood. There, in front of me, was the runway. I reduced power, made a smooth approach and landing. No sweat. Well, actually, I was sweating quite a lot.

It's a Challenge

The last week of January 1942 was a very special week in my life. My log book for January 28 has the following entry: "Inst. X–OK. Radio X–OK." I had completed the instrument phase of my training. Just three days later, January 31, the entry reads: "Aircraft SNC-1. Duration of flight: 1.0: Type of flight: Fam." I was assigned to dive-bombers for my advanced training, so I was going to the fleet aboard a carrier. That last week also brought me the following news clipping that Jean sent with just a simple comment on the edge of the story,

"Darling, I told you I would." It was from the local newspaper, the *Bremerton Searchlight*, dated January 25, 1942.

> "Mr. and Mrs. Phillip Devaney announce the engagement of their daughter, Jean Marie Devaney, to Mr. Norman Berg, the son of Mr. and Mrs. C. E. (Skipper) Berg. Both families are from our city. Miss Devaney and Mr. Berg are both graduates of Bremerton High School. Miss Devaney is employed by the U.S. Government at the Torpedo School in Bangor as a secretary. Mr. Berg is currently in training in the Naval Aviation Cadet Program at the Naval Air Station, Corpus Christi, Texas. A wedding date has not been announced."

After receiving the announcement, I wrote Jean to tell her how much I loved her and how happy I was about our future. I remember telling her that the commander of the Advanced Training Squadron said, "weather permitting," I should finish my dive-bomber training by the end of March. Also, I remember inquiring at the personnel office as to when I might expect my orders.

"What's the rush, Cadet? Getting married after graduation and your bride is getting anxious? Worried about her dress? About the church?" I acknowledged his questions, and he assured me I would have orders by the middle of March.

All I could really tell Jean was that I would be in Bremerton in early April. I would have twenty days leave, but I would not know where I would be reporting until the middle of March. I had to tell her the wedding date was up to her—I didn't have the answer.

Her next letter was typical Jean. "We're going to get married in April, and I'm going to follow you wherever the Navy sends us." I remember how she closed her letter. "Get those wings, honey, and I'll worry about the wedding."

I took Jean's advice. According to my log book, I flew over 30 hours between February 1 and 27, even though we lost six days of flying to bad weather. All my flight time was in the SNC-1, which was designated as a scouting plane built for the Navy by the Curtis Aircraft Company. It had, however, never been used in the fleet. It was a beautiful aircraft—small and sleek-looking, an all-metal, low-wing monoplane. It had two cockpits and a retractable landing gear. It was an exciting airplane to fly, very maneuverable and

The SNC-1—a sweet little airplane for gunnery, bombing, and tactical training

quick on the controls. Compared with what I had been flying, this aircraft more closely fit my image of a fighter plane.

The Navy used a letter coding system to enter the type of flight in our log books. All my flights during this period were either K (tactical) or L (navigation). The K flights were much more complicated than the simple formation flying I'd done before. The flight controls of the SNC airplane were much faster and more sensitive, making formation flying much more of a challenge.

A typical tactical flight usually involved six aircraft. In particular, I remember one flight on February 6. Our instructor assigned me as the flight leader, so I was responsible for briefing the other pilots on the flight. The assignment took me by surprise. God, so much to remember, and the instructor would be in the briefing room with us. I'd better do it right.

I started. "Listen up, guys. After I take off, I'll climb to 1,000 feet on a 090 degree heading. I want a 20-second interval between your takeoffs—just as if we were on a carrier. I'll start a turn to the port two minutes after my takeoff." I pointed, "You're the number two man and you," I pointed again, "You're number three. Join on me in a V-formation—number two on my right—number three on my left. You other two join on the number four man." Again I pointed. "Join up in a V-formation. Don't waste time joining up—in the fleet you can't afford to use extra fuel because of a sloppy join up. Watch me as you make your turn to join me. If my aircraft appears to be ahead of you, you're going to end up chasing me. If I appear to be behind you, you're going to end up ahead of me. What you want is my plane not to appear to be moving—it's a relative motion problem guys, so let's do it right.

"On our return from the training mission, I will call the tower requesting a low pass at an altitude of 500 feet. I want us to fly an approach to the field as if we were going to land aboard a carrier. We need to practice this maneuver. Remember the skipper of that carrier wants to get the aircraft aboard as quickly as possible. He has to have the carrier moving into the wind to recover aircraft, and he doesn't like staying on a steady course. That makes the carrier vulnerable to a submarine attack.

"After I call the control tower for the low pass, I want you guys to take up an echelon formation to my right. I want to look out to my right and see all of you stacked up tight, flying with your left wing tight alongside the plane on your left. I'll lead the formation past the right side of the runway—the up-wind side. As we fly by the end of the duty runway, I will fly 30 seconds more, then on the radio I'll call, 'Break!' I'll make a shallow, diving 180-degree turn to the left, descending to 300 feet. I will then be on the down-wind leg, parallel to the runway. Each of you will wait a few seconds before you break. As you turn to the down-wind leg, get your approach interval on the plane ahead by controlling your air speed. Go over your check-off lists. Don't forget, wheels down.

Make your approach to the runway. Guys, when I turn off the runway after my landing, I want to see the last plane touching down on the runway. Let's do it right. Any questions?"

The six of us grabbed our parachutes hanging on a rack in the briefing room and headed for our aircraft. The instructor stopping me at the doorway, said, "Good briefing, Cadet Berg. You're going to do fine in the fleet. Congratulations on doing a good job." I remember smiling to myself, as I walked out to the sleek, beautiful airplane that I was going to fly. I was so proud of being a Naval Aviation Cadet.

Several days later, there is another important entry in my log book: "Date: 24 February. Type of aircraft, SNC-1. Duration of flight, 2 hrs. Type of flight, K-navigation." Of all the entries in my log book, this one is easy to remember. It was a navigation (nav) training flight all right, but it was different. All my previous nav flights were from point to point over land. This flight would be over water—take off from Corpus and fly out over the Gulf of Mexico. There were six of us in the briefing room. Believe me, we were concerned about going out over water in a single engine aircraft. The instructor entered the room. We jumped to attention.

"At ease, Cadets. Take your seats." We all settled down, waiting. The instructor looked us over. "All right, listen up. This is an over-water nav flight. Do you all have your navigation plotting boards?" We all nodded our affirmative. Then he continued, "You all know from your ground school that this type of navigation is called dead reckoning navigation, DR for short. Want to know how it got its name?" We all waited for the answer. "Well, guys, if you don't 'reckon right' out there over the water, you're going to be 'dead.'" He just looked at all of us. I wondered if he was trying to be funny. He continued, "OK, let's get busy with our plotting boards and this dead reckoning nav problem."

My plotting board had a 15 by 15 inch metal frame. It was designed to fit under the instrument panel in the cockpit of the aircraft. In flight, I could pull it out to check my navigation. The plotting board looked like a commercial aircraft meal tray, only you pulled it out from under the instrument panel.

The instructor turned to the blackboard and addressed us, "Here are your latitude and longitude numbers, starting here at Corpus. Please plot them on your navigation boards."

I looked at the nav board and began plotting the numbers on the plexiglas covering the plotting board. I could see black lines through the plexiglas that represented the lines of latitude and longitude for the Corpus Christi area. When the last cadet finished plotting the numbers, the instructor continued the briefing.

"OK, now plot your compass headings and miles to each of the latitude and longitude points." He also gave us weather conditions and wind direction and velocity for the Gulf area.

It didn't take me long to determine that I was going to fly from the airfield at Corpus, out over the Gulf for 75 miles on a compass heading of 140 degrees. I would then make a turn to port (left) to a heading of 030 degrees for 30 miles. I would turn again to port to a heading of 320 degrees for 80 miles. This heading, hopefully would take me back to Corpus. As I plotted my compass headings, I considered the wind direction and velocity. I knew the wind would affect my actual flight path over the water, and I computed my flight time for each leg based on my air speed over the water and miles to be flown. Again I had to consider the wind direction because wind direction and velocity affects actual speed over the water.

"Everyone done plotting?" the instructor asked. He waited a few minutes and then continued telling us that we would be flying in two-plane formations. He wanted us to take off 15 minutes apart and told us that there would be an air/sea rescue aircraft tracking our flight. He told us to maintain radio contact with the rescue aircraft. I still remember his closing remarks.

"Just two things—you're going to be carrier pilots. Get used to navigating over water. There are no railroad tracks to follow out there. No towns with airports. Your only landing field is that carrier. And finally, watch that wind direction and velocity. You're at the mercy of the wind, guys. Keep track of it. OK, Cadets. Man your aircraft."

My wingman and I manned our airplane and were first to take off. We took off in formation. I turned to the outbound heading of 140 degrees and leveled off at 1,000 feet altitude. After about ten minutes, I looked back behind us. There was no land in sight. Suddenly, the sound of the airplane's engine and the movement of the instruments, all seemed different.

Was the fuel pressure gauge moving? It should be steady. Is the engine missing? Sounds different. Engine rpms look all right. Is my radio working? Maybe I'd better call the air/sea rescue plane. Wait a minute, all the instruments are normal.

I realized that nothing was wrong with the airplane. It was me. I was flying in a different environment and out of sight of land, with none of the visual landmarks I was used to. It was my fear of this new environment that had me hearing and seeing things that didn't exist. I took a deep breath.

Start concentrating on your navigation, Norm. The plane is performing OK. Here's the plotting board. What time are we due at the turning point? Let's see. It's 75 miles from Corpus. I'll estimate actual speed over the water at 140 knots because I have a slight head wind.

I looked down from the plane's cockpit, checking the sea conditions. I spied only an occasional white cap. The ocean appeared quite calm, with no wind streaks visible. Good, the estimate wind velocity and direction we got at the briefing are holding. I remembered my ground school nav lesson: occasional white caps and no wind streaks ... estimated wind speed eight to ten knots.

I checked my watch. We took off from Corpus at 0935. My estimated speed over the water is 140 knots. Using a small plastic calculator attached to the plotting board called an E6B, I lined up the 140 speed number with the number 75, the miles to be flown, and read off the flight time as 32 minutes. I was due at the first turning point at 1005. I called my wingman to verify my navigation. We agreed on the turning time at the first latitude and longitude point I plotted. At 1005, I made the turn to the new heading of 030.

I recall the feeling I had when I made that first turn—we were no longer flying further away from Corpus. Now we were only 30 miles away from the final checkpoint when we would turn toward home. I began to relax—all the instruments were normal—I was heading back to Corpus.

The remainder of the flight was uneventful. The wind held steady and we were over the field at Corpus on time. I knew though, that flying off the carrier would be different. I wouldn't be returning to an airport in Texas. Soon, the "airport" would be a small carrier in a big ocean. It would be moving. I would be alone with my plotting board and the ocean. It was going to be a challenge.

Gunnery and Dive-Bomber Training

On March 10, 1942, I flew my first flight in a Navy dive-bomber, the SBC-4. I had seen the plane flying in the area while I was flying the SNC on navigation and tactical missions. This was a aircraft that was still in use in the fleet. I had been told that Navy Bombing Squadron Eight was flying the SBC-4, nick-named, "the Helldiver," from the flight deck of the aircraft carrier USS *Hornet* in the Pacific. Since the war with Japan was only three months old, I was sure that Bombing Squadron Eight and the SBC-4 would probably see some action against the Japanese Fleet.

> *Wouldn't it be great if I would get orders to Bombing Eight on* Hornet?
> *I'd get to fly the SBC-4 in combat—get to land it aboard a carrier. I*
> *better do real good with the gunnery and bombing training just in case*
> *I do get orders to Bombing Eight. I'm sure going to try.*

The SBC-4 was a bi-plane with two cockpits, one for the pilot and the rear cockpit for a gunner/radio operator. It was designed as a dive-bomber built by the Curtis Aircraft Company. It had a top speed of 237 mph at 15,300 feet. It was by far the largest plane I'd ever flown. Fully loaded with a 1,000-pound bomb, it weighed over 7,000 pounds. I was very familiar with the cockpit having studied the handbook for at least a week before my first flight. I think the first cockpit items I touched when I climbed into the cockpit were the gun-charging controls and the bomb release switches. I was going to learn how to use these weapons to attack enemy ships if and when I got to the fleet. The sight of those weapon controls brought the war right into the cockpit of that dive-bomber. I remember thinking, "Boy, I hope I get a chance to attack the enemy."

My first few indoctrination flights in the SBC-4 went very well, probably because the training program had gradually taught me to fly different aircraft: first the N2S and then bigger and heavier aircraft, such as the SNV, the OS-2U, and then the SNC. These flight experiences made the transition to the SBC-4 quite easy. The remaining training experiences in the aircraft were not so easy.

An SBC-4 dive-bomber—note the gunsight

Two days later, on March 12, I flew my first gunnery flight. This was getting real now. I was going to fire my plane's machine gun with live ammunition against a moving target. There were four of us scheduled each in our own plane. Flying with me in the rear seat of my plane was our gunnery instructor. He was with us only as an observer, but I knew he would critique our flight after we returned to the base. Our mission was to join another plane out over the Gulf of Mexico in the designated gunnery area. This plane was towing a target banner. The target banner was made of heavy canvas and was about five feet wide and, as I remember, about twenty feet long. It was designed to be towed into the air behind an aircraft. Once it was off the ground, it turned to a horizontal position behind the tow plane. We had to fly our plane to a position relative to the target so the bullets from our gun would strike the target. We were firing live ammunition from a gun that was mounted on our plane in front of the pilot's cockpit.

I was leading the flight, and after about a 20-minute flight, my wingman called that he had spotted the tow plane in the assigned area. We were flying at our assigned altitude of 6,000 feet and the tow plane was below us at 5,000 feet. The tow target was visible about 500 feet behind the tow plane.

I recall thinking, "Boy, this is easy. I'm going to fill that target with bullet holes."

I was in position for my attack on the target, slightly ahead and above the tow plane. My plane was at least 500 yards on the right of the target when I rolled into a diving left turn and began my approach to the target. Sighting through the telescope gun sight mounted in front of the cockpit the tow target was suddenly visible. Rolling the plane to my right, my plane was level with the target as I squeezed the gun trigger on the plane's control stick. Now my plane was moving to a position behind the tow sleeve. Releasing the gun trigger, the firing stopped. I was in danger of hitting the tow plane. Damn, I didn't lead the target enough. Flying under the target and climbing back to 6,000 feet, I rejoined the rest of the flight.

The four of us continued to make runs on the target. Then, after each of us indicated by radio to our instructor that all ammunition had been fired, we returned to base at Corpus. We all shut down our aircraft and gathered at the operations office and waited for the tow plane to return.

There was a good deal of excitement with all of us talking and using our hands to illustrate for each other what we felt were our outstanding gunnery runs. We were all sure that we had shredded that target. Our instructor sobered the room and began to speak. I realized that these were his first words since the takeoff.

"Listen up. I'll buy the beer if any of you got more than five hits on the target." Then he said, "You'll each buy me a beer if you got less than five hits—agreed?" We all agreed, feeling we were the winners. I just knew I was. I couldn't have missed that target. We saw the tow plane make a low pass over the grassy part of the field and drop the target. We all made a mad dash for the target and quickly spread it out flat on the grass. Our instructor joined us, "OK, who had which color?"

Each plane's guns had the nose of the bullets painted with a different color. The paint was applied just before the flight so it was wet. The result, a bullet hitting the canvas target would leave a paint mark. I remember to this day—my color was blue, and I found only two hits. Only one of us had more than five hits.

The instructor had us all sit there along side the tow target. "I was watching your gunnery runs. You were all making two major mistakes. First, it appeared to me that you were using too much rudder trying to get in position. The result was that your plane was in a skid rather than in a smooth easy turn toward the target. If your gun platform is skidding, your bullets will end up off the target. Then there was your approach to the target. Too many of you ended up either 90 degrees to the target forcing you to dive under it, or you were being sucked behind so you could not fire. The ideal position is 45 degrees to the target with your aiming point ahead of the target. Then you fly a smooth approach, firing until you can break off your run flying under the target." He closed his remarks saying, "Don't worry about it. As you get used to flying that big old dive-bomber, you'll start getting hits. Besides, it's not a fighter plane. It's a dive-bomber—that's what you want to be good at."

I'm not so sure. What about shooting down an enemy plane? Or worse yet, what if one makes a gunnery run on me? Learn how to hit that target,

Norm. Don't be dead meat out there fighting a determined enemy. Besides, Jean has announced our engagement. I've got to be sure to come home to her. Can't be scared of combat. Be the best-trained naval aviator possible. Come on, Norm, you'll come back alive.

It was March 14, 1942 when I flew my last gunnery training flight. Man, was I good that day. The green-tipped bullets I was firing had a hit rate of 35 percent on the target. Pretty damn good compared to most of my colleagues. I had mastered the concept of gunnery. I was flying the aircraft smoothly and most importantly, I was getting hits.

The next morning, there were six of us, all advanced students in the dive-bombing program, sitting in a classroom in the operations building. We now had only to complete the dive-bombing phase of the training, and we would get our Navy wings. Our training would be over. We would be ready.

I've got to be careful now. This dive-bombing could be dangerous. Going straight down and then pulling out. Danger of blacking out due to the "G" pressures. Wonder if we're going to use real bombs? Probably not. One of the guys told me that we would use little smoke bombs so we could see our hits on the target.

"Morning, Cadets, I'm Ensign Brester and I'm going to make each of you dive-bomber pilots. Just a little history first. The Navy was the first service to use dive-bombing as a weapon. For example, when the aircraft carrier, USS *Lexington,* joined the fleet in 1927, there were dive-bombers aboard her. This plane you're flying now—the SBC-4—joined the fleet as a dive-bomber in 1935. So, this delivery method of a bomb has been around a long time." He paused, looking at us. "As I explain how we do dive-bombing, I'm sure you'll quickly see the advantages of the technique."

Ensign Brester continued, "Here's what you're going to do on your bombing dives. After takeoff, I'll climb to 500 feet and make an easy turn to the right. Each of you, after takeoff, join up with me. I will lead this first flight. Our bombing target is a 50-foot circle outlined in white on a small island just off the coast. Each plane will be loaded with six smoke bombs. These are small, metal-shaped objects with an explosive charge in the nose. When they hit the ground, a puff of white smoke marks the place where they hit. We'll climb to 10,000 feet on the way, then circle the target on arrival. Each of you will acknowledge, by radio, that you see the target."

He picked up a small wooden aircraft model and held it up as high as he could reach.

"Now, listen up. After you each acknowledge that you see the target, I'll signal for each of you to form a single column behind me." He backed away from us, creating a space on the floor where he drew a circle with a piece of chalk.

"Watch the aircraft model as I talk. We want to make our dive into the wind—let's say it's out of the north. Remember the wind direction. It's important. Estimate the direction and velocity so you can adjust your aiming point on the target. It will give you a better chance for accuracy in dive-bombing."

Instructor demonstrates dive-bombing with a wooden aircraft model

We watched as he moved around the chalk circle on the floor with the model. "OK, now we're downwind of the target. Notice that the model is not as high. We've dropped down to 8,000 feet. We're ready to dive. Watch the model." He moved the model, simulating a diving turn to the right; he moved it downward towards the floor. "Be sure your dive brakes are extended. The dive brakes will extend on the upper and lower sides of your lower wing. They create drag and help control your air speed in the dive. The ideal dive speed is between 170 and 180 knots at the bomb release point. The bomb release point should be no lower than 1,500 feet." He stopped, looking at each of us.

"Be careful here. You may not have the target centered in your bombsight. You want a hit, so you may want to continue the dive. You want that hit! Guys, I can't think of a worse way to die than to hit that target with your plane because you didn't pull out in time! Pull out by 1,500 feet!"

Damn! How can I keep my eyes on the target, on the air speed and the altitude, and hit the target? Maybe it won't hurt to go a bit lower if I'm almost on the target. What if it was a Jap ship I was diving on? Wouldn't I stay in the dive longer? Don't even think about it. This is training, Norm. Pull out at 1,500 feet!

After a long pause where he looked at each of us, he reminded us again. "Remember 1,500 feet! OK? Now reduce throttle as you start your dive. It will help control your air speed. What you want is a steep dive—at least 80 degrees in relation to the ground. That way you present a small target for enemy ground fire and your bombs will go almost straight down to the target. This is why dive-bombing is such a fine attack weapon. Now the pull out."

He moved the model upwards again. "Start your pullout no lower than 1,500 feet. You'll experience some Gs on your pull out. The pull of gravity is forcing your plane down. You're fighting against gravity when you pull out of the dive. Just keep a steady pressure on your controls; tighten your belly muscles to help keep your blood from moving to your lower body as it reacts to the pull of gravity.

As you level out, the G pressure will disappear. After your dive, climb back to 8,000 feet, and continue your dives individually until you complete six dives. After my first dive, I will circle the target as an observer. When the last plane makes its final dive, I will circle the target until you all join up on me and we'll return to base. Any questions? OK, let's go."

Our takeoff from the base was smooth, and we quickly joined up on the instructor and headed for the target area.

This should go OK. After all, it's like gunnery except we're diving more steeply and on a ground target rather than on a gunnery target. This target's not moving. It'll be easy compared with gunnery. Don't black out on the pull out. Be careful. Just a steady pressure on the controls. There goes the instructor on his dive. There's the smoke from his bomb—a hit! Where's the wind from? Get ready! Here I go!

First, I pulled back on the throttle, then opened my dive brakes. A metal flap extended on the upper sides of the plane's lower wing. The same kind of a flap also extended on the bottom of the plane's wing. The flaps had holes in them to allow the passage of air. The dive flaps served as brakes on the air speed as the plane went into an almost vertical dive. By controlling the speed of the dive, a pilot had time to center the target in the telescope sight located just ahead of the pilot's cockpit. By controlling the speed, the dive brakes also gave time to pull out of the dive at a controllable speed.

Man, I'm really steep! Don't let the plane skid. Fly it smooth and easy. There, the target is in my sight. Got it. What's my air speed? Check the altimeter. Got to pull out by 1,500 feet. Damn, I'm sliding out to the right from the target. Get it back in the sight. Roll this bird back to the left. Two thousand feet. Drop the fucking bomb! Now pull back on that stick. Pull! Tighten your belly. Don't black out. Where did my bomb hit? There's my smoke. Right on the edge of the target. Close the dive brakes. Let's get back up for another dive. I'll lay it right in the middle of the target next time.

Between March 15 and 26, I made 31 flights. The training program was really pushing us, most likely because of the war. The flights were either gunnery or dive-bombing. My log book shows the 17th, five flights; 18th, five flights; 19th, three flights; 22nd, five flights again. Finally, on March 26, just three flights, but they were my last ones. My training was completed.

Graduation and New Orders

There were about ten of us. We all reported to the CO's office of N.A.S. Corpus Christi, and Captain Bernard, the CO, pinned those Navy wings on our uniforms. I was designated a naval aviator and commissioned an ensign in the Navy with a date of rank of December 10, 1941. My graduation was on March 30, 1942. I had a total of 239.3 hours dual and 156.3 solo flight time.

The 1941
SLIPSTREAM
U. S. N. A. S.   CORPUS CHRISTI, TEXAS

BERG, NORMAN E.
Bremerton, Wash.
Class 6-B

This was just the last part of the good news that I had shared with Jean. I had called in early March to tell her that we had received our orders. I had orders to the Naval Air Station, Floyd Bennett Field, New York City, New York. I suggested a date for our wedding between April 10 and 15. She set the date for April 12, 1942. Our honeymoon would be in New York City. I had it made. We would be together.

I departed Corpus for Seattle by train April 1. I'd ordered tailor-made uniforms while at Corpus, and I was wearing my "aviation greens" on the train. This was a work uniform worn only by officers attached to aviation units. Dark green trousers with a khaki shirt and a dark-green jacket buttoned down the front. It was worn with brown shoes. The Navy's non-aviation officers referred to us as the "brown shoe Navy." We loved it; we were different. We had wings on our uniforms.

When the train arrived in Portland, Oregon, I was about six hours by train from Seattle. I left the train and checked into a hotel room. I had my blue Navy uniform pressed, the one with the single gold ensign stripe and the gold Navy wings. I had my black shoes shined and got a haircut and a shave. I called Jean to tell her of my arrival time in Seattle. She and my folks would meet me.

I didn't get a lot of sleep that night, but the entire effort, all the training, all the worry was over. I had made it.

I got off the train in Seattle, and there was Jean in a fur coat with a little fur hat and high-heeled shoes that complemented her lovely legs—my bride. I was home.

Chapter 3

The Ferry Command in New York

I was back in my hometown of Bremerton, Washington, as an ensign and aviator in the Navy. I'd succeeded—I'd made it. I had orders to N.A.S. Floyd Bennett Field in New York; and Jean and I were to be married April 12, 1942, and we'd leave after the wedding for New York.

As I rode through the downtown area of Bremerton with Jean and my parents, Jean seemed so excited about the future. I somehow couldn't match her enthusiasm. Our country had been badly surprised by the Japanese attack on Pearl Harbor. We were at war. My thoughts kept distracting me.

Why do I feel so apprehensive? I'm finally somebody in this little old town. I'm in love with a wonderful girl who I'm going to marry. I'm a Navy pilot. I'm a little scared—right? Maybe I shouldn't get married with the war on. Better to wait until the war is over? Am I being fair with Jean? What if I get killed? Don't even think about it! Be positive! What will it be like in New York? Where will we live? What about the new assignment?

My thoughts were interrupted by my mother saying, "You're home, Norman." We pulled up at my parents' house. Nothing had changed, including my grandmother who stood on the porch waiting to greet me. We all got out of the car and I stood there, holding Jean's hand. It was good to be home with my parents again, and especially with Jean.

The next ten days were busy. My folks invited all their friends for a welcome home party for me. They were very proud of me, a naval officer and pilot. There was no bachelor party. I guess the few high school friends I had were busy with their own lives, and it was wartime. My dad did take me to the

Elks Club for a drink where we met with some of his cronies. I heard a lot of stories about his war—the "Big War."

Funny, did I think it would be different coming home? I should have expected that there would be no bachelor party. Hell, I didn't have any male friends in high school. Jean, of course, is wonderful. I'm emotionally attached to her even in the midst of all the parties, the wedding plans, and the people who want to see me. Last night's love making was so gentle, so sweet. Go ahead with the marriage. My fears are gone. I love her so much. It's going to work out. We'll be together.

On April 12, 1942, Jean and I were married at a ceremony in the church in Bremerton where Jean had been baptized. Jean was 20, and I was 22. My younger brother, Paul, was my best man. Two of Jean's girlfriends were maids of honor. We were now Ensign and Mrs. Norman Berg. We left the next day for New York. I had managed to get tickets from Seattle to New York on Eastern Airlines for the two of us. Eighteen hours—with stops at Spokane, Washington; Billings, Montana; Minneapolis, Minnesota; and Chicago, Illinois. Jean had instructions to call her mother at every stop.

Presenting Ensign and Mrs. Norman Berg

The next day they're ready to go to New York

New York Days

We landed at LaGuardia Airport two days after our wedding. I'd made reservations at the Pennsylvania Hotel across from Penn Station in New York City. We checked in, showered, took a nap after that long flight, and took a tour of the city. I had six days before checking in at Floyd Bennett Field. Our life together had started.

Before we left Bremerton, a family friend had given me the name of a real estate agent in Rockaway Beach on Long Island. I was told it was an area close to Floyd Bennett Field. After two days in the Pennsylvania Hotel, we decided to find a cheaper hotel nearer to Floyd Bennett Field. We found a hotel room in Rockaway Beach. We contacted the real estate agent whose name I had and began looking for an apartment. The real estate agent told us that apartments were scarce, but he would continue to keep us in mind. On April 20, I reported to Floyd Bennett Field for duty. We continued to live in one room in the hotel. I knew Jean was a little unhappy living as we were, but it didn't take her long to make some friends.

The hotel was operated by the Shore family, and the family soon adopted Jean and me. Their friendship was important to Jean and certainly gave me a sense of relief. Jean had someone to turn to for help. One of the family members was a daughter, Joan, who was about 30. She and Jean struck up a friendship. I was glad that Jean had met someone who was a New Yorker. We really needed all the help we could get learning about New York. We selected the Shore's Hotel because a bus stopped on the block and I could take that bus directly to the Naval Air Station. Jean continued our search for an apartment as I reported to the Aircraft Delivery Command, commonly known as the ferry command, at Floyd Bennett Field. About 30 pilots were assigned to the ferry command on the day I reported. Our mission: delivering new aircraft to fleet bases at Norfolk, Virginia, and San Diego, California.

Delivering F4F Wildcats

I started flying again on the 23rd in the old familiar OS-2U that I flew at Corpus. Three days later, I had my first flight in a modern fighter, the F4F Wildcat. The first F4Fs had been delivered to the Navy in February 1940. They were low-winged, single-seat fighter planes designed for operations off carriers. They were interesting airplanes to fly, but nothing like the sweet little SNC I flew at Corpus. The F4F was a heavy aircraft for the horsepower of the engine. It had armor plating in the pilot's cockpit that provided the pilot protection from enemy fighters. It was very rugged; a tough little fighter, but it wasn't very maneuverable. Not a great plane for aerobatics. It had a top speed of 318 miles per hour at 19,400 feet. The armament was six forward firing .50-caliber machine guns that added even more to the weight of the plane. The F4F's landing gear was designed for carrier operations and not for operation off concrete runways. The landing gear was housed in the sides of the fuselage.

A Grumman F4F-4 Wildcat in early 1942 markings with rudder stripes and large fuselage stars   *(Courtesy of the U.S. Navy)*

When the wheels were extended, the distance between the wheels was no wider than the aircraft's fuselage. Because of the narrow distance between the wheels, the plane had a tendency to swerve either right or left upon landing. As a result, the plane would "ground loop" by making a violent turn either right or left as the wing tip dragged on the runway. It wasn't dangerous, but it was sure embarrassing.

I remember ground looping on one particular landing. I'd invited Jean to the base for lunch. The operations building had a patio overlooking the runway, and I knew she would be watching for me to land. I made a slick, smooth landing, saw Jean on the patio, and raised one hand to wave to her. Suddenly, the plane swerved to the left, and around I went in a ground loop. Jean's first words when I joined her for lunch were, "Some hot pilot."

Jean in front of the Berg's first home in 1942

By May 1, I was qualified in the F4F with 27 landings over a five-day period. So I was considered qualified to fly cross-country in both the F4F and the OS-2U. I also received a call from the real estate agent. He had found us an apartment. With help from some of the other Navy wives, Jean moved into our new apartment.

The next day, I delivered my first F4F, bureau number 02009, from Floyd Bennett Field to N.A.S., Norfolk, Virginia. The bureau number indicated that this plane was the 2,009th F4F built by the Grumman Aircraft Company. After delivering the aircraft, I would wait at the operations office until a plane from Floyd Bennett picked me up. I was carrying out the ferry command's mission—delivering aircraft to the fleet.

This isn't so tough. Nice weather and a short flight. I'll be landing at Norfolk in another 30 minutes. There's Chesapeake Bay below, I'm right on course. Wonder what it's going to be like flying all the way to San Diego. Wonder how many stops for fuel. What if the weather turns bad? The rules demand no flying on instrument. Got to fly under visual flight rules. Wonder about getting back to New York. Probably either by commercial airline or military transport. You'll be OK. Some ground school is scheduled this next week. There will be some answers. Better call the control tower at Norfolk. There's the field. After landing comes the wait for the plane from Floyd Bennett. Got to get home.

More Training!

The next few days at Floyd Bennett were filled with ground school classes and navigational (nav) training flights. The ground school phase refreshed our memory on how to read weather maps; how to file flight plans with the military authorities so as to clear us to operate on the airways; and how to plan our flights. Planning a flight involved estimating our flight time between check points, and writing the compass headings to be flown from check point to check point. In addition, I was issued a complete set of aeronautical charts for the continental United States. These charts indicated all the airways across America. The airways were designated, ten-mile-wide areas that connected airports across the country. I took the charts, drew in lines and wrote down on the map the compass headings between each airport I would be using between New York and San Diego. All ferry flights would use the southern airways through Greensboro, Atlanta, Dallas, and on to San Diego.

After the ground school phase of training came actual navigational flights. Along with two other pilots and an instructor, I was assigned to fly a navigational training flight in a GB-1. This was a single engine bi-plane Navy aircraft that carried the four of us. My log book shows the flight on May 4. The remarks read, "Floyd Bennett to Middletown, New York; Middletown to Scranton, Pennsylvania; Scranton to Floyd Bennett." Each of us would move into the cockpit with the instructor and, using our navigational charts, fly one leg of the flight. My turn came to fly the final leg from Scranton to Floyd Bennett.

After we landed at Floyd Bennett Field, we three pilots were debriefed by our instructor. Each of us had flown our leg of the flight without drifting off course and had reached our check points on time. We were told that, as of 4 May 1942, all of us were qualified for cross-country flying as ferry pilots.

Another hurdle passed. I'll soon be on the schedule to fly a plane out to San Diego, probably an F4F. Wonder how long it will take? Sure do hope for good weather. Make it a fast trip. Get back to Jean. Hope she won't be afraid about being alone. It will be the first time we will be separated since we were married—maybe she can stay with one of the other pilots' wives while I'm gone. At least she knows I'll be back in a few days. It's not like being out in the Pacific on a carrier. Think about those three days off when I get back. Take Jean to a Broadway show.

The Coral Sea Battle

The eighth of May was a busy flying day for me. But it was more than just flying. I had made two trips in the GB-1 to the airfield at the Grumman aviation plant with another pilot flying. The GB-1 was the plane I flew in for my navigational training flights. On each trip, I flew an F4F back to Floyd Bennett Field. When I landed at Floyd Bennett after the last flight, I headed for the locker room to change from my flight gear into my uniform. Just as I entered the locker room, I saw a group of pilots standing around reading an article from a New York newspaper. I remember joining them and, for the first time, I heard about a carrier battle between U.S. and Japanese carriers. It was the Battle of the Coral Sea, which had taken place on that very day—May 8, 1942. The newspaper article said that we might have lost a carrier in the battle. There was a lot of talk as the news of the battle sunk into our consciousness in that locker room. We were all flying carrier aircraft, the F4F. All of us had been trained as pilots in either fighters or dive-bombers. As I left the base and caught the bus that would take me home to Jean, my thoughts were about Jean and our marriage.

Wonder if Jean has seen a paper about the carrier battle? Sure she has. The paper usually gets to the apartment by late afternoon. What am I going to say to her about us? Our staying together? What are the chances of staying here in the ferry command? Kind of slim. I'm trained as a dive-bomber pilot. Fleet is going to need pilots. Don't volunteer for an assignment to a carrier squadron. I can't do that to Jean, but if orders come ... well, I go—that's it! How will I react to combat? Being shot at? Dropping bombs on people? Try to stay here in New York. Hell, don't know—anyway, the Navy will decide.

I left the bus and walked the two blocks to our apartment.

Damn that carrier battle! It might change Jean's and my life. Just got our apartment. First place of our own. Three rooms, kitchen, living room, bath and bedroom. Just two blocks from the beach. Wonder if Jean is still in her swimming suit? She loves the beach. Guess we're still on our honeymoon; she's usually just taking off her swim suit as I get home. She's so beautiful. I love her so. Just wait. All I can do is wait. That's all, just wait to see what the Navy will do.

I walked up the path to our apartment and climbed the stairs, wondering how Jean would greet me. I opened the door and called her name.

"I'm in the living room. Did you hear the news out at the base?"

I joined her, and before I could answer her question, she handed me a newspaper. I saw the headlines.

U.S. FLEET IN SOUTH PACIFIC BATTLE
5-DAY BATTLE IN CORAL SEA HAS HEAVY TOLL FOR BOTH SIDES
**Allied Nations Report Sinking or Critical Damage to At Least 13
Jap Warcraft While Tokyo Makes Similar Claims of Allied Losses**

I looked at Jean and saw the worried look in her eyes; her lips were pressed tightly together. She looked so grim and, in a way, so sad. I reached for her, enclosing her tense body in my arms. I remember reassuring her that I was there with her—that I'd be needed for a long time in the ferry command, telling her that the fleet would be needing aircraft and that was what I was trained to do.

Slowly, she pulled away from my caress and her question came very softly. "What if you get orders to sea duty? Won't they need pilots too?"

We talked a long time that evening as I tried to assure my Jean that everything would be fine, that our marriage would survive no matter what effect the war or the Navy might have on our lives. I promised her, too, that I would not volunteer for an assignment to a carrier squadron.

The next morning over breakfast, Jean seemed relieved as she described a shopping trip she had planned with Joan, her friend from the hotel. They were going into Manhattan to shop for kitchen cookware. I kissed Jean good-bye and left for the base.

That ferry flight to San Diego will be coming up soon. I'd better hope nothing else hits the news while I'm gone. Jean needs my reassurance that everything will be OK. After all, she's going to be alone ... away from her folks for the first time and I know she worries about me and the war. She was really upset about the Battle in the Coral Sea reports. I know what Jean wants ... stay here. But the idea of combat is exciting, flying off a carrier, hitting the enemy. Forget it. Just do my job here. Enjoy New York with Jean.

The next few days were routine. I delivered an OS-2U to Norfolk, had another navigational training flight and then on May 10, I saw that I was on the flight schedule to deliver an F4F to San Diego. It would be my first long flight. When I arrived home that day, there was more news about the Coral Sea Battle. I decided to wait to tell Jean about my upcoming flight to San Diego until later.

We sat the dinner table, side by side, looking at a newspaper map where the battle was fought. There were also news stories announcing the loss of the aircraft carrier, USS *Lexington,* and an interview with a commander of a Navy torpedo plane squadron whose unit was involved in the battle.

LEXINGTON WAS SUNK BY BLAST FROM GASOLINE

"The United States American pride in its Navy and in the airmen soared to a new high yesterday as the first full story of the Battle of the Coral Sea fought early in May, revealed that seventeen Japanese ships were sunk or damaged at a cost of only three American vessels—the aircraft carrier *Lexington,* the destroyer *Sims* and the naval tanker *Neosho.* ..."

TORPEDO PLANES IN THE BIG BATTLE OF THE CORAL SEA
**As Told By the Commander of an
American Torpedo Plane Squadron**

"SOMEWHERE IN THE Southwestern Pacific (AP)—At 8 a.m., our scout planes loom out of an overcast sky and come aboard. The word quickly spreads through the ship that they have sighted an enemy aircraft carrier and that we are to attack. The date is May 7—five months after Pearl Harbor. ..."

At one point, Jean stopped reading the article about torpedo planes and asked if I was flying that kind of aircraft. I told her no, I was only flying the F4F fighter. I did tell her that the Grumman aircraft plant was building a new torpedo plane, the TBF-1, and I'd soon get checked out so I could deliver them to the fleet. She finished reading the article on the torpedo planes and turned to me. I could see her tears. "Honey, I'm so scared! Please don't let them send you to a carrier squadron. Please!" All I could do was hold her, telling her that I loved her, and promising that I'd never volunteer for carrier duty. Then I had to tell her about my next flight on May 12 to deliver

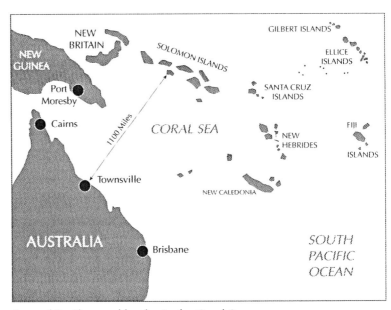

Area of Pacific naval battles in the Coral Sea

an F4F to San Diego. Jean cried herself to sleep as I held her trembling body in my arms.

Flying New Planes

May of 1942 was a very active flying period for me. I left New York on the twelfth in an F4F, bureau number 02030—the 2,030th F4F built by Grumman. I was delayed for two days in Atlanta because of bad weather, and finally arrived in San Diego on May 17. I returned to New York in style after that trip. No government aircraft was available, so I was issued a travel voucher: Los Angeles to New York onboard a Super Connie sleeper plane! The Connie was a four-engine propeller aircraft. After dinner on board, berths were made up. I slept in a berth, which was quite comfortable, and was awakened in time for breakfast! I remember thinking, "Not a bad life for a Navy ensign."

I had three days off after my ferry trip, and Jean and I had a wonderful time in Manhattan. The Navy was pretty good about paying us our per-diem soon after a trip. As a result, we had extra money for fun. We again stayed at the Pennsylvania Hotel, had dinner at Jack Dempsey's restaurant, saw Olsen and Johnson in the Broadway show "Hell's A-Poppin," and danced to the Glenn Miller Band with Helen O'Connell and Bob Eberly. A big weekend.

After those three days, I felt that Jean had passed a milestone in our relationship. Our lovemaking was exciting, tender, and fulfilling for both of us. She seemed to have reached an understanding about our future and the war. I think she knew that the Navy and the war would control our lives for the foreseeable future, but the present was ours to enjoy to the fullest in our love for each other.

I left on May 24, again delivering an F4F. This time to the Naval Air Station, Alameda, California, arriving on May 28. It was a quick trip, just four days, with great flying weather. I expected to be back with Jean in just a couple of days. But there was a dispatch waiting for me at the operations office at Alameda, when I reported my arrival with the F4F. I read the dispatch as I was driven out to the flight line.

> ENSIGN NORMAN BERG 112307 USNR HEREBY ORDERED TO
> DELIVER AIRCRAFT BREWSTER BUFFALO SERIAL NUMBER
> 01516 TO N.A.S. SAN DIEGO

What the hell is a Brewster Buffalo? Never seen one before. Wow! A single cockpit, low-wing fighter! Hot damn! This baby is just back from the fleet. Better sit a while in the cockpit. Got to figure how to start the damn thing. No sign of a pilot handbook. Cockpit looks normal. Kind of dirty, controls are standard . . . throttle, flaps, gear handle, prop control, instruments. Better get a mechanic over to show me how to start this bird.

I called to a sailor who was standing by the plane, asking him to climb up on the wing and point out the ignition switch and starter controls to me. I started the aircraft, taxied out and requested clearance from the control tower for a familiarization flight. I received my clearance, checked my engine instruments and rolled down the runway.

A Brewster F2A Buffalo

Gear up, flaps up, reduce take off power, now, easy climb out over the bay. Boy, Frisco is sure pretty today! Take it on up to 6,000 feet. Sure turns nice and smooth. Not a very good rate of climb. The F4F does better. OK, level off. Let's see where this baby stalls out. Wings level. Ease back on the power. Control stick back; get the nose a little higher. There, don't let it spin. Air speed about 60 when it wants to quit flying. OK. Let's go down and shoot a couple of touch-and-go landings.

I shot a couple of landings, parked the plane, went to operations and got my flight clearance. Twenty minutes later, I was airborne for San Diego. My log book shows a flight of one hour and 20 minutes to San Diego. In San Diego, I caught a military transport flight going to New York, and was back home enjoying New York and Jean on June 2.

Thinking back today on that experience, I realize how really simple flying was in those days. All single-engine aircraft were very similar. Some flew faster than others; some were a little heavier; some had different stalling speeds. The problems arose when the pilot found himself in dangerous weather. Clouds, rain, fog, thunder storms—pilots of single-engine aircraft just didn't have the type of flight instruments needed to operate safely in adverse weather conditions. As long as the weather was CAVU (ceiling and visibility unlimited), flying single-engine aircraft was a walk in the park.

The Battle of Midway

On June 5, 1942 I headed out again for San Diego with an F4F. I landed at the Atlanta airport that evening and stayed overnight in a hotel in downtown Atlanta. That night at the hotel, I heard the news of another carrier battle. This one at Midway. The news was incomplete, but I decided I'd better call Jean at our apartment.

She sounded calm and yes, she'd heard the news and yes, she would save the papers for me and, yes she loved me. We hung up—long distance calls were expensive. After a two-day delay due to inclement weather in the Atlanta area, I headed again for San Diego. I was back in New York via a military transport plane on June 12. That night, Jean and I read over the news stories in a Brooklyn paper Jean had saved. The stories were dated June 5, 1942, and headlines read:

JAP FLEET IN MIDWAY REGION
NIMITZ REPORTS "TOO EARLY TO CLAIM JAPANESE DISASTER"
Enemy Damage Very Heavy, With Crippling Blows Inflicted on Several Ships — Tokyo Claims Control of Two Oceans

JAP ARMADA NEARLY WIPED OUT BY U.S. FLEET
NIMITZ REPORTS ENEMY FLED SO FAST IT DID NOT SEEK TO RESCUE DROWNING

I recall talking with Jean, explaining why we had no news about our losses. We didn't want to give the Japanese any information. Then she showed me an article about Ensign George Gay, a pilot with Torpedo Squadron Eight.

U.S. PILOT TELLS OF BURNING OF JAPANESE SHIPS
Eye Witness Was in Rubber Boat for Hours After His Plane Crashed
The first eyewitness account of the Battle of Midway came Monday from a naval aviator, who, floating in the sea, saw a line of burning Japanese ships pass by.

God! I know about Ensign Gay, his story. Heard it out in San Diego at the officers' club. The whole fleet knew the story. Gay was the only survivor of the 13 planes that attacked an enemy carrier. They had all been shot down. All killed except Gay. They were flying the old TBD, a plane with a top speed of less than 200 mph. It had to be a slaughter. They had no fighter planes with them for protection. Jean is going to ask me again not to go to a carrier squadron.

She put the paper down and asked me if I had flown the Grumman torpedo plane yet—she had seen them flying along the beach on their way to Floyd Bennett Field. I recall my surprise that she would ask such a question after reading about Ensign Gay. I told her that I would have my first flight that next week.

It seemed as though she had no desire to talk about Ensign Gay and the fact that he was a torpedo plane pilot. She seemed reconciled with our situation. She understood the story about Gay. I was a Navy pilot. I'd fly the planes I was told to fly, and she knew too that I must accept any orders I might receive—even ones to a carrier squadron.

God, how I love her—she understands—I know she loves me.

The TBF-1 by Grumman

On June 18, I flew TBF bureau number 00480 for one hour. I flew one again the following day for 30 minutes, and the day after that, I left for San Diego in TBF bureau number 00481.

The Grumman-built TBF-1 was the largest carrier-based plane flown in World War II. It was almost 18 feet from the top of the cockpit to the ground. The wingspan was 54 feet 2 inches and had a gross weight of 15,905 pounds. I can still recall my thoughts as I walked up to the TBF-1 for my first flight: This bird is too damn big to fly off a carrier. It turned out to be a wonderful airplane—very stable in flight, plenty of power with a 1,700 hp engine. It stalled at about 60 knots, with no tendency to fall off on one wing. When it stalled, the nose would just drop straight down and immediately pick up air speed again. It was really a joy to fly.

A Grumman TBF-1 Avenger being prepared for takeoff

Especially satisfying was the flight range of the TBF-1. My log book shows that I made the trip from Floyd Bennett to San Diego in just four days. One leg was 4.1 hours of flight time and another 5.7 hours. That was a lot different from flying the F4F with its short flying range. With an F4F, it usually took five or six days because of fuel stops.

I returned to New York and had some time at home with Jean. I flew locally for the rest of June, picking up aircraft at the Grumman plant on Long Island and bringing them back to Floyd Bennett Field. I couldn't help but notice how my flight time was building up. During the month of May, I flew 56.2 hours and in June, 40.3 hours. I was averaging more than an hour a day. I was getting valuable experience, not only in flight time but also in flying different types of aircraft. Most important, I was building my confidence as a pilot. I was getting the job done and I was doing it alone, just me and the airplane.

Jean and I celebrated July 4 with a beach party by the ocean on Rockaway Beach. The next day, I left for San Diego with a TBF. I made the trip in five days, due to weather delays, and was looking forward to a quick trip home.

Oh no! Not another old clunker to fly to some training base. BT-1. Jesus, flew one of these at Corpus. Deliver it to N.A.S. Miami. That's going to take a week. Might as well get started. Let's see how you start this old bird.

Looking at my log book, it took me ten fuel stops and 11.4 hours of flight time for the trip. I returned to New York on the 14th. So much for Miami.

The TBD Torpedo Plane

The scheduling office must have taken pity on me because I stayed in New York flying locally. My log book shows 18 flights between July 11 and 25. All of them were under one hour in duration. Then, on June 29, I headed out again for San Diego. I must have had good weather nationally, because instead of flying the southern route, I made the flight via Indianapolis, St. Louis, Dallas, and on to San Diego. The trip took just four days. Then it happened again—operations had a plane for me to deliver to N.A.S. Corpus Christi—a TBD torpedo plane.

This was the type of aircraft that Torpedo Eight was flying at Midway. Everyone was killed except George Gay. Thirteen planes shot down. Those guys didn't have a chance. Japanese fighters got them. That .30-caliber machine gun in the rear cockpit of the TBD was no help. God, those guys had guts. I wonder if I could have faced it? Our dive-bombers got the enemy carriers though, while the Japanese were busy defending against the torpedo planes. If I do ever get orders to a carrier squadron that has torpedo planes, at least I'll have a great airplane to fly . . . the TBF!

The flight to Corpus was routine, but my arrival did cause some problems. I considered myself a hot ferry pilot, and I no longer used a helmet and goggles. I wore a baseball cap, a headset for the radio and sunglasses. Since it was bright sunny day, I decided to get some sun while flying. I

A Douglas TBD-1 Devastator

stripped my flight suit free of my shoulders and bunched it around my waist. I was naked from the waist up.

I called the tower at Corpus for clearance, made my approach, landed, and taxied up to the operations building. I shut down my engine and stood up in the cockpit. Then I saw a very large group of officers and sailors standing in formation. God! There was a personnel inspection going on. The next thing I saw was a Navy captain stopping and looking directly at me standing there—half-naked. Suddenly, another officer came running out of the operations building yelling, "You! Get your ass out of that airplane. The captain wants to see you."

Twenty minutes later, I was standing at attention (my flight suit in place). I responded with "Yes, Sir" and "No, Sir" and the captain told me never to land again at his base.

I returned to New York by military transport and was flying again on the 15th, picking an F4F at the Grumman plant and flying it back to Floyd Bennett. When I returned, there was a message to report to Commander O. J. Whitney, the commanding officer of the ferry command. I reported to his office. He handed me my orders to a carrier squadron based at N.A.S. Norfolk, Virginia. My reporting date was 23 August 1942.

> *Well, Jean's greatest fear has come true. I'm going! So little time. Jean will have to stay here and pack our gear. It takes time for the Navy to arrange for a move. Maybe Jean should go back to Bremerton now. No, she will want to come to Norfolk to be with me. Wonder what kind of planes a VGS (composite air group) squadron has? Hope they have dive-bombers ... TBFs would be fine too—what carrier will we get? Wonder how long before we leave? I hope Jean understands. I know she will. It's orders. She knows, though, that I didn't volunteer ... I kept my promise.*

Chapter 4

Squadron Duty in Norfolk

I didn't have much time after Commander Whitney handed me my orders on August 15. I did take some leave to help Jean with the packing and to enjoy New York City with her before reporting to my new assignment in Norfolk.

My log book shows a flight on August 23, 1942, in an F4F to Norfolk. I was reporting for my new assignment with Escort Scouting Squadron 28 at Naval Air Station, Norfolk, Virginia. I didn't even know what an escort scouting squadron did—all I knew I was going to the fleet and I would be a carrier pilot.

I had said good-bye to Jean that morning at our apartment. We both knew it would be only for a short time. She was very excited about joining me in Norfolk. There was going to be a slight delay though, before she would join me. Jean's younger brother, Ed, was coming east for a visit. He had just graduated from Bremerton High School, and this visit was his graduation gift from Jean and Ed's parents. Jean didn't want to ask her folks to cancel his trip because of my orders, so she decided to remain in New York until Ed left. Then she would finish packing and join me in Norfolk.

As I flew from New York to Norfolk, my thoughts took over as I guided the plane through the sky.

You're on your way, and this is no routine ferry flight. There will be no plane from Floyd Bennett to pick you up, Norm, and fly you back to Jean. No complaints. This is what I really want, isn't it? I haven't been completely honest with Jean about my hopes for the future. Well, I got my wish, and now she's going to join you. Watch those clouds! Better fly around them. Get back on course for Norfolk. There, I better pay a little more attention to my flying. OK, so Jean's coming to Norfolk and

I'll have to find a place to live. First, though, I've got to report to the squadron for duty. Wonder if there will be some time off to hunt for an apartment. Well, I'd better ask. I've got a wife to take care of too.

I landed, checked in at operations, did the paperwork to transfer the F4F to N.A.S. Norfolk, and asked directions to the offices of Escort Scouting Squadron 28. I can still recall the response of the young sailor behind the counter at operations.

"Sir, VGS-28 is in hangar three. Catch the bus just outside. It will drop you off. Good luck, Sir, and get a Jap for me."

I stood at the bus stop, waiting.

So much for your welcome to the fleet. Well, I'm just a lowly ensign. What did I expect? Someone from the squadron? Wonder what a squadron will be like? How many pilots? Hope the squadron has dive-bombers. Funny remark that sailor made. Wonder if the squadron is assigned to a carrier. Hope the squadron won't be leaving right away. Maybe Jean should go back to Bremerton? Here's my stop.

I reported to the squadron duty officer with my orders, and after a day devoted to checking out with the medical and personnel departments to be sure my personal papers were in order, I reported to the number two man in the squadron: the executive officer (XO), Lieutenant Poutant. After declaring, "Ensign Berg reporting, Sir!" he asked me to sit down in front of his desk and proceeded to fill me in on the history of VGS-28. (VGS means "composite air group.") We were one of four newly commissioned carrier squadrons at Norfolk, scheduled for deployment aboard four newly commissioned carriers. I felt excited about going aboard a new carrier. The XO, as I remember, quickly dampened my exuberance. In fact, I still remember his words.

"Mr. Berg, this outfit is scheduled to deploy on a converted oil tanker previously owned by the Esso Oil Company. It is now owned by the Navy and has a flight deck built on it so it can fly aircraft off the deck. Our ship is USS *Chenango*, Auxiliary Aircraft Carrier (ACV-28), named after a river in New York State. It's not much of a carrier—top speed 18 knots as compared to the Navy's four remaining fleet carriers, *Enterprise*, *Saratoga*, *Wasp*, and *Hornet*, which all can do 30 knots! Our carrier will still carry fuel oil, so we'll be refueling other ships as well as operating our aircraft."

After describing our carrier, he asked, "Mr. Berg, you're married, aren't you? Is your wife with you?"

I quickly explained my situation about Jean's brother visiting and how I'd been checking the apartment rentals in the Norfolk area.

USS *Chenango* (CVE-28). Photo taken in Eniwetok Harbor on July 9, 1944

Original photo by Paul Madden, photographer, (CV 6), USS Essex

"Mr. Berg, unless you have a car, I'd recommend that you look for a room for you and your wife in a private home that's on the bus line. Apartments are usually a long way from the air station and you'll need a car. I'll ask my wife to keep a look out for a room for you and Mrs. Berg."

It was clear that the interview was over. I stood up, thanked him, saluted, and left his office. I walked down the passageway to the pilots' ready room where we had lockers to stow our flight gear, got a cup of coffee and sat down.

God! A room in someone's home! Housing is really tough in this town. Did he say only four fleet carriers left? Let's see, Yorktown *was lost at Midway in June. I remember reading the story with Jean—a room! Jean is going to be so disappointed. Maybe the XO's wife can help. Got to find something soon. Then we lost* Lexington *at the Battle of Coral Sea in May. Why wasn't Jean home when I called last night? No answer. She may have disconnected the phone in the apartment. Maybe she'll call here so I'll know when to meet her. Ed must be about ready to go back to Bremerton. Wonder when the squadron will leave for the Pacific? Bet there's a pilot shortage right now. That's why the hurry to get this outfit ready to go. I'm already on the flight schedule tomorrow, in a TBF for a practice bombing flight—a bombing flight! How in the hell do you bomb with a torpedo plane? I've got to find a place to live. Wonder when Jean will get here. Bombing with a TBF?*

My thoughts were interrupted as a group of pilots walked into the ready room. "You're Berg, aren't you? We're going to the officers' club and since you're the newest ensign in the squadron, you get to buy the first round." My squadron life started—at the bar.

I'm the "Bull Ensign"

The next morning, I walked the short distance from the bachelor officer quarters (BOQ) where I was staying to the squadron's hangar. I wasn't exactly a bachelor, but I was an officer and eligible to stay in the BOQ until Jean arrived. Walking along, I realized that I'd learned a great deal about the squadron last night at the bar. VGS-28 was designated as a composite squadron. In addition to the torpedo plane squadron where I was assigned, there was a dive-bombing squadron and a fighter squadron. The aircraft complement for the three squadrons was nine TBFs for my squadron; nine SBD dive-bombers; and twelve F4Fs in the fighter squadron. My squadron had a complement of 12 pilots as did the dive-bombing squadron. The fighter squadron had 15 pilots. This total of 39 pilots was small compared with the larger, faster fleet carriers like *Enterprise*. The limiting factor was the number of aircrafts our ship could operate. The larger fleet carriers could carry more than twice the number of aircraft as *Chenango*.

As I approached the squadron's hangar, I felt that this assignment was certainly going to be an exciting experience. It was already apparent that a sense of togetherness and bonding was occurring between the pilots. It had been obvious last night at the officers' club. All the junior torpedo squadron pilots were at the club. We were all ensigns and, with the exception of myself, all the pilots had just graduated from flight training. The only exceptions were two lieutenants who were also in the squadron. I learned later that they were married, so they didn't usually show up at the club with ensigns.

I remember, though, that I was welcomed into the group. In fact, as I recall, I took a good deal of friendly razzing. First of all, I was the new pilot and I had to buy the first round of beers. But then there was the issue of seniority. One of the pilots asked me what my date of rank was. When I told him that I'd been commissioned an ensign on December 10, 1941, the entire group lined up in front of me, came to attention and, raising their beer bottles, saluted me as the "Bull Ensign." I had no idea what bull ensign meant. All I knew I was the senior ensign by date of rank. I soon learned that, although the title didn't bring me any power, it did put me into a leadership position with the senior officers in the squadron—the lieutenants, the XO and the CO, Lieutenant Commander Spence Butts. They saw me as the leader of the rest of the ensigns. Little did I know that those leadership demands would occur much more rapidly than I was prepared for.

I arrived at the squadron hangar and headed for the ready room to check the flight schedule. There were six of us scheduled for a practice bombing flight in the TBF that morning. Lieutenant Olsen, one of the lieutenants assigned to the squadron, was scheduled to lead the flight. I had already met the XO, Lieutenant Poutant, so I introduced myself to Lieutenant Olsen.

"So, Mr. Berg, I hear you're the bull ensign. You're also the pilot who's been in the ferry command. How much flight time do you have in the TBF?"

"Sir, I have about 50 hours—all of it flying the plane either locally at Floyd Bennett Field or cross-country from New York to San Diego."

"Ever put the bird into a dive to see what it felt like—a big airplane like the TBF?" I acknowledged that I had. "Well, Mr. Berg, with 50 hours in the TBF, you're the most experienced TBF pilot in the outfit. We're still taking delivery of the TBFs, so until we have our full complement of TBFs, flying time for some of the pilots has been limited. Now, I'll lead this flight to the practice bombing target. Then I'll move into the tail-end Charlie position—the number six position—and you take over."

Damn it! Take over the lead at the target area? I haven't done this since flight training. It can't be dive-bombing. The TBF won't take a vertical dive. No dive brakes. The wings would probably come off. What's the lieutenant saying? Glide bombing? OK, some of the guys at the bar told me of the commanding officer's plan to develop a glide bomb technique to make the TBF more than just a torpedo plane. OK, what's that? Altitude 8,000 to 1,000 feet, 40–45 degree dive; landing gear extended to slow the plane down; reduce the throttle; damn! With power off, the bird will be gliding. It sure as hell won't be flying! Don't exceed 250 knots on the pullout. Be out of the dive by 1,000 feet. Release the bomb on pull out from the dive. This will insure that the bombs will fall clear of the bomb bay. Hell! It's just like dive-bombing, except not so steep. You can do it. Just like in training. Do it!

The six of us took off, joined up on the lieutenant and headed out over the ocean from the air station. We were in a steady climb, leveling off at 9,000 feet. As we leveled off, I received a radio call from the lieutenant ordering me to take the lead. He moved to the back of the formation and I assumed the lead. I spotted the practice bombing target, a barge anchored off the coast from Norfolk. The barge appeared to be about 100 feet long and had a white bulls-eye painted in the center of the deck.

We were using practice bombs made of metal, the same size as a regular 500-pound bomb, except these were filled with water. This was done to approximate the weight and give the practice bomb almost the same aerodynamic behavior through the air as a bomb filled with explosives. Pilots wanted to be sure, too, that the practice bombs would drop clear of the bomb bay, even though the plane was not in level flight. The TBF carried four bombs in a bomb bay in the lower part of the fuselage. We each made four runs. I remember I got one hit, but the others hit close to the barge. It was very easy to see the misses when the practice bomb hit the water. Since it was my first time, I wasn't bothered—none of us did very well. At the debriefing back in the ready room, the lieutenant agreed that we needed more experience with the bombing technique, but we were relieved. By releasing the bombs on pull out from the dive, all practice bombs dropped clear of our aircraft when released. As we all changed from our flight gear to our uniforms and got ready to leave for lunch, the squadron duty officer called to me.

"Hey, Norm. A telegram came for you this morning right after you took off on your flight. Here it is."

I ripped open the yellow envelope and read:

ENSIGN NORMAN BERG VGS-28 N.A.S. NORFOLK VIRGINIA. ARRIVING NORFOLK BY TRAIN TWO PM 30 AUGUST. STOP. HAVEN'T HEARD FROM YOU. STOP. PLEASE MEET ME. STOP. LOVE YOU. STOP. JEAN.

Damn! I forgot to write her to tell her about the housing. Jean's coming, and I don't have a place for her to live yet. What about the XO? I haven't even asked him if his wife has a lead on the room. I'm such jerk! I've got a wife! Did I just forget? Why didn't I write? Didn't I want her to come? No, it's just that so much is happening . . . no damn excuses. Go catch a bus and get to the train station. Better let the XO know about Jean coming. Come on, get with the program. I'm married . . . love her . . . go meet her.

Jean Arrives in Norfolk

I knew when I caught the bus to downtown Norfolk that it took only about 20 minutes, but it seemed like an eternity. I knew also that I'd let Jean down; I'd failed her by not staying in touch. I was sure glad it was Friday. I would have the weekend to try and explain my behavior to Jean. Also, after we got together, we'd have some time to look for a place to live. I was sure we'd find a room somewhere. Suddenly, the bus driver called out, "'Ensign, here's your stop. The train station is just down the block."

I jumped off the bus and started up the block toward the train station. Then I saw her. She was wearing the suit she wore at our wedding. A little pill box hat was perched on her head, and she was lugging a big suitcase. I remember running toward her and calling out her name as she dropped the suitcase and stood waiting for me. I took her into my arms and I remember her words as they spilled out.

"Oh, Norm! I didn't know what to do! The rent on the apartment was due. I tried to call you, but the Navy said that your location was confidential. Why didn't you call me or write? I just didn't know what to do. It was awful!"

I held her close as I whispered my apologies, trying to express my feeling of guilt, my shame in my failure to stay in contact with her. After a few moments, Jean pushed me away from my embrace. I could see the tears glistening on her face. I took her hands in mine, and a quick little smile crossed her face when I told her that I had the weekend off and suggested we get a hotel room. Then I had to tell her that we should start looking for a room.

Her smile disappeared as she pulled her hands free of mine.

"So, we have no place to live! What on earth have you been doing? I know. It's those damn airplanes! Well, you hot pilot, do I go back to Bremerton or do I stay here with you? You'd better decide damn quick—the train station is right here!"

My response was to hail a cab and check into the best hotel in Norfolk, The Grady. I left her to freshen up while I got a newspaper to look at rooms for rent section. I returned hoping to go with her to the hotel room. To my chagrin, she told me that she would join me in the lobby later. When she returned, I received her brief kiss of welcome. She hardly gave me time to return her kiss before she asked for the paper. I told her about the advice the XO had given me about getting a room near a bus stop.

She looked at me as if to say, "A room in somebody's house!"; but she quickly pulled the paper open and found the section listing "Rooms for Rent."

We got a map of the city, a bus map and spent most of Saturday looking at rooms for rent. We decided on one that was about half a mile from the base figuring that I could walk to work. There was also a shopping area a few blocks away where there was a restaurant. There was no place to cook in our rented room. Jean would have to go out for meals. The landlady and I agreed on a weekly price for the room after Jean and I underwent a close inspection by the very suspicious landlady. I remember wondering if she would demand to see our marriage license. Since we'd found a place to stay, I suggested we walk over to the air station and go to the officers' club for dinner before going back to the hotel. We walked along a quiet street holding hands on our way to dinner.

Wonder what Jean's thinking? She sure can't be very happy about the room. No place to stay except in the room sitting on one of the beds. No place to eat. She's sure quiet. What do you expect? Do something—can't ask Jean to live like this. Hope there are some of the squadron guys at the club. Maybe Bill Austin and his wife will be there, how about the Cliff Johnsons? He's one of the other married ensigns. If Jean could meet some of the other wives.... Damn it, I want her to stay. Sure hope she will understand. New worries about fitting in. Leadership worries. She must know I love her. Maybe back at the hotel ...

alone in our room, I can convince her that I love her and want her to stay. Got to try.

That evening at the officers' club, chance again entered my life. It came in the form of two young Navy wives who were at the club with their husbands, two of my squadron mates. They welcomed Jean with warmth and understanding as we sat together, enjoying cocktails before ordering dinner. As we husbands listened, our wives began exchanging horror stories about living conditions in Norfolk and being married to naval aviators. As the stories got more outrageous, so did the laughter. The three women continued to point out the often macho and stupid behavior of their husbands. Jean was especially vocal that evening about my behavior. One story she told was her response to me telling her that we had no place to live. I remember that her comments evoked the greatest laughter from the two other couples. I just had to sit and take the kidding from the group.

Jean and I left the club after dinner, a little mellow from the cocktails and dinner. A cab dropped us at the Grady Hotel. This time Jean took my hand in hers, and as we entered the lobby, she whispered her invitation to me. I knew she would not be going back to Bremerton. Our life together would continue.

Gunnery Training with the SNJ

According to my pilot's log book for September 1 to 10, 1942, I flew 31 hours. There were five practice glide-bombing flights, six gunnery flights, four tow flights and six field carrier practice flights.

A typical day would appear in my log book as three separate flights.

Sept. 3 – Aircraft: TBF Duration 2.5 hr. Type of flight: Bomb

Sept. 3 – Aircraft: TBF Duration 1.4 hr. Type of flight: Gunnery

Sept. 3 – Aircraft: SNJ Duration 1.4 hr. Type of flight: Gunnery-tow flight

Each flight required a minimum of an hour for briefing and debriefing time as well as different skills and extreme concentration on the pilot's part, especially the bombing and gunnery flights. Training pilots for carrier operations meant practicing multiple skills under stressful conditions. The result—a very tired and often emotionally drained pilot.

Of the three flights on September 3, the gunnery-tow flight was the least stressful. I had passed a written exam and flown the SNJ, the airplane that was used by the squadron as a tow plane for gunnery training. This procedure qualified me to fly the aircraft solo. The SNJ was a low-wing, single-engine plane with two cockpits that was built by North American Aviation as a training plane for the Navy. My job as the tow plane pilot started as I taxied the SNJ out on to the take-off runway. There, two sailors would attach 500 feet of rope to the underside of the plane's fuselage. At the other end of the rope was a canvas banner laying flat on the runway. It was about 25 feet long and 6 feet wide. I waited until I saw four TBFs begin to taxi out to the runway where I was waiting with the tow target. These were the pilots who would join me in the gunnery area for gunnery training. I pushed the throttle to full power and started to roll down the runway. I was airborne with the tow target without a problem. The SNJ had plenty of power and speed to tow the target.

As soon as the target left the runway, it rolled into vertical position, and I began a steady climb out over the ocean on a heading for the gunnery area. The four TBFs joined me, staying well clear of the towline. The gunnery practice area was an air space over the Atlantic Ocean about 50 miles from N.A.S. Norfolk The shipping charts designated it as an area closed to ship navigation. The air space set aside for gunnery training was 50 miles long and 20 miles wide. My first task was to keep the tow plane within the perimeters of the gunnery air space. After reaching 8,000 feet of altitude and checking my navigation to be sure I was in the assigned area, I would call the lead plane and clear the flight to commence gunnery runs. I also warned all pilots at that time.

"Stop firing if you drift behind the target. Remember, I'm not the target!"

The four TBFs were in a position ahead of the tow plane, to my right and at an altitude above my plane. Each plane would commence a diving turn towards the tow plane, fly past the tow plane and then turn again toward the target and begin firing. The flight path of the aircraft would look like the letter *S*. The top of the *S* was where the plane would start the diving turn. The bottom of the *S* was where the target was located. After completing a firing run,

each plane would recover by flying under the tow target and climbing back above the tow plane for another gunnery run. After the fourth pilot completed his run, I would reverse course with the tow plane and again tell the pilots to commence the gunnery runs. This would continue until all ammunition in each plane was gone.

The TBFs would then join up and head for the base. The SNJ was much slower, so by

Like Canada, Africa, the United Kingdom, the United States, and several other countries, New Zealand relied heavily on the Harvard (the British designation of the North American T-6 Texan, also known to U.S. naval aviators as the SNJ) as an advanced pilot training and basic air weapons training aircraft from March 1941 until they were finally phased out in 1977 the time I arrived over the field, the TBF pilots would have landed and would be standing by the aircraft parking ramp waiting for me to drop the target. I would fly slowly over a grassy area between the cement runways and release the tow-line and target. A truck would be waiting to pick up the target and towline. The truck would drop the target off by the pilots. All of us would be like a bunch of kids after the gunnery flight—counting bullet holes. Hits on the target were important—low man bought the beer at the club. Scoring was still done as it had been in training at Corpus—the bullets were pained with different colors that left a mark on the target. Hits were few, though. The TBF in 1942 had only one .30-caliber machine synchronized to fire through the propeller. Plus, a pilot only had about eight to ten seconds of actual firing time against the target. Pilots kidded one another about feeling like being in WWI and flying against the Red Baron. The training was important, though. We were all learning the necessary skills to fly the TBF under combat conditions.

A Night to Forget!

That evening after dinner at the officers' club, Jean and I, along with five of our bachelor friends, decided to go to a nightclub that had a dance band. The club we found also had a bar. When the club closed at one o'clock, Jean and I, along with George Hartman, one of the bachelors, were the only ones left of the original group of pilots. George and I were both pretty mellow; in fact, we were both quite drunk. So the three of us got a cab, and when we arrived at our rooming house, we all piled out of the cab busy talking about the evening. I paid the cabby, but forgot about George. The cab left and there stood all three of us. I insisted that it was too far for George to walk to the base. In a moment of drunken clarity, I suggested George stay with us. Why not? There were two twin beds in our rented room. He could have one and Jean and I would use the other one. We tiptoed very quietly to our room. Jean undressed in the bathroom and quickly got into bed. George and I stripped to our skivvies and I joined Jean as George got into the other bed.

The next morning, George and I were up early. It was a workday and we had to get to the squadron. I got into my robe and used the bathroom first. I noticed that the landlady was having her morning coffee sitting in the kitchen. She sure was nosy, I thought—always up early checking on Jean and me. Back in the room, George was up and dressed. Before I could say anything about the landlady, he said, "I'm leaving, Norm, but I've got to go to the head (Navy word for bathroom) first. I'll see you later at the squadron." I knew the landlady would see him.

I got dressed and tried to sneak out of the room. She was waiting for me.

"Mr. Berg, who was that man who just left your room?"

"A friend, Ma'am, just a good friend."

"Is your wife with you in the room?"

"Yes, Ma'am, but . . . ." She interrupted me. "Mr. Berg, I want you and your wife out of my house by tonight. I won't tolerate such behavior!"

I woke Jean before leaving. She was still half-asleep, but she awakened quickly when I said, "Honey, please see the landlady. She's really upset about George staying with us. She's kicking us out as of tonight. I've got to get to the base. Will you call Betty Austin and see if there's room in the boarding house where they stay? Sorry about George staying, honey. Call me at the squadron if we get a room at the boarding house. I'll meet you and help with the move."

She just sat there in bed, her hair tousled from sleep. Then, as I left the room she replied, "OK, I'll call Betty. Go fly your stupid airplanes—and will you please grow up! Stop acting like a high school kid!"

Field Carrier Landing Practice

I left the room quietly, avoiding our irate landlady, and started walking down the street towards the base. I had left Jean—my very unhappy wife—sitting in bed.

> *God! You are a master at doing dumb things. Having George stay with us was so stupid! I hope Jean can find a room for us in that boarding house with the Austins. That would be better for her since Betty's her friend. I should've taken some extra aspirins; got to quit partying on work nights. No fun flying with a hangover. No sweat though, it should be an easy day. I'll get a strong cup of coffee at the squadron and then check the flight schedule.*

I walked into the squadron ready room, poured myself a cup of black coffee and saw a message written in chalk on the blackboard. "Mr. Berg, report to Lieutenant Malanosky." Malanosky was the squadron's landing signal officer (LSO). It wasn't going to be an easy day.

Every carrier squadron, while preparing for deployment, was assigned an LSO. I'd met the lieutenant before. He was an older man with plenty of experience flying off carriers. I'd also talked to other squadron pilots about him and about FCLP, field carrier landing practice.

As I walked down the passageway to his office, I knew what was coming—my training was starting—learning to land aboard *Chenango*, our carrier. I entered his office, saluted, and said, "Ensign Berg reporting as ordered, Sir!"

He acknowledged my salute and told me to sit down as he continued going through some papers.

Suddenly, I knew that this man would control my future as a carrier pilot.

This was *déjà vu*—just like primary training when I got those down checks. I had to get the lieutenant's OK in the field carrier landing training before he would approve me for actual landings on the carrier. Without his approval, I'd be transferred out of the squadron.

What if I failed and couldn't qualify for carrier duty? What if I am transferred out of the squadron? Maybe Jean and I would be together. No, that wouldn't happen. I'd probably go to a noncarrier squadron. Hell, I've got to make it!

I heard the lieutenant ask, "Is this your first FCLP training flight?"

When I responded it was, he stood up and moved out away from his desk. He picked up two paddles—each about twelve inches in diameter—looking like large ping-pong paddles. Attached to wires on the interior of the paddles were strips of bright pink cloth that fluttered as he moved the paddles back and forth.

"Mr. Berg," he paused, looking into my eyes. "These little paddles are your lifeline. They will get you back aboard the carrier. You let me help you, and I'll get you back home to your pretty, young wife. Ignore my signals and you'll end up a dead naval aviator."

He paused, still looking at me, then he reached across the desk and handed me the two paddles. "Do you know the signals I will be giving you as you make your approach to the carrier?" I indicated that I did. My fellow pilots had demonstrated the signals to me at the bar often enough. Damn! After what he just said I'd better know the signals.

"OK. You're too high on your approach. What's the signal?"

I raised both paddles over my head in the shape of a *V*.

"You're fast. Reduce air speed."

I held one paddle in my right hand straight out from my shoulder. The paddle in my left hand was moving up and down between my waist and the floor.

"You're too slow. Add power."

I held both paddles waist high and moved them both forward and then back again—like swimming the breaststroke, I thought.

"You're OK. Good approach!"

I held both paddles straight out from my shoulders. This was the semaphore signal for alphabet letter *R*. A perfect approach was known as a "Roger Pass." I knew I would need plenty of these to satisfy the LSO officer.

"Now show me the two mandatory signals—the ones you must obey."

I raised both paddles above my head moving them rapidly back and forth. This was the signal for "wave off," add power and gain altitude, and most of all, "Do Not Land!"

The final signal was a "cut." The paddle in my left hand was pointing down to the floor. The paddle in my right hand made a swift motion across in front of my face—cut the throttle and land the plane.

"OK, Norm. It's Norm, isn't it?" He had a slight smile on his face as he looked at me. "That was real good. You know your signals. I've got your pilot log book here. With the amount of flight time you have in the TBF you should have no trouble." I could feel a wide grin splitting my face. But then he continued. "I know you're scheduled for a FCLP training flight this morning. Since this is your first experience with field carrier landing practice, here's what I want you to do. Take off 30 minutes ahead of the rest of the flight. Fly out to Rogers Field, a satellite field to N.A.S. Norfolk. When you see the field, you'll notice a large white square painted on the end of the runway. It's 85 feet wide and 150 feet long. That represents the size of the flight deck you will have for landing on *Chenango*. Any questions?"

Damn! The wing span on the TBF is 54 feet! Not much room for error . . . and speed control. It's critical. Don't be too fast or too high. Just hope you walk away from a crash, or swim away if you go over the side. Jesus! He's right; he's going to save my ass. I need him. Pay attention to those paddles!

"No questions, Sir. Anything else, Sir?"

"Yes, Norm, just a couple of more things. I don't want you to make any landings today. Before you practice your first landings with me, I want you to practice some slow flight. Climb to 3,000 feet, put your wheels and flaps down. You'll be in a landing configuration. Then reduce power until you're flying about five knots above stalling speed. What will that be for the TBF?"

"Sir, depending on the weight of the plane, it should be about 73 to 75 knots."

"OK, Norm. I want you to spend about 30 minutes practicing slow flight. Make some turns—control your air speed and altitude. Get the feel of the airplane. Think about the signals you'll be getting from me on an actual approach. How will you respond to the various signals? OK? I'll see you after the flight."

I got into my flight gear, climbed into my assigned aircraft, and taxied out to the duty runway. I was cleared for takeoff by the tower, and about 20 minutes later, I saw the white painted outline of the landing area on the runway as I flew over Rogers Field. I was at 3,000 feet.

Sure is small. At least it's not moving. The carrier sure as hell will be. Now, landing gear and flaps down; reduce power; control stick back;

get the nose a little higher; watch the air speed … 80 … 75 … add some power! Steady. Hold it right there. Now an easy turn. Add power! Air speed is dropping below 70. There, back to 75. Damn! The plane is almost ready to quit flying. Ready to stall. Settle down, Norm, remember you're going to be flying only 50 feet above the ground on your approach to the landing area. Come on, the LSO said practice for 30 minutes. Come on, you can fly the damn box this plane came in!

I finished practicing slow flight procedure and started back to the Norfolk Air Station. I was a little disappointed that the LSO had not let me make some landings, but I figured he knew best. I was wondering, too, if Jean had found us a place to live.

Hell, I wonder if she's even talking to me! I hope there's a message from her at the squadron. There's the field. Better call the tower for landing clearance. I'll call her when I get back to the squadron. Am I letting my fear of failure interfere with my feelings for her? I do want her with me. I need her. Got to do something to show her I love her. Come on, do something!

I received my landing clearance, made my approach and landed at the Naval Air Station. As I taxied to the squadron area, shut down the plane and headed for the squadron ready room, I was hoping for a message from Jean. I wondered if she had found a place for us to live. I stopped by the duty officer's desk and he handed me two messages. One was a memo of a telephone call from Jean. The other was a written memo from the skipper's office. I opened Jean's message first.

"NORM, WE'RE ALL SET AT THE BOARDING HOUSE. THE GIRLS HELPED ME MOVE. FLYBOY, I HOPE YOU ENJOYED YOUR FLIGHT WHILE I WAS LEFT TO SOLVE OUR PROBLEM! WE HAVE BOARD AND ROOM, SO I EXPECT YOU FOR DINNER. NO OFFICERS' CLUB TONIGHT. JEAN."

Then the duty officer spoke, "Norm, that second message is from the skipper. He wants to see you."

The skipper was Commander Butts, the squadron commanding officer. As I walked down the passageway to the skipper's office, I thought, Now what? I've got enough problems with Jean and carrier landings! I don't need anything else! I knocked at the skipper's office door and as I entered, I heard him say, "Come in."

"Ensign Berg, reporting as ordered, Sir!"

"Sit down, Norm." He came right to the point. "I understand that you and your new wife are having housing problems. In fact, I heard you've been evicted from your present living quarters. Something about having another man staying overnight in your room with your wife present."

As I stammered out my explanation of what had happened that night with George Hartman, his expression softened. By the time I finished, a slight smile replaced the grimness around his mouth and eyes that had greeted me when I first entered his office.

"Mr. Berg, you must remember that our Southern women are very delicate, especially the older generation." He started to laugh. "I bet she said to you, 'I don't tolerate such behavior in my home!'"

I nodded my head.

"Well, Norm, what are you going to do now? Do you need the afternoon off to find another place to live?"

"Sir, I have a message from my wife. She has moved us to a boarding house a few miles from the base. There are three other married squadron officers living there. In fact, their wives helped my wife move. There's bus transportation to the base area, so we're all set."

There was a long silence as my skipper seemed to study me—staring at me, and then finally he said, "Norm, I sense that you're having some problems. The LSO tells me that you're ready to start your FCLP training. It appears too, that your relationship with your wife is what—difficult? Perhaps I can help make things a little easier. I don't want you under any unusual stress as you start your training for carrier work. I have a lot of confidence in you, Norm. You're the senior ensign."

He paused. "Starting today, you'll have custody of my official sedan. You may use it only for transporting yourself and the other squadron officers from the boarding house to the base—no evening trips to the club, only official business. Understood? Any questions?"

The skipper's car? What a privilege! No more buses. He trusts me and believes I can do the job. I can set the example as the bull ensign. Does he think I can become a leader? He must, giving me the official car to use. I won't let him down. I can do it. I've got to do better with Jean. Stop resenting that she's here with me. Remember I'm nobody without her help. She's my anchor. I've got to put her first in my life. Put the airplanes second. Do it!

I left his office feeling that I was ready for my afternoon flight. I was scheduled for field carrier landing practice, and this time I would be answering the signals from the landing signal officer. God! What a jubilant feeling! I had the respect of the skipper. I knew I could live up to his expectations.

I grabbed a quick sandwich and a soda from the Navy Exchange food truck that sold snacks outside the squadron hangar and joined the three other pilots scheduled for the afternoon FCLP flight. When I told them about the official car, it seemed that I saw a new look of respect from all of them. They kidded me, too, about brown-nosing the skipper, but I just replied, R.H.I.P. (rank has its privileges).

By one o'clock, we were taxiing out to the duty runway and, after takeoff, we joined up and headed for Rogers Field. As we approached the field, I could see the landing signal officer standing at the end of the runway. The painted outline of the carrier deck was highly visible. The LSO was in position to direct my approach and landing. He would be on my left when I made my first approach to the landing area.

I was the number four man in the flight—the "tail-end Charlie." The lead plane signaled us to move into an echelon to the right as we flew parallel to the left side of the runway. We were flying at an altitude of 1,000 feet, air speed 140 knots. As the formation passed the upper end of the runway, the lead plane descended with a 180 degree turn to the left. Each of us, after a five-second delay, followed the lead plane making our turn to the left. We were all now on our downwind leg with the runway on our left. I was at 500 feet of altitude as I lowered my landing gear and landing flaps. My air speed was about 90 knots. I could see the other three planes ahead of me. I could see the lead plane making his first landing on the runway.

OK, get ready. What's my air speed? Eighty-five, too fast. Slow down; reduce throttle. I'm high; get down to below 100 feet. Lower the nose a little. Start the final turn to the runway now! Air speed! Get it down below 80. I'm still high. There's the LSO. The paddles are up above his head. I'm too high! Now he's moving the left hand paddle up and down. I'm too fast! Now both paddles are down below his waist . . . I'm low! Shit! Add power! I'm too slow. Don't let it climb. Damn! A wave off! He's waving both paddles above his head! A wave off—add power . . . get the gear up . . . ease up the landing flaps. Damn! It's hot. I'm sweating. Get back in the landing pattern. Try again and get it right!

The four of us were now flying what was called a racetrack pattern around the field as we continued the FCLP training. Each pilot was scheduled to make six approaches to the runway, responding each time to the LSO's signals.

After I took the wave off from the LSO, I climbed to 1,000 feet and made a slight turn to the right. I was now to the right of the runway. Flying straight ahead, I maintained altitude until I saw the number three plane ahead of me make a 180-degree left turn to the downwind leg of his approach. After waiting about five seconds, I made my left 180-degree turn to the downwind leg, altitude 500 feet, the runway on my left. I was ready to make my second landing attempt under the control of the LSO. I made my final turn towards the runway, saw the LSO and got another wave off! That day, I made three more attempts, but was waved off each time. I just couldn't seem to slow the plane down.

I remember that I finally got a cut on my sixth and last approach. I sure welcomed that cut signal as I saw the paddle in the LSO's right hand cross in front of his body. I closed the throttle, landed the plane, quickly raised the landing flaps, added power and took off again—a touch-and-go landing. The FCLP training was over for the day. I saw the rest of the planes orbiting the field waiting for me to join the flight. I added power and took my position again as tail-end Charlie. We headed back to the air station.

Damn! With the exception of my last approach, the rest were rotten. Only got one "cut" signal out of six attempts.

After the flight, we four pilots gathered in the squadron ready room with the LSO. I remember he had a little brown book where he had evaluated each of us. The rest of the guys had done pretty well. Only a few wave offs. Unlike my situation, this had not been their first FCLP training flight. I was still the new kid on the block when it came to FCLP. I knew I was rationalizing, finding an excuse for my lousy flying. I knew I should have done better. I had the most experience in the TBF airplane. The LSO turned to me.

"Berg, what in the hell were you doing out there? If I sound pissed, I am! High and fast, high and fast. Is that the only way you know how to fly? Your last pass was good though—a Roger all the way. But you were still a little fast. Now, I always find it necessary to speak, especially to you married guys, about carrier landings. You always tend to add a few extra knots of air speed in honor of your pretty new wives! Then, after that, you start adding extra knots for each kid! Believe me, guys! If you're fast on the approach, I won't give you a cut. Why? Because you'd be heading for a crash! That plane of yours will float right up the deck, your tail hook will miss the arresting gear, and you'll be a crash waiting to happen. That's all! Let's secure for the day."

I got out of my flight gear and into my uniform. No civilian clothes for us—Navy regulations required us to be in uniform when leaving the air station. Bill Austin and the other two guys living at the boarding house were waiting for me. I picked up the keys to the skipper's official car from the squadron duty officer, and after a few lewd remarks about my status as the senior ensign, we headed for the boarding house and our wives.

I wondered what the boarding house would be like, and was glad Jean would have company. I knew it had been lonely for her with so much flying. I had seven days on, and one day off. I wanted some privacy and hoped the room had a double bed. Jean had been giggling about trying to get some rest in a single bed and claimed I kept waking her up in the middle of the night. I reminded her I was a hot Navy pilot, and maybe it was the danger and the excitement of the flying, but I had a hard time keeping my hands off her and wanting to make love to her. She said she wanted a baby, and I guessed we would probably have one.

I love her. I know she wants a baby. I know I'll survive this war . . . I'll make it.

The Boarding House and Ready Room

After work, Bill and I gathered up the other two officers and headed for the officers' club. We stopped for a couple of beers and then left for the boarding house. Suddenly, Bill said, "Turn here, Norm! The boarding house is just down the street." I followed Bill's instructions and turned, heading down the street to the boarding house. As I pulled up in front of the house, I saw Jean standing on the front porch. The house was old. I guessed it had probably been built in the 1890s. The broad front porch ran the full length of the three-story house. It appeared to be well-cared for. I got out of the car and went up onto the porch, gave Jean a warm hug and whispered my thanks for finding a place for us to be together.

Then I said, "What do you think of our car?" as I pointed it out. "The skipper let me use it to get back and forth to work. Not bad for an ensign, right?"

Jean turned to look at the car and pushed me away, saying, "So you and the guys have a car. Can you take me any place tonight? And don't be so sure with your thanks. You haven't seen our room yet."

As we walked onto the porch, I had to explain that the car was only for transportation to work. Jean's response was, "Big deal."

We opened the front door and walked into an entry hall. "What's that odd smell?" I whispered to Jean.

"It's our landlady's cooking. The girls tell me she cooks things like ham hocks and cabbage, eggs and brains, kidneys, beef tongue, even tripe, whatever that is. But wait till you see our room and the bathrooms—no showers, just tubs."

I looked in on a living room as we headed for the stairs and saw some bookshelves filled with books that all appeared to be bound in leather. There was a large upright radio standing along one wall and a card table was set up next to the radio. The furniture, a couch and three overstuffed chairs, were old and worn-looking. The drapes were pulled, so the room was dark. It reminded me of an old funeral home. Not a very hospitable room, I thought, as Jean and I started up the stairs.

"Where's our room, honey? What's it like?" I reached over and patted her gently on her bottom. "Does it have a double bed?"

"Norm, can't you keep your hands to yourself? You leave me to find a place to live and when you see me, all you want is the usual. Go pat one of your airplanes!"

We reached the second floor and, as I moved away from Jean, we started up another flight of stairs.

"Sorry, Darling, it's just that I missed you today. The FCLP was real tough flying—flying so low and slow takes so much concentration. I'm fighting my fear all the time making those approaches."

We reached the third floor and Jean led the way to a door. She opened it. "Here's our love nest, flyboy. Try fighting your fears here. The bathroom's down the hall, and we share it with Joe and Alice. If you listen—there, hear them talking? They're home, and they fight a lot. Then, the worst part—you can hear them making up."

Jean stepped aside as I entered the room. There was a double bed that sagged towards the middle, one old dresser, a desk with one chair and one worn-looking easy chair. I noticed a closet door, and one wall had a small window. There were throw rugs on each side of the bed. The rest of the floor was covered with linoleum. I walked over to the window to look out. All I could see was the back alley with a couple of dogs nosing through the garbage.

I turned back to Jean and moved quickly to her as I saw her tears. Then, through her sobs, I could hear her, "Oh Norm, it's just awful! How can we possibly live here? It's no problem for you—you're gone all day." She pushed me away and, looking at me through her tears, she said, "And then you come home, you pat me on my behind and think everything is all right. Well, it's not all right and I want to know what you're going to do about it! It's either that or I'm going back to Bremerton where I still have a decent place to live!"

When I attempted to put my arms around her, she resisted. I couldn't believe that we were having our first argument. I knew, though, that she was right. I promised her right then that I would contact the housing office at the base first thing the next morning. I would also ask the XO for some time off so we could search the newspapers for rentals. She seemed to feel a bit better. She indicated she realized that all the other wives were in the same situation. None of them were very happy in the boarding house.

I knew I had been wrong. I'd been ignoring Jean's concerns. She must have felt that I resented her being there in Norfolk, and my behavior certainly supported her feelings. She must have thought that all I wanted from her was to take her to bed. I had my flying during the day, and I had her in bed at night. Maybe that night, when we went back to our room, she would accept my apology for my behavior.

Later that evening, we four couples all had our first supper together at the boarding house. It was a ham dish with okra. The ham was quite salty and the okra—well, it was slippery and a little slimy. The green salad was good though. We all ate; after all, we were paying for the food. After dinner, two of the couples started a bridge game. I sat listening to the news on the radio. The battle for Guadalcanal was underway. The Marines had landed and were fighting the Japanese.

I bet that's where we'll be going. Wonder what it's going to be like being shot at—dropping bombs on people?

I looked around for Jean, and when I asked, one of the girls indicated that she had gone upstairs. I decided to wait a while before joining her. I wanted to collect my thoughts before facing her. I was ashamed of my behavior, but I needed to convince Jean that I was truly sorry, that I loved her and wanted her with me.

When I got to our room, Jean was in bed. She had left the small desk lamp on for me. I quickly undressed, turned off the light and slipped quietly into bed. I very carefully kissed the back of Jean's neck and whispered, "I'm sorry, Jean. I'll see you in the morning before I leave. Love you." The only sound was Jean's quiet breathing.

I lay there in the dark, remembering Jean's comment. "It's no problem for you, you're gone all day."

She was right. My life was centered around the squadron ready room, my flying and my flying buddies. That ready room was like a home for me. One wall was all windows with a view of our flight line and our planes. We each had a leather-covered chair with a small desk-like board that we could move up over our laps to write on. Along one wall was a cabinet holding our navigation chart boards. Of course, we had a coffee-making machine, and doughnuts were always available. The blackboard in the front of the room had the daily flight schedule posted. Safety posters on the walls reminded us to fly safely. Hanging from the ceiling were wooden models of various Japanese planes. We had to be familiar with each of the planes because we were given weekly quizzes on enemy aircraft identification. In the back of the room were our flight gear lockers, helmets, flight suits, gloves, and life jackets, called "Mae Wests."

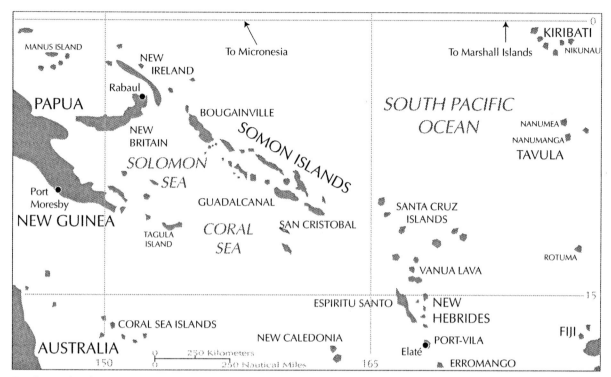

South Pacific Theater

It was here, too, the air intelligence officer (AIO) gave us a weekly briefing. We all knew that our forces had landed on Guadalcanal and that the battle was continuing. During the past week, he told us the Japanese had taken control and established a major base at Rabaul, New Britain. They were now moving down the Solomon Islands setting up bases on the islands of Bougainville, Munda, and Guadalcanal. The Japanese goal was to cut off Australia and take control of the sea lanes in the South Pacific. The Japanese forces had started to build a landing strip on Guadalcanal. On September 15, he told us Japanese aircraft had sunk the carrier USS *Wasp*. Planes from *Wasp* were protecting a supply convoy of ships heading for Guadalcanal. He reminded us that this was secret information. It had not yet been released to the public.

I lay there in the dark, sensing Jean's warm and lush body next to mine.

I know I'll be going to the Pacific. Our carriers will be needed. We only have three large carriers left in the Pacific. I'll be leaving my loving Jean. For the first time since high school, she will not be close by, my anchor. I won't wake her when I leave for the base. We'll talk tonight. Maybe I'll have some good news. I've got to find an apartment for her. Maybe the Austins will join us and help pay part of the rent for an apart-

ment. Jean likes Betty. Got to get some sleep ... on the schedule for
FCLP ... I'm doing better. Got some good "Roger Passes" last time.

I awoke to the sound of rain pounding on our one window. I didn't wake
Jean as I dressed and joined the guys for coffee in the dining room of the boarding house. There were even some sweet rolls ready for us. As we drove to the
base, we all knew there would be no flying because of the weather. It was a little after eight o'clock when the executive officer came into the ready room.

"Norm, is everyone present? Are all your charges bright-eyed and bushy-
tailed?"

"Yes, Sir! All present and accounted!"

Next, we all heard the command, "Attention on deck!" We jumped to our
feet as Commander Butts, our skipper, entered the ready room.

"As you were, gentlemen." We all took our seats as he stood in front of us.
We waited, wondering what brought the skipper to the ready room. It was
unusual. Something important? Were we shipping out early?

The skipper turned to the AIO. "Have you told them about *Chenango*? You
haven't? OK, I'll cover it. Two things, gentlemen. This morning, *Chenango*,
our carrier, left for the Mediterranean with a load of Army pilots and their airplanes on board. They will be engaged in the invasion of North Africa against
the Germans. Those Army guys will fly their fighters off our carrier and land at
captured airfields in Morocco. I know we wish them luck. Don't worry, though,
Chenango will be back for us when our turn comes to deploy. One more thing.
On September 21, the torpedo squadron will fly to N.A.S. Quonset Point,
Connecticut, for torpedo training. We will be dropping live torpedoes without
explosive heads. We'll be there for about a week. For you married officers, you
have my permission to live off base during the period we're at Quonset Point.
There's a very nice hotel in town." He looked directly at me. "Perhaps some of
you might like to have your wives come to Quonset Point. I know Mrs. Butts is
coming with me. That will be all, gentlemen." We all stood as the skipper left
the room.

A week at Quonset Point in a hotel for Jean and me! I still have a week
before we leave to keep looking for an apartment. I'll get over to the
housing office right now. I've got to find a place! I promised Jean.

When all four of us ensigns arrived at the boarding house after work, we
were greeted by four very excited wives. They were all on the front porch like a
welcoming committee.

"Guess what, Norm?" Jean said. "The skipper's wife called me. She told
me about the squadron going to Connecticut for training. Then she asked me, as

the senior ensign's wife, to let her know if any of the wives living here would want to go to Connecticut. All four of us want to go!"

I took both her hands in mine. "Of course, darling, call her back and let her know." I knew our very first argument was over. I knew too that I had to be more understanding of Jean's feelings. Though this may be a great adventure for me, for Jean, it was a fear of the future, of what the war might do to our lives.

That evening after supper, Jean and I took a long walk. The part of Norfolk we lived in was part of the old town. Large, stately homes with spacious lawns, all with large front porches and the customary rocking chairs, lined the streets. Walking along, we could almost imagine horse-drawn carriages clattering along the cobblestone streets. As we strolled along under the old trees, Jean spoke to me about her fears—of my being sent to sea and not returning from the war. She explained to me her deep desire for a child—our child. I responded with my apologies for my behavior and my promise to be more understanding of her worries. I also promised her that we would find an apartment.

We stopped, and I took her in my arms and looking into her green eyes, I told her that we should have a child and that I hoped she would look just like her mother. We were both laughing then as we faced our future together. I knew I would make it home—I had to, we were planning to have a baby!

Quonset Point and Torpedo Run

I felt so relieved about Jean as I drove to the base the next morning. Our relationship was back on an even keel. I had learned a valuable lesson and hoped that never again would I take Jean for granted. I knew that our love had to be nurtured, if it was to last. The stress of the war, of our separation, would offer an even greater challenge. I knew, too, that our decision to have a child would help strengthen our love for one another.

As I drove up and parked at the squadron hangar, I thought that all I had to do now would be to find an apartment for us. That would really help our love affair! Jean hated the boarding house. Maybe when we got back from Quonset Point, the Navy housing office would have something for us.

On 21 September 1942, my log book shows a flight from Norfolk to N.A.S. Quonset Point, Connecticut. Another phase of my training was beginning. The flight schedule had nine of us listed, each flying one of the squadron TBFs to Quonset Point. The rest of the pilots, and some of the key enlisted personnel, were traveling in a Navy transport airplane. Enlisted personnel included the plane captains; and the men who maintained our aircraft, refueling and inspecting each plane before flight. Also on board the transport were the sailors from the squadron ordnance division. These were the men trained in loading our aircraft with ammunition for the guns and bombs. They would be loading the torpedoes aboard our aircraft at N.A.S. Quonset Point for the torpedo training.

We all manned our planes and, one by one, departed for Quonset Point. The weather was clear all the way. Cruising along, I found myself wondering if the wives had departed yet. The skipper's wife had made train reservations for Jean and the other wives. We were all going to meet at a hotel in Quonset. What a week we were going to have!

The training went extremely well. On our first day, we did coordinated torpedo runs. After takeoff, the nine planes joined up, first in a three-plane group. Each group would have a lead plane with the two other planes flying on the left and right side of the lead plane. The formation would look like an inverted *V*. Then the three-plane groups would join into a nine-plane group. In Navy terminology—we would have three, three-plane sections and then, after join up, one nine-plane division.

We climbed to an altitude of 10,000 feet and proceeded to the target area. The purpose of this training flight was to learn how to make a coordinated attack on an enemy ship. In this exercise, the enemy ship was a rock formation out in Long Island Sound. At about eight to ten miles from the target, the lead plane of the nine-plane formation gave a visual hand signal by pumping his arm up over his head. That was the signal to the leaders of each of the three-plane sections on his left and on his right. I was leading the section on the leader's left. When I saw the leader's signal, I began a shallow diving turn to my left and signaled my two wingmen to spread out from our tight formation. I saw the three planes on the leader's right begin their descent as they turned to the right. The leader held his course straight ahead as his section began to descend. When I reached a point where the target was bearing about 45 degrees from my position, I made a sharp turn toward the target. I was at an altitude of about 2,000 feet. I could see the other aircraft spread out, all heading for the target—all of us at about 2,000 feet. The planes looked like a spread-out fan approaching the target. We were covering an ark of about 180 degrees. We had the target bracketed! I had my air speed down to 130 knots and was flying at about 100 to 150 feet above the water. Although we were not carrying a torpedo for training purposes, altitude and air speed were critical to insure a good entry by the torpedo. Too much speed or altitude and the torpedo would break upon entry to the water. We had all arrived at the target within 30 to 40 seconds of each other and all at about the same altitude—50 to 100 feet—and all flying toward the target from slightly different directions. The air space around the target was filled with airplanes! All we had to do now was to follow the procedure we had been briefed on before the flight. The three-plane lead section held its altitude crossing the target. My section of three planes lowered its altitude, just skimming over the target. The other section increased its altitude over the target. There was very little space over the target for the nine planes to clear the target and not collide midair with another aircraft. It was hairy!

We joined up for a second coordinated attack, made one more run, joined up again and headed back to the base.

I hope I'll never have to make a real run. It would be tough flying against an enemy ship, catching heavy AA (anti-aircraft) fire. Low and slow. Of course, using a coordinated attack would increase our luck. All those planes attacking at the same time. If the dive-bombers were attacking too, that would be great. That's what happened to Torpedo Eight. They were the only target. No dive-bombers. Well, don't worry about it now. Just be ready if it happens. There's the field. Hey! We're going to do a low pass over the runway. All nine of us, in formation! Hot stuff!

That evening, we were with our wives for dinner. The skipper and the squadron lieutenants were with their wives at another table. We had all met earlier in the bar for drinks where we met the senior officers' wives. I had to explain to Jean that the Navy was rather formal. Senior officers rarely mixed socially with junior officers. The senior people soon left, but the skipper stopped by our table. He congratulated us for our performance on the torpedo training flight and hoped our wives would enjoy this little holiday. I thought for minute Jean was going to kiss the skipper. She seemed so happy to be there with me.

After dinner, we all went to the nightclub in the hotel. Most of the single guys were there. A small dance band was playing as we and our wives sat down at a table. Soon, the single guys joined us, pulling over an extra table. The party had started! Jean danced with every one of the bachelor pilots. I was told that it was a rule: the bull ensign's wife was expected to dance with all the single pilots. Jean loved it!

We all left the club when the band stopped. All the married couples headed for our rooms off the base. There were a few ribald remarks from the single guys who had to return to the base, but Jean and I didn't care; we were in love and we were going to make a baby!

We were in ground school for the next two days learning about torpedoes. Then on 25 September we went to the flight line to observe our ordnance guys load our TBFs with torpedoes. They were deadly-looking weapons: about 20 feet long and shaped like a cigar. They were made of steel with a compact alcohol-fueled engine that powered a small propeller at the back of the torpedo.

They weighed over 1,200 pounds. These practice torpedoes, of course, did not have an explosive attached to their heads.

When my assigned plane was loaded, I prepared for takeoff. I taxied out, highly aware that my plane was heavily loaded. I would need more runway length for takeoff. After takeoff, I headed out to the torpedo range area. When I arrived in the area, I contacted the range officer by radio. He was located on a small boat charged with retrieving the torpedoes after they were dropped. The drop area was outlined by a series of buoys on each side. I could see more small boats at the end of the marked area; they supported the underwater nets that were designed to stop the torpedo at the end of the drop area.

The range officer's voice suddenly came through on my radio. "TBF approaching the range. The range is clear. You are cleared to make your approach and drop."

I could see the entrance to the range. A line of buoys marked it.

OK, get lined up. What's the compass heading? Check the chart—140 degrees. Altitude: 200 feet. Air speed: 128 knots. Steady now. Bomb bay door open. Hope the damn thing drops out ... there! I'm past the entry buoy. Press the torpedo release switch. There it goes! This plane is a hell of a lot lighter. I can feel the difference. God! What a helpless feeling ... low and slow ... if I was making a run on the enemy ship ... hell! There's no place to go! How would I even avoid the ship I was attacking? No wonder all those guys died in Torpedo Eight, except Ensign Gay.

Then I heard my radio again. "Good approach, TBF. You have a hot run. The weapon is running true and straight. You're cleared to return to base." The next day was our last day of training at Quonset. I flew a TBF back to the air station at Norfolk. I expected Jean, along with the other wives that evening, so I was planning on meeting her at the train station. I would pick them up with the official car and take them to the boarding house. I headed for the ready room, opened my travel bag, got my uniform, and changed from my flight gear. When I stopped on the way out to check my message box, there was a note from the housing office. They said they had an apartment for me to look at. I knew we would take it. Anything would be better for Jean than that boarding house!

I talked with Jean that evening after we returned all the other wives to the boarding house. We agreed we'd take the apartment. Bill and Betty Austin agreed to join us. The apartment was described as a two-bedroom apartment, furnished, with a kitchen and bath. I called the housing office the next morning, agreeing to take the apartment and told them my wife would be moving that day. That evening, Bill and I joined our wives in our new apartment after dropping off the two guys who still lived at the rooming house. I told the guys that I would continue to pick them up at the rooming house and take them to the base.

The four of us sat on a dingy, old couch in a tiny livingroom. Bill and I had just inspected the apartment. The two bedrooms were very small with just enough room for a bed and a dresser. The wallpaper in our bedroom was stained from some old water damage. The kitchen was of ancient vintage. A small four-burner gas stove, a sink that looked like it was made of stone and an icebox, the kind that held ice in the top were the only appliances we could see. There was a pan under the icebox to catch the melting ice water. On the linoleum covering the floor, there was plenty of evidence that water had overflowed many times. Again, like the boarding house, the bathroom had no shower, just a tub and the sink and toilet.

Sitting there, I turned to Jean and Betty, asking, "Did you two girls inspect this lovely little hovel we're going to live in before you paid the rent?"

Both to them started to giggle, and finally Jean said, "Sure we did. It looked like paradise after the boarding house." Both girls stopped giggling, and Jean continued, "Norm, Betty and I are going to fix this place up, get some curtains, some pictures on the walls. We'll be able to fix our own meals. Norm, it's home. Don't you guys worry about us. We're going to be real happy here. And you guessed right, Norm, we did close our eyes when we signed the monthly rental lease."

The next two months were wonderful. Jean was happy with a place of our own. The Austins were wonderful friends and the girls related very well to each other. Betty had told us she was pregnant, and Jean insisted on going with Betty to the hospital for her check-ups. A learning experience, Jean called it.

As for Bill and me, we were very busy getting ready for deployment. We didn't have a date yet, but we knew it wouldn't be long. During the month of October, I logged 27 hours of flight time in 11 days. A great deal of flying time was lost that month due to bad weather. In November, however, the weather improved and I got 59 hours of flight time in 18 days of flying. We were continuing to gain proficiency in glide bombing, gunnery, FCLP, and navigation.

The flight syllabus we were flying was dictated, not by our commanding officer, but by a Navy staff called COMFAIRLANT (Commander Fleet Air Atlantic). A Navy admiral headed the staff. All TBF squadrons training on the Atlantic Coast used the same flight syllabus, and it was designed to ready us for carrier operations in the Pacific. In November, a new element was added to our flying. My log book recorded eight hours of night flying.

Night Flying

I was surprised when, on November 8, my name appeared on the daily flight schedule: "Berg: TBF. Time 2000 hrs. Night Familiarization. That evening, I sat in the ready room with three other pilots. One of the lieutenants was scheduled to brief us on the flight at any moment.

> *Jesus! I haven't done any night flying since Corpus Christi back in 1941! What's the weather like? Sure hope it's clear ... need to see that horizon. Better replace the white lens in my goggles with red lens. I'll get them from my flight gear locker. They will cut out the white lights here in the ready room. Give me better night vision; got to keep bright light out of my eyes. This is just a familiarization flight to help us get the feel of flying at night. Bet we'll be doing night formation flying pretty soon. What about night carrier flying? No, we're not trained for that. No night FCLP; just daytime. Here's the lieutenant.*

I was right about the formation and about the night carrier work. The briefing officer gave us the schedule for the next five nights. We would be practicing joining up, first in three-plane sections and then joining in a nine-plane division. He also told us we would not be landing aboard the carrier at night, because our carriers were not equipped for night operations. What a relief, I thought; day carrier landing will be tough enough. Well, I still had that to look forward to.

The next five nights went smoothly. The weather was cooperative with a big, full moon the last two nights. No mid-air collisions on join-ups. Actually, it was a fine example of teamwork and precision flying. I remember feeling that we were ready for the Pacific. All we had left to do were the carrier landings. Each pilot had to make six carrier landings to be considered qualified to perform all missions from the carrier. I felt I was ready.

When the Thanksgiving holiday arrived in late November, the Austins, along with the other two couples from the boarding house, and Jean and I were all in our tiny apartment for a feast. The turkey was cooked in a baby's bathtub borrowed from a young family living next door. Our celebration had to wait, however, until we could also borrow an extra table and chairs from the same neighbors. We all toasted one another with a Chianti wine poured from a bottle encased in a little straw basket. Jean took the empty bottle and promised to use it as a candleholder at our next Thanksgiving. I remember that she looked at all of us and said, "No matter what happens in the future, let each of us remember this first Thanksgiving together."

The celebration ended soon as four of our friends headed back to the rooming house, and the rest of us helped clean up. There was no shop talk that day, no flying stories. We pilots knew that the skipper had scheduled an all officers' meeting for the day after Thanksgiving. I think we each knew the reason for the

Chapter 5

Heading for the Pacific

The day after Thanksgiving 1942, Bill Austin and I left the apartment before seven in the morning to pick up the other two pilots at the boarding house and head for the base. When we arrived, conversation centered around the meeting with the skipper, although we all agreed it was about deployment. We were concerned about how much time we had there in Norfolk with our wives.

None of our wives was planning on staying in Norfolk, and we were all thinking about making travel arrangements for them. I knew Jean would be going back to Bremerton, but then there was the apartment. I had to help Jean pack our belongings and arrange to have them shipped to Bremerton. We also had to return the dishes and linens that the Navy Relief Society had loaned us to set up the apartment.

Last, but certainly not least, there was one final concern: none of the squadron pilots, including the four of us, had yet to make our first carrier landing. We'd done a lot of FCLPs, but none of us had actually landed on the deck of a carrier.

By eight o'clock, all the pilots from TBF squadron and the dive-bombing squadron were in the ready room. The room was filled with the odor of coffee, cigarette smoke, and sweaty flight suits. The murmuring of conversation continued as to why we were there. It was on everyone's mind. Suddenly, we heard the order, "Attention!" as Commander Butts entered. We quickly stood and came to attention until the skipper said, "As you were, gentlemen."

He stood before us, a big, burly man with rusty-reddish hair that matched his ruddy face. He was chewing on a cigar. Looking at him, I thought, "This is the man we're going to follow into combat, into war." We could all sense his confidence, his willingness to lead us wherever our carrier would take us.

He laid his cigar down in an ashtray on the desk in front of him. "Good morning, gentlemen. Have a good Thanksgiving?" There was a buzz of responses mixed with a few "Yes, Sirs!" He continued. "I guess you're all aware that we lost *Hornet* last month. Her planes were protecting a convoy taking supplies to Guadalcanal when the Jap bombers found her. Her fighters got most of the bombers, but not before she was hit." He paused. "Well, gentlemen, we're not another *Hornet*, but we're heading for the Pacific!"

There was a sudden burst of cheers, of pent up excitement from all of us. Finally, we were going to the war! I remember being just as excited as the rest of the guys. It seemed as if we'd been training forever.

> *But what about Jean? She won't be cheering; she'll be frightened and worried. And she's pregnant; she told me just last night. Sometimes I feel so guilty. Maybe we should've waited until after the war to get married—hell! All I can do is my best. I'm a damn good pilot. I'll come home to Jean and Bremerton a hero ... I'll make it.*

The skipper's voice broke into my thoughts. "Our major problem is getting all of you carrier-qualified. You know that *Chenango* has been supporting the invasion of North Africa. What you don't know is that she was damaged in a storm on her return to Norfolk. She's in the shipyard for repairs. In view of our problem, COMFAIRLANT has made USS *Ranger* available for our carrier qualifications. If you young ensigns don't know, *Ranger* was the Navy's first carrier. As a matter of fact, she was the ship I did my carrier quals on, and I don't feel obligated to tell you how long ago that was!" He stopped, waiting for our laughter to subside. "She's not considered a combat carrier any longer. She's now a training carrier and here are the dates we have for you 'torpecker' pilots." (My pilot log book has the following dates for carrier qualifications: December 10 and 12.) "Now one final thing—the date we've all been training for. We are scheduled to deploy on *Chenango* on December 20. We will be transiting the Panama Canal heading for the South Pacific. May I remind you that our deployment date is secret? Go ahead though with your planning for your wives' departures, but do not tell them the date of our departure. You married officers should make your wives' travel arrangements with our deployment date in mind."

He paused, picked up his unlit cigar and stuck in his mouth. It seemed as though he was looking at each one of us. Then, speaking around the cigar, he said, "It seems to me that you guys are ready. Let's always remember we are a team and we'll face the enemy as a team. I expect each of you to do your duty as a naval officer. We're going to win this war! XO take over."

As we heard the command, "Attention," we all stood again and the skipper left the ready room. As he departed, there was only a low sound of voices. It was as if we were no longer just practicing war. We had a responsibility, a duty to our country to win the war. I stood there among my friends, those men with whom I flew, partied, and had just shared Thanksgiving.

Am I afraid of dying? No, I'm not afraid! I'm too good a pilot ... too well-trained. It can't happen to me. It won't! I have Jean and our baby. It won't happen to me ... it just won't!

The meeting broke up as the pilots from the bombing squadron left for their ready room in another area of the squadron hangar. We all had a flight schedule to meet. I saw that I was on the schedule for FCLP right after lunch. After that morning meeting though, the rest of the day was just routine. All I could think about was Jean leaving for Bremerton.

On the drive home, Bill and I decided we'd tell the girls about the squadron leaving for the Pacific right after dinner. Both the girls took the news quietly. There were no tears, only an acceptance of what they both knew was going to happen. Bill and I were going to the war.

The evening dissolved into a planning session: train reservations for the girls to go home, Jean to Bremerton, Betty to Spokane, Washington; closing the apartment, all the little details that had to be done; packages to be sent via Railway Express; clothes to be carried on the train. Jean and I agreed on a departure date. We decided on December 8, 1942. I felt this would allow us extra time in case reservations were hard to get. I told Jean I would arrange for the tickets through the Navy, as Bill would do for Betty.

Before Norm leaves, a formal photo

That night, as Jean and I slowly undressed each other for bed, holding one another, we realized it would be like this for only a few more days. So little time to express how we both felt: our excitement about our baby, our enduring love for one another, and my promise that I would return to Jean and our child.

Good-bye to Jean Again

Before we knew it, it was time for Jean to leave. I took her to the train station in the official car. It didn't seem possible that it had been only ten days since our Thanksgiving party. We still laughed, though, about the skipper's car. "Is this official business, Norm?" Jean asked, but I could see a few tears as we parked the car. I said good-bye to my Jean that morning. As I waited on the train platform looking at my love waving good-bye from a train window, I felt my tears come. I had to make it back to her. I had to! I missed Jean, but I was relieved, too. I sensed Jean may have felt the same way. She was going home to have her baby and that was her priority. Now, I could concentrate on flying off a carrier and coming back alive. I would miss her and I loved her, but I had a job to do. I wanted to get it over with and to get back home.

According to the telegram I received at the squadron, Jean arrived safely in Seattle three days later. I was relieved she had had such a good trip. With so much military activity, train travel was often difficult. I didn't learn until I received my first letter from Jean how she'd managed it. She had an uncle who worked for the Great Northern Railroad and he lived Seattle, so she called him from Chicago, which was as far as her Norfolk train reservation was valid. He arranged a bedroom for her on a train from Chicago to Seattle. Her letter read, "Norm, I traveled with twelve Army Air Force pilots. They took turns taking me to the dining car. Darling, I had a great trip. They were properly impressed when I told them I was married to the best naval aviator in the fleet." I remember how much I loved her first letter.

A Date with an SBD

The next few days were hectic. I had two more flights of FCLP. Man, I was ready for that carrier! I was getting all "Roger passes." I also received an unexpected opportunity. Lieutenant Malanosky, our LSO, asked me if I'd like to fly the SBD, which was the type of plane that sank the Japanese carriers at the Battle of Midway. My log book showed two flights on December 5, 1942. I took that bird up to 10,000 feet and really did some practice dive-bombing. It was sure different from glide-bombing with the TBF! With the SBD, my dives were straight down, not the shallow dive we used with the TBF. I remember thinking, as I landed the SBD, that maybe I could get transferred to the dive-bomber squadron. No, I think the skipper wanted me in torpeckers [torpedo pilots].

An SBD – Navy dive bomber, Douglas Aircraft Co.

Getting Carrier-Qualified

Finally, on December 10, 1942, I was on the flight schedule for carrier quals. There were six of us scheduled for the afternoon flight. We were all in the ready room in the squadron hangar at the Naval Air Station when the morning flight returned. What a bunch of hot pilots. All six had qualified on USS *Ranger*. Bill Austin was one. "A real breeze, Norm. Nothing to it," he yelled at me from across the room.

The ready room quieted down as the morning flight left for lunch. I didn't feel like eating—a little nervous I guess. We'd been briefed about USS *Ranger* and the procedures we would follow for our carrier qualification flights. I decided to review my notes on the briefing before flying out to *Ranger* for the actual carrier qualification landings.

Ranger's flight deck was 634 feet long. The deck area used for landings took up about one-third the total flight deck. The landing area had nine arresting cables stretched across the deck. These cables were designed to stop the aircraft on landing. All our carrier planes had a tail hook attached to the back and at the bottom of the fuselage. As a plane landed, the hook would engage one of the cables. The cables were held about three inches off the flight deck by curved metal lifts. Each cable was attached to a hydraulic piston located below the flight deck. Each of the nine cables was set at a different hydraulic pressure. The first cable, for example, would give a fairly soft stop on landing; however, if the ninth cable was engaged because the plane landed long, the plane would stop like it had hit a brick wall. Just past the ninth cable were two barriers that could be raised or lowered by personnel standing at the barrier controls. When aircraft were landing, these barriers were raised. They were designed to stop any aircraft that failed to hook an arresting cable. If the aircraft landed safely, the barriers would be lowered. I knew, when my chance came to qualify aboard, my goal was to land so the plane would engage the first arresting cable.

As I turned to another page in my notes, I felt I needed to review the procedures I would follow after my first landing. I knew I would be expected to get ready to make a takeoff from the carrier. Each pilot needed six landings to be carrier-qualified. Flight operations would continue until all six of us had made our six landings.

After landing, the first action would be a flight deck sailor would detach the tail hook from the arresting cable. The pilot would then retract the plane's landing flaps, retract the tail hook, and unlock the plane's tail wheel. A flight deck director would approach the aircraft, signal the pilot to taxi ahead to the take-off spot. Once at the take-off spot, the flight deck director would signal the pilot by raising his arm and holding up two fingers. The pilot would stand on the plane brakes by pushing on the top of the rudder pedals, go to half power on the throttle and go over the take-off checklist, which consisted of about six items listed on a metal plaque on the instrument panel. The pilot would then give a thumbs-up signal to the flight deck director that he was ready for take off.

Control of the aircraft was then passed to the flight deck officer. This officer, wearing a bright yellow shirt, would take a position to the right of the aircraft where he had a clear view of the pilot in the plane's cockpit. He would confirm that the flight deck was clear and would then raise his arm and start to twirl his hand with three fingers extended. This was the signal to go to full power on the plane's engine. One final check of the instruments, and the pilot would salute the flight control officer to indicate, "I'm ready for take off." The flight control officer would then turn and point his arm toward the bow of the ship. The pilot would release the brakes and fly the aircraft off the deck, making a slight right turn and begin to climb to 500 feet where he would then re-enter the flight pattern around the carrier and prepare for another landing.

Suddenly, I heard, "Hey, Berg, better get your flight gear. It's time to get those landings in and you're our mighty leader. Let's go!" I tossed my briefing notes aside and quickly got into my flight gear, which was all in my locker at the back of the ready room.

We each had a navigation chart board at our chairs as we did the navigation planning to take off from Norfolk and rendezvous with *Ranger*. She was operating about 65 miles due east of the air station at Norfolk. I called flight operations to check the weather and was given a report of: ceiling 2,500 feet broken; visibility twelve miles; wind from the southeast at twelve knots. When I asked about a weather report from *Ranger*, the reply was, "Sorry, we don't have a weather report from *Ranger*."

Despite this, I decided to launch, assuming the weather at *Ranger* would be OK for carrier work. All six planes were airborne and joined me in two three-plane sections a little after 1300 hours. I set up a heading of 087 degrees and headed for *Ranger*'s estimated position. After about 15 minutes, the ceiling began to lower. To stay clear of the clouds, I reduced altitude until we were flying about 500 feet above the ocean. Visibility was dropping too, and some raindrops began striking my wind screen.

Using my call sign and *Ranger*'s call sign, "Papa," I radioed the rest of the flight. "Alpha flight, this is Bull. Close up. Contacting Papa One now." The five other planes tightened up the formation. My two wingmen practically had their wing tips in my cockpit!

"Papa One, this is Alpha flight. ETA at Papa twelve minutes. Request weather conditions. Over."

Very quickly, I received a reply, "Alpha flight operations canceled due to weather. Return to base. Out."

"Alpha flight, this is Bull. Returning to base due to weather. Turning to a heading of 267 degrees. Maintaining 500 feet. Turning now."

By the time we got back to the air station, the ceiling was down to 1,000 feet, and it was raining. I made the landing, taxied up our flight line and shut down. I just sat there for a few minutes. So much for carrier quals.

It was kinda of hairy out there. The guys did good. Nobody panicked. No one broke away on their own. Good discipline. We're all home safe. I'll buy the first round tonight. I must admit I'm looking forward to being with the guys. Squadron spirit is so important and so is discipline. This outfit has both. It's going to be a great cruise!

The squadron's next scheduled carrier quals were set for 12 December 1942. This time I rode as a passenger in the radio compartment of George Hartman's TBF. George was a classmate from Corpus and the ferry command and a fine pilot. I trusted him. There were six planes in this flight. I was in the radio compartment of George's plane as the flight headed out to *Ranger*, which was still operating off the coast of Norfolk. The plan was that after George completed his first landings, I would get out of his plane and wait on the ship until he completed five more landings. Then we would switch places and I'd take his plane and do my landings. George dropped me off after his first landing. I headed for the flying bridge, one deck below the ship's bridge where *Ranger's* captain controlled the flight operations. I watched the landings until I saw George make his sixth landing. It was time to head down to the flight deck.

As George made his sixth landing, he followed the directions of the flight deck director to the take-off spot where I was waiting. We were ready to switch pilots. A flight deck sailor quickly put wheel chocks in front of the plane's landing gear to keep it from moving. The plane's engine was not shut down as George and I quickly changed places. I got settled onto the parachute and the seat belt and hooked up the plane's radio to my helmet. The flight director gave me the signal to add power, brakes on, tail hook up, wing flaps down. The wheel chocks were removed.

Then the flight deck officer in his yellow shirt raised his arm above his head and he began rotating his hand, three fingers extended. He was looking at me, waiting. I checked my instruments, all OK. I flipped him a hand salute, his arm dropped, pointing forward as I went to full power and released the plane's brakes. Man, that ocean looked mighty close as I cleared the flight deck and made the slight right turn and climbed to 500 feet. I was ready for my first carrier landing. I turned to the downwind leg: gear down; tail hook down; landing flaps down; altitude 300 feet; air speed 85 knots.

Next, I saw a plane on final approach. The pilot appeared to take the cut signal from the LSO, but he drifted to the right of the flight deck. As he hit the deck, the plane bounced to the right as the hook engaged a cable. I watched the plane go over the side of the flight deck. The landing gear dropped into the catwalk alongside the flight deck. That, and the fact the tail hook was still engaged with an arresting cable, kept the plane from going over the side into the ocean. I could see the pilot scrambling out of the cockpit. My radio crackled. *Ranger* was calling, "This is Papa One. Flight operations canceled. All aircraft return to base. Out."

There were five of us in the pattern. I climbed to 1,000 feet, flying upwind and passing *Ranger* on the starboard side. "This is Bull. Join on me. My position, upwind leg passing Papa's starboard side. Turning to a heading 270 degrees, altitude 1,000 feet. Bull out."

As we headed back to the base, I thought, so much for carrier landings! I guess I'd go to sea without being carrier-qualified. The squadron was scheduled to board *Chenango* in eight days. I guessed Joe Johnson, the guy who went over the side, would have nice ride home, along with George who was supposed to fly back with me after I made my sixth landing. The ship would return to Norfolk to remove the crashed plane. I wondered if the chow (food) was good on *Ranger*. Eventually, I saw the field and requested a low pass and a carrier break, thinking I might as well have some fun. Tomorrow was another day.

Loading the Carrier

For me, squadron flight activity had almost ceased as the squadron completed the planning to board *Chenango*. My last flight before deployment was on December 15. It was field carrier landing practice (FCLP). The landing signal officer (LSO) was determined to keep me ready for landing aboard *Chenango*, even if it was after we left for the South Pacific. It was obvious to me that I'd have to qualify after we were at sea. That raised some interesting questions. What if there was a deck crash like the last time I tried to qualify? All I did then was fly back to Norfolk. We'd be a long way from land and heading for Panama. What if the ship couldn't get the deck clear for a landing? What then? Land in the ocean after running out of fuel? It was going to be interesting to say the least.

My thoughts were interrupted when I heard my name called. "Mr. Berg, the executive officer would like to see you in his office." I followed a young sailor down the passageway to the XO's office. The office door was open; he saw me and said, "Come in, Norm. Sit down." He's certainly informal today, I thought. I took a chair in front of his desk, but without the usual, "Reporting as ordered, Sir."

He came right to the point. "Norm, I have a job for you. Normally I'd assign one of the lieutenants to this task, but the skipper has granted them leave until we deploy on the 20th. Their families are remaining here in Norfolk, and he wanted to give them as much time at home as possible. I know you're married too, but I understand that your wife has left for her parents' home."

I nodded my confirmation that Jean had left.

"Norm, you're well aware of the difficulties we've had getting our pilots carrier-qualified. In fact, you're one of them. I know, too, that you're very aware of the problems we've had with weather and deck crashes. The weather forecast for the 20th, our departure date, is marginal for flight operations. Yesterday, the skipper had a conference with the captain of *Chenango*. The decision was made that we will hoist our planes aboard the ship at dockside. Our TBFs will be towed by tractor to the dock where *Chenango* is moored. Using the ship's crane, each plane will be hoisted aboard. The boarding date is the 19th commencing at 0800 hours. Norm, I want you in charge of the loading. Crews have been assigned to supervise the towing of the aircraft from the squadron area to the dock area. You will meet each aircraft and insure that it is safely loaded aboard the carrier. I have every confidence in you, Norm. Now, any questions?"

"Just one question, Sir. Who's in charge of having the planes towed to the dock?"

The executive officer told me it was Chief Petty Officer Williams.

"He's a top man, Norm, plenty of experience. He'll get those planes to you for loading right on time. And don't worry about the ship; they will be ready for you. Anything else?"

I responded with. "Yes, Sir! I'll get them aboard."

"OK, Norm. I'll see you on the 20th aboard ship."

Damn it! This loading job! I don't know anything about loading airplanes on ships! And Chief Williams. He's the most senior enlisted man in the squadron. I'm a pilot. I don't load planes on carriers! How do you order an enlisted man to do something? Do you say, "Please do this?" Well, all I can do is be at the dock and do my best.

That night, the officers' club was quiet. I guessed that everyone was on leave except me. None of the squadron guys were there. I left the club and headed for *Chenango*. I had checked out of the bachelor officers' quarters (BOQ) when the ship tied up at the dock, and I had a bunk in a space with five other squadron guys. We called the area "Boys' Town." We each had a locker for our clothes. It was pretty primitive, but we knew it would serve us well throughout the cruise.

I was at the dock at 0730 on December 19. *Chenango* was moored alongside. My home away from home for—hell, I didn't know. Then I saw the first TBF approaching the dock. Sitting on the tractor towing the plane was the chief. When he saw me, he signaled the tractor driver to stop. He got off the tractor, approached me, saluted and said, "Good morning, Mr. Berg. Nice to see you, Sir."

I returned his salute and, in my deepest voice, I said, "Chief, I'm here to supervise the loading of our aircraft. Please get on with it now."

He looked at me, "Sir, may the chief make a suggestion?" I responded with a nod. "Sir, may I suggest you go aboard ship and have a cup of coffee? I will carry out your order, Sir."

I looked at Chief Williams, then at the four gold stripes on the sleeve of his uniform representing 16 years of service in the Navy. He wore the Good Conduct ribbon on his chest, with three stars on the ribbon. He had never been involved in any disciplinary action. "Hells bells," I thought, "let the chief do it! He sure as hell knows what he's doing."

A smile broke out on both our faces. "Chief, that's a fine suggestion. Coffee would taste good. Please carry on. I will check with you after lunch. I suspect all aircraft will be aboard by then."

"They certainly will be, Sir. I'm planning on having a nice dinner with my family tonight. It's going to be a long cruise, Sir."

Anchors Away

On December 20 at 0800, the officers and men of *Chenango* and all the aviation squadron personnel were on the flight deck. We were in formation, long lines of sailors and officers standing at attention as our ship moved away from the dock. A Navy band was on the dock. As we pulled away, we could all hear the tune of "Anchors Away" and then the "Navy Hymn." Some of the words came to me: "Oh God, care for those in peril on the sea." The slowly disappearing dock was filled with wives and children. Everyone was singing the "Navy Hymn" as they waved good-bye to their men of *Chenango*.

It was a very emotional moment for me as the ship moved away from the dock. All the excitement of getting ready to leave seemed to evaporate. I looked down and saw the space between the ship and the dock widen. The water was oily-looking, grayish, but as the space widened, I knew I was moving into a dangerous environment. The sea was unforgiving, and I was going there. I felt a moment of fear, fear of the future. I turned away from the view of the water. To hell with it! I was going to make it! I headed down the catwalk, a walkway just below the level of the flight deck. I was going to our pilots' ready room. I needed some company.

The ready room was crowded, but I found a chair in the back of the room. A lot of conversation was going on as we all waited for lunch. The spaces looked very similar to our ready room back at the base—leather chairs that reclined, a coffee maker, the smell of cigarette smoke, a blackboard. There was a significance difference though. We now heard the low hum of the ship's engines and the sound of the ocean moving along the hull of our carrier. Plus, there were the sounds of the ship itself. As the ship rolled due to the wave action, we all heard the creaking sounds of metal rubbing together; of things moving in work spaces and on the flight deck, aircraft tie downs; everything scraping together. The sounds of a moving ship; sounds we would learn to live with.

An announcement came over the ship's P.A. system: "The officers' ward-room is now open for lunch." With that, we moved quickly to the ward room, which was the officers' dining area. The food was served family-style at tables for eight. There were actually three dining areas on the ship: the officers' ward room, the chiefs' mess, and the ship's galley for the sailors. As pilots, we soon discovered our daily lives centered around the ready room and the ward room. The ward room became an area for reading, for bridge games, and for socializing. The ship's executive officer, who was the senior officer of the ward room, had just one rule: Officers did not discuss women, politics, or religion in the ward room.

After lunch, I wandered back to the ready room. Some of the guys were in their assigned bunkroom, stowing their clothes, trying to get settled. I sat there adjusting to the sounds of the ship, the wind moving over the flight deck, the sound of the water along the hull, when Lieutenant Shyrock, the squadron operations officer, entered the ready room.

"Hi, Norm, waiting for tomorrow's flight schedule? You're on it—the morning flight for carrier landing qualifications."

I watched as he wrote the schedule on the blackboard. There I was: "0800 Berg: TBF number 00862. Carrier Quals." Finally, I was going to land aboard the carrier.

"Norm, the pre-flight briefing will be at 0630. The LSO will do the briefing along with the ship's flight deck officer. See you in the morning."

Carrier Quals at Sea

I didn't get a lot of rest that night. Too many strange noises from the ship and then all the procedures I would have to follow trying to land aboard were not conducive to sleep. I still felt rested, though, as I arrived at the ready room at 0630. Three other pilots gathered in the ward room for breakfast before the briefing.

The LSO began the briefing. "OK, guys, you've all done well with the FCLP. You all know the landing signals that I'll be using. Berg, you still tend to be a little fast on the final. Get set up on the downwind leg, with your altitude and speed correct for a landing. Now, one word of warning. You're not landing on a runway like in FCLP. This is a moving landing platform. The runway where you've been doing FCLP was not 60 feet above the surface, and it was not moving forward and up and down. You may feel a bit disoriented on your first pass. Guys, just follow my signals, and I'll get you aboard. OK, I'll turn you over to the flight deck officer."

Damn! What's this disorientation stuff? Just follow his signals he says. "Berg, you're fast" ... well, what's my choice? OK, calm down. Hundreds of Navy pilots have made carrier landings. Just go do it!

We listened up as the flight deck officer reviewed the signals we would receive after landing and preparing to take off again. "Tail hook retracted; landing flaps down; taxi to take-off spot; go over take-off checklist; hold brakes; turn up full power; salute when ready for takeoff."

He continued, "Remember pilots, we want each of you to make six landings. Flight conditions are near perfect. We have 12 to 15 knots of wind from the southeast. The carrier will turn into the wind for flight operations. The carrier speed will be 14 knots. This combination will give us an average of 26 to 29 knots of wind over the deck for landings. Any questions? OK, I'll see you on the flight deck. Good luck."

I quickly calculated my final approach's air speed by estimating my plane would be going around 80 knots as I approached the flight deck, subtract the wind over the deck of 26 to 29 knots from my 80 knots of indicated air speed, and my actual speed on final approach would be between 51 and 54 knots. Damn! He was right—perfect conditions. This was going to be a snap!

The order came over the intercom in the ready room, "Pilots, man your planes." As the four of us headed for the flight deck, I thought of those pilots at the Battle of Midway, old Torpedo Eight; they all had heard the same message. For me, this time it was just for carrier quals. For them, it was death in battle.

My thoughts quickly shifted back to the situation at hand as I arrived on the flight deck. My plane was spotted second for takeoff. A young sailor helped me strap on my parachute and hook up the radio cords to my helmet. I checked my fuel switches and flight controls. Then I heard, "Pilots, start your engines." This command came from a loud speaker mounted on the ship's bridge above the flight deck. Not only did it tell the pilots what to do, it warned the deck crew to stand clear of the planes.

Within a few seconds, all four of us had our plane's engines started. I began going over my take-off checklist: flaps down, engine mags checked, all engine instrument normal. I felt ready for takeoff—my first one from a carrier. I watched as the plane ahead of me got the take-off signal from the flight deck officer. I could hear his plane's engine roaring at full power as he began moving toward the bow of the ship. As I watched, he was airborne well before he reached the end of the flight deck. It's all that wind over the deck, I thought. Nothing to these carrier takeoffs.

I slowly taxied my TBF to the take-off spot. Holding my brakes, I responded to the flight deck officer's signal, and went to full power by advancing the throttle. My plane was shaking as I held my brakes on. One final check of the engine instruments—all OK. I saluted the flight deck officer and released my brakes as I saw his arm point to the bow of the ship. I was rolling! As soon as I was airborne and clear of the ship's deck, I made a slight turn to the right, and raised my landing gear. Flying straight ahead, I reduced power, raised my landing flaps and leveled off at 500 feet. I had to set up to make my first carrier landing.

A sense of calm swept over me. All the hours of field carrier landing practice (FCLP), my trust in the LSO and perfect flying conditions, gave me all the confidence I needed. The plane that had taken off ahead of me was off to my left. He was on the downwind leg of his approach, ready to turn toward the carrier for his first landing. Lowering my landing gear and my tail hook, I made a 180-degree turn to the left. Reducing power and losing altitude, I stopped my turn. The plane was now level at 200 feet. My plane was flying the downwind leg of my approach, with the carrier about 400 yards to my left. My landing flaps were lowered, and when the plane was abreast of the stern of the carrier, I began an easy turn toward the carrier. My altitude was only 100 feet above the ocean, air speed 78 knots. Rolling out of my turn, the plane was directly astern of the carrier on final approach for my first landing.

Suddenly, the LSO came into view out of the left side of my cockpit. He was giving me a high signal! Ease off a little power, lower the nose. There's a Roger! Air speed right on. There's my cut. Cut the throttle—ease back on the control stick—the flight deck came rushing up at me. The plane hit hard, caught a wire and threw me forward against my seat belt. I was aboard! Only five more to go.

My pilot log book has an entry for December 21. "One point seven hours of flight time. Purpose: Carrier Qualifying on *Chenango*; Six landings." I made it! I was a Navy carrier pilot.

Protecting the Ship from Enemy Subs

After my sixth landing, I switched places with another pilot, helped him get the chute on and hook up his radio, and then I headed for the ready room. It was apparent that carrier quals were going to proceed until all the torpecker pilots were qualified. After grabbing a cup of coffee in the ready room, I slumped down into a chair. I felt drained—mentally I was still flying that plane, 100 feet over the ocean.

Jesus, a couple of times I got too slow. The damn airplane was shaking ... it almost quit flying! The LSO sure can't complain that I was too fast! That last landing was a bitch. I was too fast and the plane floated up the deck after the cut. Lucky I caught a wire. I stopped damn quick—damn! Six landings one after the other are too many! I sure feel good though ... I did it!

When the announcement came over the squawk box, "Secure flight operations," all the TBF pilots were in the ready room. The last plane had landed, and we were all waiting for the LSO. We had all qualified, but we knew our LSO would have a few choice words for each of us. He walked into the ready room, the signal paddles still in his hand. He started with me.

"Berg! What's this signal mean?" He moved the paddles rapidly back and forth out in front of his body at waist level.

I stood. "Sir, it means I was slow. But Sir, you always tell me I'm too fast on my approach. I was just following orders, Sir!"

He just stood there looking at all of us. "OK, guys, you all did good. You answered my signals, and I saved your butts. I got you all qualified, and Berg, you buy the first round of beer when we get to Panama. Don't you ever scare me like that again. You were *too* damn slow! God himself must have been holding your plane in the air. That's it. Let's go to lunch."

Following lunch, most of the squadron pilots wandered back to the ready room. We were still talking about our approaches and landings, trading information, sharing some tips on carrier approaches, asking about how best to respond to the LSO's signals, helping one another. It was part of being a squadron pilot.

Our bull session was interrupted by the ship's intercom. "Now hear this! All torpedo squadron pilots report to the ready room."

In a few moments, the remainder of our pilots came in, along with the operations officer, Lieutenant Bill Shyrock, and our air intelligence officer, Lieutenant Joe Anson. Lieutenant Shyrock opened the meeting congratulating all of us on qualifying aboard.

"Fellas," Lieutenant Shyrock continued, "perhaps some of you have noticed that the ship is now constantly changing course and speed. There's a damn good reason for this—German submarines! A carrier is most vulnerable when it maintains a steady course and speed. That's when it becomes an easy target for a sub. The ship's captain expects you pilots to launch and recover in the minimum of time. Believe me, he hates keeping the ship into the wind on a steady course while a pilot messes up an approach and gets a wave off. He really gets upset if the same pilot gets a second wave off!" He paused for emphasis and then continued, "Before I turn this meeting over to Lieutenant Anson, who will brief you on the German and Japanese submarine situation, there's one more point I must make."

I was watching Bill Shyrock. He was over six feet tall, blond, and looked like he could play football as a pass-catching end. What surprised me was that he was usually very relaxed

Landing signal officer (LSO) waving an aircraft aboard with a Roger Pass signal

around us junior pilots. Right now, it appeared that he hated what he was going to say. He seemed to take a deep breath. "Gentlemen, as of this moment you will maintain radio silence on all flights from the carrier. The ship will also maintain radio silence. The risk of enemy submarines homing in on radio transmissions is too great a risk to the ship. Visual flag signals from the bridge will be used to control aircraft recoveries. Gentlemen, your navigation plotting board, the ship's YE, the carrier's homing beacon, and your skill as a pilot will keep you alive. Any questions?" (A ship's YE system was Morse code letters that identified itself as belonging to that ship. Each carrier would have different Morse code letters.)

There was one question from the back of the room. "Sir, what if we have an engine failure—have to land in the water? Can we transmit our position to the ship?"

"Yes, if it were me, I'd transmit. The ship's captain would have to make a decision. Does sending one of the accompanying destroyers to your last position hazard the position of the carrier? I don't know what his decision would be. Anything else? OK, Lieutenant Anson, take over."

As Joe Anson started his briefing on the submarine problem, my thoughts drifted.

Radio silence. No transmissions. It's tough to understand. A pilot's life possibly being traded for the carrier being hit by a torpedo. Be sure that the plane's engine is operating properly. Can't risk an engine failure. Watch my navigation. No mistakes. Got to stay concentrating on

the wind direction ... a wind change could blow the plane off course.
Wonder when I'll get my first flight off the ship. Jesus! Radio silence.
The captain has to do it; can't risk the carrier ... what's Anson saying?

I began to listen as Anson continued the briefing. "Fellas, this sub danger is real. The Germans have sunk over a hundred merchant ships in 1942 alone. These losses have occurred all along the East Coast as well as in the Gulf of Mexico. We have to expect that German subs will join the Japanese in the Pacific. We are finding ways to cut our losses. We are using a convoy system here in the Atlantic, rather than having single ships sailing alone. By doing so, we can concentrate our defenses against the subs. The best defense we have will be our own planes, our TBFs armed with depth charges. Currently, long-range patrol planes from bases in Florida are flying antisub patrols in our area. Their mission is to keep any sub from getting a visual sighting on us using their periscope. The very presence of aircraft in our area is a real deterrent to a sub commander. Any questions?"

"Joe, how in the hell can that periscope be spotted if the sub has it extended?" someone asked.

"Well, if the sea is fairly calm and wind force is under twelve knots, the periscope will cause a 'feather' of white as it moves through the water. A higher wind speed makes it more difficult to see the feather. Of course higher wind conditions give the sub commander a problem too. It cuts his visibility through the periscope. Any more questions?"

Bill Shyrock now stood. "As of tomorrow at 0600, we take over our own antisub patrols. The land-based patrol planes mentioned earlier will no longer protect us. He paused and looked at me. "Norm, your first off at 0600—briefing at 0500." He named three other pilots also flying the early flight. "Just a word about the ship's YE. I mentioned before that it can save your life. It will get you back to the ship. I'm sure you all remember how to use it, but let me review how it works. The ship does have one of the first experimental radars aboard. However, even if the ship has your plane on radar, with radio silence in effect, the ship won't contact you. The radar can't help you, the YE will."

Bill drew a circle on the blackboard. He then drew a series of lines from the center of the circle to the outside of the circle. He divided the circle into a series of roughly 15-degree pieces so that it looked like a pie ready to be cut. Next he inserted a different letter of the Morse code into each piece. The drawing now had a series of dots and dashes in each segment. He turned back to us.

"Now guys, imagine the ship at the center of the circle. The YE is nothing more than a radio transmitter mounted on the ship. It continually broadcasts a series of Morse code signals, a different letter in each segment. The range is about 30 miles at sea level. The range increases with your plane's altitude. OK, so far?

"Let's pretend you're flying the inbound leg of an antisub search. Your navigation plan indicates you're about 40 miles from the ship. You're flying at 1,000 feet. You flip the switch on your YE receiver—compass heading is 070 degrees. You hear 'dit da, dit da' on the YE—Morse code for *A*. You hold your heading. Now you begin to hear a different Morse code signal. You check the YE chart on your navigation board. It has all the Morse code letters entered on the chart. You begin to hear an *S*. You're drifting off to the right from the *A* quadrant to the *S* quadrant. You adjust your heading by turning a few degrees to the left until you get a solid *A* again. Now you're on the correct bearing for the ship. After a few minutes, you see the ship. Home again!

"One more important point. The sequence of the Morse code letters is changed each day. This prevents an enemy ship from getting a radio fix on the ship. If you don't have the correct codes for the day on the YE chart, all you will hear is a series of meaningless Morse code letters. Believe me guys, that's all you'll get if you don't change the code on the YE chart each time you're on the flight schedule. That's all for today. See you all in the ward room for dinner."

The pilots drifted off, some to their bunks for a nap, others to the ward room for a bridge game. I went to the ship library to check it out. It was going to be a long cruise! I hoped there would be some recent books aboard. There was not much to fill the time other than flying or getting ready to fly. Of course, we didn't fly every day. The antisub flights were shared with pilots from the dive-bombing squadron too. There were occasions as well when the weather prevented flight operations. Low visibility, rain or high winds would cancel flight operations.

Sometimes there were evening movies on the hangar deck, but the choice was limited. With no exercise equipment on board, most of us would jog on the flight deck to get some exercise. Most of our time, however, was taken up in bull sessions about flying. Flying was our life, and we spent a lot of time talking about it.

I turned in early that night. I wanted to get some rest before that 0600 launch in the morning. I was not anticipating any problem with the navigation. The squadron executive officer had been holding refresher sessions with all of us. I felt very confident that my navigation planning would get me home. As I lay there in my bunk, though, a tiny, nagging issue remained.

Radio silence. I would be out of touch with the ship for the entire flight. No matter how good my navigation was, I still might have engine trouble. I might fly into bad weather or the YE might fail. What if the wind changes and I don't see it? God! Two or three hours flying over that big, lonely ocean with no land within flying range. Just the carrier. It's going to seem like a damn long flight. To hell with it! Get some sleep, Norm.

I got to the ready room right at 0500 after coffee and rolls in the ward room. The other three pilots were already there. We got all the info we needed to do our navigation from the information on the blackboard. The four search sectors, all ahead of the ship, covered a 180-degree arc. The outbound leg was 75 miles for all the sectors. We copied the YE information onto our navigation boards. All we needed now was a weather report from the ship's aerology department, and the ship's course and its speed for the next two hours. The ship's navigator came up on the intercom from the bridge with information on the planned course and speed of the ship. We all plotted this information onto our navigation plotting boards. Then came the weather: Scattered clouds, visibility twelve miles, wind three to five knots from the southeast.

The wind is sure no factor in the navigation planning I thought, as I began laying out my compass headings and flight time for each leg of my flight. I had just finished entering the figures when the ship's catapult officer came into the ready room.

We all looked at him. He had a big smile on his face.

"Gentlemen, I'm your friendly cat officer, and you pilots are about to meet my favorite toy, my catapult. It's only about 80 feet long, but it will give you a real kick in the butt! As you might guess, there's insufficient wind to launch you with a deck take off. With the ship's top speed of 18 knots, we'd only get a max of 22 knots over the deck. That's not enough for the TBF, especially when each of your planes has four depth charges hanging in the bomb bays. You know, you just might see a sub!"

I sat there a bit stunned—a catapult shot! What next? Well, I was a carrier pilot! No choice but to get on with it!

He continued. "Here's how it's going to work. After you man your aircraft and get your engines started, you'll be passed to my control. I'll direct you to taxi your plane into position on the cat. Then one of my crew will attach a small copper ring to the back of your plane and to a hold-down bar on the deck of the carrier. Another man will attach the catapult harness to brackets on the inside of both your landing gear struts. Now we're ready. I'll be standing to your right where I can see you. I'll give you a two-finger turn up." He stopped to be sure he had our attention. He sure did!

"I want to hear your engine at full power. Go over your check-off list. Be sure all engine instruments are normal. Now, be sure your feet are off the top of your rudder pedals. You don't want your brakes on! That little copper clamp will hold your plane from moving, believe me. There's a headrest behind you. Pull it out until you feel the back of your head resting against it. Now, when you're ready, toss me a salute, and I'll give you the ride of your life!"

The next thing we heard was the order: "Pilots, man your planes."

I got my plane started and quickly received the signal to taxi to the catapult area.

Goddamn it! Don't hurry me! I'm getting frantic signals to get in place on the cat. There's the signal that I'm in place and hooked up. There's the two finger signal from the cat officer ... OK ... go to full power ... feet off the brakes. Everything looks good. Hope that little brass ring holds. Take-off checklist completed. Go ahead ... give him a salute. Let's go flying!

When I gave the catapult office my salute, he began the action to fire the catapult. This was a hydraulic catapult. Hydraulic pressure forced a piston forward. Attached to the piston were the cables that were hooked to my landing gear struts. I was airborne in about ten seconds! It worked just like a kid's sling-shot!

What a ride! Get the nose down. The plane wants to climb. Gear up ... reduce power ... milk the flaps up slowly. Damn, that cat shot really jerked my head back. Next time, I'll rest my head against it before the shot. I really hit the back of my head on that head rest. Everything seems fine. What's that heading for the first leg? Might as well shut off the radio; got to do it alone. Engine sounds fine. Just pay attention to the navigation; remember you want to get home to Jean. Better check the YE. Wonder if I'll find a sub. Where are the switches for arming those depth charges?

I had two crewmen aboard the plane. I met them at the plane and briefed them on the flight. I told them I would give a warning on the intercom reminding them to brace themselves for the cat shot. I reminded them, too, that their job during the flight was to keep a sharp lookout for any evidence of a sub. Smitty, who was in the ball turret with the .50-caliber machine gun, and McElroy, who was in the radio compartment, both had windows, so they could observe the ocean as the flight progressed. I also reminded them about radio silence. I told them both that I would talk with them throughout the flight. I felt that at least I had someone to talk to even if I couldn't call the carrier.

Once we were airborne, the flying time was totally uneventful. In fact, it was quite boring. Weather was perfect. The engine was operating smoothly. My navigation was accurate. I saw the carrier exactly at the time and place planned by the navigation calculations. Within about five minutes, the other three planes arrived. Since I was already orbiting the carrier, the other planes quickly joined me, one on my left, the other two on my right. I noticed that the wind speed had increased. I could see wind streaks on the surface of the water and a few white caps. I knew that the carrier would turn into the wind to recover the four airplanes. I checked my altimeter; we were at 1,000 feet. Then I saw the "Charlie flag" stream from the signal mast on the ship's bridge. It was a large red flag and it was my signal that the ship was preparing to recover us. The ship began its turn into the wind, and I led the flight down to 300 feet.

When the carrier steadied on its new course into the wind, I had the four of us flying past the carrier on its starboard side in a right echelon formation. Five seconds after I flew past the bow of the carrier, I gave a hand signal to my wingman, by touching my hand to my mouth and throwing him a good-bye kiss. I made a diving turn to my left and set up the approach pattern for the carrier landing. It was just like carrier quals. I turned into position just astern of the ship, saw the LSO, got a cut signal, caught a wire and was aboard. I taxied forward and by the time I was out of my plane and in the ready room, I heard the fourth plane land. I sat, calming down with a cigarette and cup of coffee, when the ready room intercom squawked, "This is the captain. All aircraft were aboard in under two minutes. Well done. Out."

I heard someone in the back of the ready room yell out, "Pretty hot stuff, Norm. I'll fly wing on you any time." I know I had a big grin—I couldn't hide it!

Christmas in Panama

On December 24, 1942, our maintenance people discovered that a few of our aircraft had suffered some minor damage on landings. Some wrinkles had appeared in the skin of the fuselage where it joined the tail assembly. Our people believed the damage was caused when the aircraft landed with the depth charges aboard. The extra weight was causing the damage. Our skipper decided to fly all our TBFs to the Naval Air Station at Coco Solo, Panama, to repair the damage. The ship was only about 100 miles from the air station and there were facilities there to do a quick repair on our planes.

Following lunch, nine of us packed an extra uniform and shaving gear in our travel bags. We were all in the ready room waiting for the call of "Pilots, man your aircraft." All the squadron pilots were going with us, so one of the pilots with his spare gear flew as my passenger in the radio compartment of the plane. When the call did come on the intercom, we all rushed pell-mell to our assigned aircraft. I was spotted number three on the deck with two planes ahead and the rest behind me.

My passenger got into the radio compartment with our travel bags. I climbed into the plane's cockpit and got ready to start my engine.

Then I heard, "Pilots, start your engines." Quickly, props were turning and exhaust smoke from the engines drifted across the flight deck as all nine planes got their engines started. I sat there, my parachute tight on my shoulders, my safety belt snug across my lap.

Not a bad deal ... the officers' club at the air station for Christmas Eve ... a nice Christmas dinner. Wonder what Jean is doing? Those were wonderful times with her Norwegian grandparents for Christmas. How they would tease me by speaking Norwegian and then looking at me, laughing. Jean would tell me later, though, that only nice things were being said. Jean and I were still in high school. There goes plane number two. I'm next. Take-off checklist; engine instruments look OK; there's the three-finger turn up. Brakes off ... nice and smooth ... stick back a little ... let it fly off. I'm clear of the deck. What's wrong? I'm losing power—settling toward the water. Get the gear up! Try to ease this bird to the right. Get clear of the ship! It'll run right over us if we go in ... milk up the damn flaps slowly! There, engine sounds better, engine rpms are back to normal ... God! It seemed it took forever to get full power from the engine ... I'm going to make it! That was too damn close!

I heard a frantic call from my passenger, "Norm, what the hell are you doing? I thought you could fly this bird!"

After all planes were airborne, we joined on the first plane, which was the skipper's, and we headed for the Coco Solo air station. After landing and delivering the planes for repair, everyone checked into the BOQ and headed for

The author skimming the water on take off in a TBF from the light carrier USS *Chenango*, which after leaving Norfolk in December 1942 was headed for Panama

the officers' club. Although we had a good Christmas, we all felt the distance from our loved ones.

On December 26, two days after we had arrived, with each aircraft repaired over the Christmas holiday, all nine of us flew across the Isthmus of Panama using the Panama Canal as our map. *Chenango* had transited the canal while we were at the air station. Radio silence was still in effect, but the ship's YE led us right to her.

The nine TBFs orbited the carrier waiting for the red "Fox" flag to signal that the ship was ready to take us aboard. As we circled, I thought about the strange Christmas we had experienced at the officers' club in Panama. There was a lot of drinking and the dinner was good, but it wasn't Christmas. Maybe next year I would be with Jean and our new baby.

As we approached the ship for landing, we were in a nine-plane division of three, three-plane sections. As we flew past the starboard side of the carrier, the first three-plane section moved into an echelon to the right. Then each plane made a diving turn to the left, entered the downwind leg and prepared to land on the carrier. The two remaining sections made one circle of the ship and then the second section followed the first three planes into the landing pattern. I was leading the third three-plane section. I quickly made one circle of the ship, got into position on the starboard side of the carrier and followed the second three-plane section into the landing pattern. I only saw one wave off, as eight of us got aboard on the first pass.

We were all together that night for dinner in the ward room. We were still talking about the great job we had done getting aboard the ship. We were in our only home—USS *Chenango*. We were on our way to the war and finally in the Pacific.

Guadalcanal

It was a long trip from Panama to our initial destination. Again, bad weather limited flight operations during the transit of the Pacific, but it also protected us from submarine attack. Bad weather, especially rain squalls and low clouds, would hide the task force from a sub trying to find our ship.

We finally arrived and anchored in the harbor of Noumea on the island of New Caledonia on January 7, 1943. The island of New Caledonia was a major outpost in support of the action on Guadalcanal. It was also the headquarters of the South Pacific Naval Command. Geographically, New Caledonia was located about 800 miles northeast of Brisbane, Australia.

From 26 December 1942 when we left Panama, until our arrival at Noumea, my flying time was very limited. The daily flight schedule consisted of three, two-plane antisub searches. These searches were designed to protect the carrier from enemy sub attacks. An enemy sub had to use its periscope to locate a target. If a plane spotted the periscope, the sub was highly vulnerable to attack.

To meet this daily flight schedule, only six pilots each day were required. Since our squadron shared the flights with the dive-bombing squadron pilots, that meant 24 pilots were available for flights; 12 from each squadron. We also faced possible flight cancellations due to weather. The result was that I didn't fly very often. It was January before I was on the flight schedule. My log book entry for 2 January 1943 reads, "TBF 2.5 hrs. dusk patrol." That was my first flight since landing on the carrier on December 26.

The dusk patrol consisted of one aircraft circling our task force at a range of five to ten miles. Our task force consisted of *Chenango*, four destroyers and one light cruiser. The greatest concern of the task group commander, *Chenango*'s Captain Ben Wyatt, was the threat of Japanese subs. The aim was to keep an enemy sub from attacking the carrier or any of the rest of the ships. The thinking was that dusk would be the ideal time for the Japanese to attack. For me, flying the patrol was complete boredom. The only real concern I had was to get back aboard the carrier before dark.

While in Noumea, we ensigns received some good news. Among all the messages the ship picked up at Navy Headquarters, there was a promotion list. All of us had been promoted to lieutenant, junior grade. My title was now Lieutenant (jg.) Berg.

The news we were really waiting for though, was mail from home. No such luck. Our mail hadn't caught up with us yet, although I did manage to mail three letters to Jean. My mailing address was "Ensign Norman Berg, USS *Chenango*, c/o Fleet Post Office, San Francisco." We all thought it was rather vague. We were over 2,000 miles and 13 days from Panama. We were even farther from the United States and home.

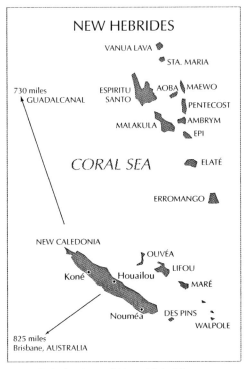

New Caledonia and New Hebrides

Heading for Guadalcanal

After two days in port, we were under way again escorting a convoy of supply ships headed for Guadalcanal.

I flew a four-hour antisub patrol on January 11. It was much different from the dusk patrol. My search pattern took me over 150 miles from the carrier. This would take me well out of the normal shipping lanes and ship traffic. The thinking was that I might spot an enemy sub on the surface recharging the sub's electric batteries. The submarine commander might get careless feeling that he was safe away from the normal antisub patrols.

I was on the schedule again on January 23. I flew another four-hour, 150-mile antisub search. I'd been off the flight schedule since my flight on the 11th. This was normal squadron policy. When a pilot completed one of these long antisub flights, it was usually a week before he went back on the flight schedule. The type of flights were much different from the dusk patrol. The chance for a navigational error was greater, since the wind direction and velocity 150 miles from the carrier could be much different. The possibility of bad weather from what the ship was reporting was always a threat. All these factors meant both physical and mental strain in the pilot. Some time off was helpful for a pilot to unwind.

Then, on January 25, we were put on alert for possible action against a Japanese battle fleet. We had all heard the scuttlebutt about a possible sea battle in the Guadalcanal area. That evening, the squadron skipper, Commander Butts, using the ship's intercom system, called a meeting in the ward room of all pilots, including pilots from the fighter and dive-bombing squadron, as well as the torpedo pilots. The ship had two ready rooms, one for the fighter squadron and the other we shared with the dive-bombing pilots. Neither ready room was large enough for an all-pilots meeting.

After the announcement, we were all in the ward room. There was none of the usual banter between the TBF pilots and the dive-bomber pilots with the fighter pilots. We all thought the fighter pilots were "prima donnas" and highly overrated. They all thought we were just "truck drivers." Instead of the friendly jokes, though, we were all quiet. Any conversations were very subdued. I could feel the tension in the room. We were damn nervous. Was this going to be the action we had trained for? How many ships did the Japs have? What was our strength? Was it just our carrier? What about the carrier *Enterprise*? She was in the area too.

The skipper, chewing on his usual cigar, entered the ward room. We all stood until he announced, "Seats, gentlemen."

"Well, gentlemen, here's the scoop. Two days from now, on the 27th, the heavy cruiser *Chicago* will leave Noumea en route to the Guadalcanal area. There, she will be joining a U.S. battle force of battleships and cruiser operations in the area. She will be moving at 25 knots. *Chenango* will set up a course tonight, the 25th, to be in position to give *Chicago* antisub coverage as well as long-range search protection. *Chenango* is leaving two days ahead of *Chicago* because of the speed difference. Our flight operations will commence today with our searches covering the area ahead of *Chicago*'s course." He turned to Joe Anson, our air intelligence officer (AIO). "Joe, go ahead and cover the intelligence briefing you had at Navy Headquarters in Noumea."

Lieutenant Anson took over. "Guys, the Japanese are still contesting our occupation of Guadalcanal. They are determined to stop our convoys from supplying our troops there. But it's more than the Canal. They know that by our controlling Guadalcanal and the airfield there, we can eventually attack Rabaul, their major base in the South Pacific. We will be able to invade the Japanese-held islands of New Georgia and Bougainville, take over their airfields and, with our aircraft, we can neutralize Rabaul. By doing this, we will neutralize the Japanese threat to Australia." [See South Pacific map in Chapter 4, page 77.]

Joe paused for a sip of coffee.

"Now, about *Chicago*. We have good intelligence from the Navy Command at Guadalcanal that the Japanese are moving aircraft to the field on New

Georgia. When the Japanese invaded the Solomon Islands, they took control of the islands of Bougainville, New Georgia, and Guadalcanal, and the non-native population—mostly Aussie and French nationals—left the islands. However, on the islands the Japanese did not invade, a few Aussies remained with the native population. They are known as coast watchers. They have radios powered by hand generators and are constantly reporting the movement of Japanese forces. Even more important, they have saved numerous Marine and Navy pilots that have been shot down flying out of Henderson Field on Guadalcanal." Joe paused, as if for emphasis.

Our skipper stood and interrupted Joe, saying, "Thanks, Joe. Good briefing. Now gentlemen, what is our part in all this? For now, we're ordered to protect the convoy and *Chicago* from submarine attack. However, after meeting with Captain Ben Wyatt, the commanding officer of *Chenango*, I've requested that the Navy Command in Noumea be informed that our air group is ready to supply air support to *Chicago*. The fighter squadron is available to supply fighter cover for the convoy. In addition, our dive-bombing and torpedo squadrons' attack capability is also available if the Japanese ships attempt to attack. That message has been passed to the Navy Command in Noumea with Captain Wyatt's concurrence. Gentlemen, that's where we stand. Our first job is antisub protection. Let's do a good job starting tomorrow. There's one thing more. Effective at midnight tonight, the order for complete radio silence is canceled. The new order allows radio transmissions in case of emergency. Gentlemen, be damn sure it's an emergency! That's all. Good night."

I headed for the bunk room and laid there in the darkness.

That build up of Jap planes means there's going to be a battle. They're going to try and get the convoy. Wonder how many ships the Japs will have? Maybe we'll attack their airfield on New Georgia. Bet they've got heavy AA guns protecting the airfields. Got to do my job; wish I could forget Torpedo Eight. Poor bastards. Didn't have a chance. Shit. I'll be all right ... I'll make it ... got to ... come on ... turn it off ... get some sleep.

I wasn't on the flight schedule again until January 28, but what a day it was! I remember that I first heard the rumor at breakfast—we were scheduled for a practice torpedo attack. I headed for the ready room. There it was; the schedule was on the blackboard. I was leading the third three-plane section. Commander Butts came into the ready room right behind me, so I called the group to attention.

"Seats, gentlemen." That chewed cigar came out of his mouth. "OK, Captain Wyatt had a response from Navy Headquarters in Noumea. You recall that I told them we could supply air support to *Chicago*. Gentlemen, we're ordered to prepare to launch a torpedo attack if enemy targets become available." He paused, looking at us, waiting for the sounds of surprise, the audible sound of voices, "A torpedo attack!" Then he continued. "It's been a long time since we practiced a squadron torpedo attack. It was at the Naval Air Station at Quonset Point. I remember some of us had our wives with us for that week. We did real well that time. We were all over that rock we used for a target. Now it's time to practice again. For this practice run, we'll launch nine aircraft. I will lead the flight. Our practice target will be *Chenango*. No weapons of course!" There was some rather forced humor from the pilots. We were still thinking torpedo attack!

The skipper continued. "Join on me after launch. We'll start our attack from 10,000 feet. The procedure will be identical with the practice runs we all made at Quonset Point. I want you leaders of the other two sections to plan your attack so we'll arrive over the ship together. Let's show the ship's skipper how good we are! Any questions?"

Later, I sat in my plane. Seventh in line to launch for the practice torpedo attack.

Damn! When is this tension going to stop? Boy! Do I ever remember that week at Quonset. Jean was so sweet. Damn it, just when I get a little relaxed, the fear starts again. God! I hope we really don't have to do this; let's just practice. Hope the Japs keep their ships in their harbors. What are my odds? One out of nine. Hell, if the skipper can do it, I've got to do it, too. No choice. There's my taxi signal. Get this bird moving, let's go!

The practice torpedo attack went well. All nine TBFs roared over *Chenango* within 20 seconds of each other and we got aboard without a wave off. We gathered in the ready room—everyone talking at once. We were one bunch of hot Navy pilots. We'd all make it back to the States—we knew it!

On the evening of January 30, *Chenango* passed the word on the ship's P.A. system that *Chicago* had been hit by Japanese torpedo bombers. There had been a night battle at Rennel Island just south of Guadalcanal. The next day, while she was under tow, she was hit again with four torpedoes from Japanese planes.

Chicago had been sunk.

That evening, we torpecker pilots were all in the ready room talking, wondering if we could have saved *Chicago*, or at least protected her while she was under tow. Well, our skipper had offered to help—we had tried. There was a sense too, at least on my part, of disappointment. I guess most of us wanted to be heroes. I wondered if the farther away one gets from danger, the greater the enthusiasm is to face danger? We had to prove that we were not afraid.

We all learned the facts a few days later, when Joe, our AIO, briefed us. The Navy Command at Noumea had notified the admiral commanding the U.S. Task Force during the attack on *Chicago*, that *Chenango* was available to join his task force. Joe said the admiral commanding the task force had declined the offer. Joe read directly from the message. The admiral had said, "... I cannot command a task force of battleships and cruisers that fight battles moving at 30 knots and include *Chenango*, a carrier with a top speed of 18 knots."

USS *Chicago*, CA-29, before her sinking

For most of February, I flew seven flights totaling 18 hours. All were anti-sub patrols. *Chenango* was assigned to convoy duty. That decision not to use *Chenango* to help protect *Chicago* seemed to have sealed our future. We were safe, but God, it was looking like it was going to be dull.

Flying to Efate

On February 26, the ship received orders to proceed to the harbor at the tiny island of Efate. Efate was one of the many islands in the New Hebrides group located about 200 miles northeast of Noumea. Our three squadrons were ordered to fly off the carrier and proceed to the airfield at Efate. The fighter squadron left first, then the dive-bombers, and last, the torpedo pilots. All planes arrived safely at Efate. None of us knew what the hell was going on.

Efate was a French-controlled island. The Marines had constructed an airfield there in support of the invasion of Guadalcanal. The Navy had moved in after the Marines. There was a mess hall, metal Quonset huts for living quarters, an officers' club, and an enlisted club for our crewmen. It seemed like the entire island had been a coconut plantation before the war. The only trees we saw were coconuts, but it was a marvelous change from the ship. Best of all, we torpedo plane pilots were not flying those damn antisub patrols. Most of us were convinced that the Japanese had no submarines! We were all prepared for a nice change from the ship and some partying at the officers' club. The day after our arrival, however, that all changed when the skipper called an all-pilots meeting at the officers' club.

"Well, good morning, gentlemen. I hope you were pleased with your accommodations. I noticed too that some of you really enjoyed the officers' club." He stopped and shifted the cigar in his mouth. "Gentlemen, we have just ten days before we get back into the war." He seemed to look at each of us as his eyes roamed around the room. There were some obvious groans. Even some "Oh, damns" could be heard. He turned to Bill Shyrock, the operations officer. "Bill, pass out that flight schedule for the next six days."

As torpedo pilots, we each got one labeled, Torpedo Squadron. I saw that every torpedo pilot was scheduled for five glide-bombing flights and one gunnery flight. The entire officers' club was buzzing as the pilots tried to absorb the meaning of the flight schedule. We torpedo pilots had not practiced glide-bombing or gunnery since Norfolk.

"All right, gentlemen, settle down." He paused, waiting for us to quiet down. Then it came. "Yesterday, I received orders from the Navy Command in Noumea. We will deploy our three squadrons on March 10 to Henderson Field, Guadalcanal. We will fly our aircraft and our crewmen to the Canal. A Navy transport aircraft will move selected enlisted personnel for maintenance support. *Chenango* will remain at the harbor of Efate. That's all, gentlemen. We're going to war. God go with each of us as we face this challenge."

The anticipated pleasures of Efate—the beaches, having a chance to discover the beauty of the island and yes, the officers' club vanished from my thoughts. The Canal would not be a pleasure visit to a tropical South Seas island. I was getting my wish. I would be fighting the enemy. There were moments when I wished I'd stayed in Bremerton with Jean and worked in the Navy Yard, but I'd never admit to such a thought. I was a Navy pilot—I could do the job!

The next ten days were devoted to getting ready to make the flight to Henderson Field on Guadalcanal. By March 4, I had flown my four glide-bombing flights and the one gunnery flight. Our sojourn on the lovely little island was about over, but at least we had some time off. Just a few days after our arrival at Efate, the mail finally caught up with us. I spent a good deal of time re-reading the stack of letters I received from Jean and the two from my parents.

For me, the best news was that Jean was expecting our baby in June. She said that there was no problem checking in at the naval hospital at the naval shipyard in Bremerton. Her doctor was a civilian who had recently left his practice and volunteered to serve with the Navy. He had specialized in obstetrics. I felt relieved that Jean was getting good care while I was gone. I didn't know, though, what my life would be like with a baby in the family. I was sure that Jean and I would work it out.

We had some opportunities to do some sightseeing on the island. We visited a small village within walking distance of the airstrip. George Hartman and

I wandered in one afternoon and found a little bar run by a French couple, Mr. and Mrs. La Pierie. Between George's fractured French and the owner's little English, we found ourselves being invited to stay as their guests and enjoy some local cheese and their own wine. They closed the bar every afternoon. Local custom, we guessed. The couple lived upstairs over the bar, and the two of them seemed genuinely pleased that we had agreed to stay. We kept hearing how glad they were to have the *amis* (friends) there.

Their apartment was quite small with a tiny kitchen, and a combined living and dining room. I noticed two closed doors off the livingroom. Bedrooms, I guessed. The apartment was beautifully furnished with what appeared to be antique pieces and everything was sparkling clean. An oriental rug covered the floor. Mr. La Pierie offered us a chair at the dining table as his wife rustled around in the kitchen. Then he moved to one of the closed doors and knocked. The door opened, and I could see the figure of a person. He motioned with his arm as he said, "*Amis*, my daughter." George and I both jumped to our feet. She appeared to be about twelve, dark hair hanging loosely around her cameo-shaped face. She was dressed in a dark skirt and a white blouse. And then, in an accented English, she said, "Speaking for my Papa, we welcome you."

The afternoon moved quickly. Our host's wife brought out a plate with a chunk of cheese and a knife. There was a loaf of bread and a bottle of wine. With some ceremony, our host opened the wine, as his daughter explained that he had made the wine. George and I and the La Pieries sat around that old table, a thousand miles from home. Those strangers welcomed us as family. Their daughter was our translator. We talked about America and Efate. I sat silently as I listened to George tell about his family in California.

> *God! On the 10th, we'll fly off the Guadalcanal into ... I just don't know. Bombs dropping; the enemy trying to kill me. I feel so lonely and homesick. Missing Jean so much. Glad she's home and doing so well. Her letters are so positive. Now I know when our baby is due. Jean said June. Feels so safe here, cheese and wine ... friendly people.*

Gradually, we emptied the wine bottle. George and I were saying our good-byes and our thanks. My last memory of that day is the vision of a lovely, young girl with long dark hair waving good-bye to George and me.

Flying to Henderson Field

On March 10, 1943, our air group left for Henderson Field and Guadalcanal. The fighter squadron left first with the dive-bombers leaving next and then the torpedo plane pilots. Our route took us from "Roses" (the code name for Efate) to "Button" (the radio code name for Espiritu Santo). Espiritu Santo was an island about 160 miles north of Efate. An airfield had been built there in support of the invasion of Guadalcanal. As we landed at the airstrip, we caught sight of the carrier *Enterprise* anchored in the harbor. She had been damaged while supporting the landings at the Canal earlier in the year and was being repaired at Espiritu Santo.

USS *Enterprise*, CV-6, underway in the Pacific in 1941
(Courtesy of the U.S. Navy)

Our aircraft were quickly refueled as we pilots completed our flight planning for the flight to the island of Guadalcanal. It was almost a 600-mile flight, all over open ocean. It was there that Henderson Field airstrip was located. The radio code name for Guadalcanal was "Cactus." My log book shows a flight of 4.5 hours. Our nine TBFs flew in a loose formation, staying in visual contact with each other. More than once on that flight, I mentally thanked Pratt and Whitney, the company that had built the engine for my TBF. I sure didn't want any engine problems on that flight!

About 30 minutes from our estimated time of arrival at Guadalcanal, I began looking for the island. This was every pilot's instinct—where the hell was a place to land this plane? I was tired. I noticed a dark kind of blur on the horizon. Then as we continued flying, the blur began to take shape. There was Guadalcanal, rising out of the ocean. It looked lush and green.

My radio crackled. It was Bill Shyrock, the flight leader. "TBF flight, close on me. We'll make a low pass over the airstrip. Make the usual carrier break to landing. All pilots meet at the operations building after landing for a briefing. Out."

We all heard the control tower give us landing permission. As I circled the landing strip waiting for my turn to land, I looked down at the landing strip. So this was Henderson Field. It looked to be about 4,000 feet long. It had been built by cutting a swath in a grove of coconut trees wide and long enough to accommodate the strip. The strip was covered, side to side, with steel planks about 12 inches wide and 20 feet long. All the planks had two-inch diameter holes in them. The planks were fastened tightly together by steel cables and covered the landing strip from beginning to end. These planks, called Marstin Matting, stabilized the soft sandy soil and were used throughout the Pacific Theater to construct airstrips. (The Pacific Theater applied to the ocean areas west of Hawaii to Japan, including the Philippines and Australia.)

USS *Santee*, ACV-29, one of four Sangamon-class carriers that were converted from Esso tankers in 1942. She flew Grumman F4F-4 Wildcats and TBF-1 Avengers as well as Douglas SBD-3 Dauntlesses

(Courtesy of the U.S. Navy)

Our entire air group arrived safely at Henderson Field. Traditionally, our Navy squadrons could now be identified as part of the "Cactus Air Force." We became part of that very proud name. It was first used by Marine fighter and dive-bombing squadrons defending the landing of the First Marine Division in August 1942 on Guadalcanal. That bunch of courageous pilots called themselves the Cactus Air Force. The next group who earned the name were pilots from the carrier *Enterprise* while relieving the Marines. Now, it was our turn, the Torpedo Squadron 28. Joining us were squadrons from two sister ships of *Chenango* class carriers: *Sangamon* and *Santee*, both operating in the South Pacific. Air groups from those two carriers had also flown into Guadalcanal. This would be the first time we had all operated together. Our three carriers had never worked together. Now, at least, the carrier squadrons would fight the enemy together. This gave the Cactus Air Force over 36 fresh fighter pilots with their Grumman F4F fighters, 17 SBD dive-bombers, and 27 TBFs, all with freshly rested pilots.

We landed in quick order and were directed to an aircraft parking area just off the airstrip. The aircraft parking area was also covered with the steel planks. There was only one building visible near the airstrip. We learned later that it was called the "Pagoda" and had been built by the Japanese when they occupied the area. Our forces were using it as an operations office and a pilot briefing area. Two trucks pulled up to our aircraft parking area. Each had benches in the back for us and we all boarded with our parachute bags. Since

The Pagoda, built by the Japanese, was the operations center

our parachutes remained on our planes, the parachute bags were used to carry our personal gear. The trucks moved off the matting and onto the sandy road as we headed for the Pagoda for our briefing.

My first impression of Guadalcanal was the sickening sweet-sour smell of rotting coconuts. The entire area had been a large coconut plantation. Since the Japanese invasion, and now with our forces present, there had been no harvest of the coconuts. Thousands of them were rotting on the ground, and the odor was overwhelming.

As we drove down the dirt road, we could see tents on both sides of the road. We could see groups of men lounging around. A few of them called out, "You'll be sorry!" I heard the driver holler back to us. "Those were Army guys waiting to ship out. This is how we all live—tents with no floors, drinking water from the Tenaru River. A lot of Japs died trying to cross that river. See those canvas bags hanging between those two palm trees? That's so-called drinking water. It has so much chlorine in it for purification, that all you can do is hold your nose when you try to drink it! See there," he pointed with one arm. "That's the mess tent. Only go there when you're so hungry you can't stand it. Powdered milk and eggs. Terrible pancakes. Spam three times a day, instant potatoes and soups, rice, and coffee that smells like chlorine. At least the stuff is hot. Sirs, you're going to be sorry leaving that nice, clean ship."

The trucks pulled up in front of the Pagoda. We jumped out and found the pilots' briefing room. The dive-bombing pilots were waiting for us along with our skipper, Commander Butts.

As we listened to an Army sergeant brief us, we soon learned what our living area would be: four-person tents with canvas floors. There was a four-hole latrine in our area, but no showers. The bathing and clothes-washing area was the Tenaru River. Cots, with mosquito netting and one blanket, were placed in each tent. The mess tent was a short walk down the road from our area. The squadron was assigned one truck and a jeep. We were to supply our own driver for the truck.

As I listened there in the briefing room, I looked out a dusty window. Black—like the color of the soil throughout the area. I wondered what it would be like if a thunder storm hit the island. Black mud? Then for the first time, I noticed that many of the coconut trees around the area had no tops, and I wondered what caused that.

As the sergeant finished, our skipper stood to address us.

Operations office and briefing room, in the Pagoda

"Gentlemen, welcome to Guadalcanal. You are now part of the Cactus Air Force. It's sure not *Chenango*, but we'll do OK. One word of caution. A supply of pills to prevent malaria is placed in each tent. You will take one pill a day. Understood? We can't afford to have pilots sick with malaria.

"I noticed many of you looking at the shattered coconut trees. This damage occurred during the height of the battle for the island. Japanese ships would regularly shell the airfield. The shells from the ships' guns shattered the tops of the trees." He stopped, looking at our anxious faces.

"Presently, Guadalcanal is considered a secure island. The Army is still pursing a few remaining Japanese soldiers in the north of the island. There's been no shelling for the past two months, so relax. We do have a regular night visitor, however. A single Japanese bomber that flies down from the Japanese-held island of Bougainville. The Army calls him "Washing Machine Charlie" because of the sound of his engines. He will drop one bomb every time he flies over our area. He usually leaves after ten bombs. Between the bombs and our anti-aircraft guns firing at him, sleep becomes difficult.

"You'll find a bomb shelter in our living area. It's a deep hole big enough for ten or twelve people and it's covered with coconut logs. It's not a pleasant place, but it's safe. It's your choice."

Wonder how long we'll be here? It's going to be tough. Did he say some Japs were still on the island? Bombing every night by a Jap bomber? No showers and washing our own clothes. Just wear shorts or a flight suit. That truck driver said the food was bad too. Malaria. Better be careful and take those pills. Nothing yet about flying ... probably will start in the next few days to give us some time to get settled in our living area. Who's that coming in? A Navy guy....

We saw a naval officer enter the briefing room. "Gentlemen," the skipper said turning towards us, "this is Navy Commander Williams. He is assigned to the staff of the commanding general here at Guadalcanal. When we arrived here, control of our operations shifted from the Navy to the general's staff here at Henderson Field. The commander is now our flight scheduling officer and he will be working with me on the scheduling of our pilots. Commander, the floor is yours."

He was a short, stocky officer, slightly bald with deeply set eyes ringed with dark circles. He wore a khaki uniform, and we could all see the Navy wings pinned to his shirt. "Well guys, welcome to the Cactus Air Force. What we do here is not fun and it's not easy." He paused. "What the staff does is schedule the daily flight operations of the squadrons assigned to our control. Flight operations are controlled by the need to attack a wide range of enemy targets based on intelligence reports of enemy activity. Now, some of these reports are long range, while others require immediate action." He stopped, looking at Commander Butts, and continued, "Your skipper has been briefed on the current intelligence report and concurs with the staff plan.

"This morning we received a report that the Japanese are moving a large number of aircraft to their field on New Georgia Island. Our staff believes they are planning an attack on Henderson Field. We are sure they are aware of the arrival of our three new air groups. We intend to attack first."

There wasn't a sound in the briefing room, except for one sudden gasp of surprise. The commander turned to a map on the wall. "Here's the target." He pointed out an airfield marked on the map of New Georgia, "The distance is about 200 miles." Then he looked through the wet, dust-streaked window on the side of the briefing room. "As you can see, it's raining out now. This evening's forecast calls for clearing by tomorrow afternoon with clear skies by evening. Because of the weather, it doesn't appear that we can commence flight operations until tomorrow evening. But neither can the Japanese.

"In my opening remarks, I said that this job is no fun and it's not easy." Again, he paused. "Gentlemen, we will launch six TBFs at 2100 hours on the 12th for a night attack on the Japanese airstrip on New Georgia. The bomb load will be four 500-pound bombs in each aircraft. Briefing will be at 1900 hours here in this room. Commander Butts, it's all yours, Sir." The commander left the room as our skipper stood facing us.

He was slowly chewing on his cigar as he looked at a group of stunned torpedo pilots.

A night attack against a target in an area none of us had ever flown in! There was another problem too—we hadn't flown at night since Norfolk! Jesus! There, the bomber pilots are leaving. Lucky guys ... 200 miles. That's 400 miles round trip, at least a four-hour flight. Can't use our planes' running lights after we join up because the Japs would see them when we reached the target. Got to have clear weather. Maybe I won't be on the flight, but join up after the attack will be tough. We'll be spread out after our pull outs. Here's the skipper.

His voice was soft, almost gentle. "Fellas, this is a tough one, but I agree that we've got to hit them first. With clear skies and good visibility, the flight to the target shouldn't be a problem. OK, here are the lead pilots I've scheduled: Bill Shyrock will lead the first three-plane section. Norm Berg will lead the second section. You leaders, pick your wingmen and crewmen. That's all gentlemen. Bill and Norm, ride with me in the jeep. I want to talk with you both. The truck is outside for the rest of you. Rest easy, guys. The weather is too bad for Charlie to pay us a visit tonight."

I sat in the jeep with Bill and the skipper thinking, this is what I've been waiting for—a chance to attack the enemy. Well, it's time to prove myself. My first combat mission. Riding in the jeep, I thought I'd like to wait a little longer. I didn't know if I was ready for it.

First Attack

The next day, March 11, and most of the following day, were spent trying to organize the tent area where we were living. I kept plodding through the various tasks, getting some tables and benches for the area, hanging up an extra water bag, and trying to bail the water out of our bomb shelter after the rain. The work and the companionship of my friends kept my mind off the upcoming mission. It wasn't even brought up. I figured no one wanted to talk about it, not even the two pilots who were going as my wingmen.

Bill Shyrock and I, along with the other four pilots who would be our wingmen, met after lunch, which had been the usual canned meat called Spam served with rice. We wanted to plan the navigation and study the maps of the area. After all, none of us had ever flown in that part of the world. There were so damn many islands in the Solomons. We couldn't even pronounce half the names on the map.

Later, the six of us had supper together—some kind of soup with hard crackers and the usual "bug juice," water with fruit flavor to hide the smell of the chlorine in the water. After we ate, we all sat around in the mess tent—our wingmen along with the rest of the squadron pilots. The talk was about how long we would be at Henderson Field and about flying. There was no conversation about the mission the six of us were going to fly that night.

After a while, a truck pulled up outside the mess tent. Bill Shyrock stood. "That's us, guys. Let's go do it!" The rest of the pilots followed the six of us out to the truck.

The guys were yelling, "Go get 'em! Good luck!" and "We'll be waiting for you guys when you get back!"

The six of us clambered into the back of the truck. We were wearing our flight suits and "Mae Wests" and carrying our navigation boards and maps. (The Mae Wests were yellow life preservers pilots wore that could be inflated if the pilot had to land in the ocean because of enemy action or aircraft mechanical problems. They covered the pilot from neck to waist, and when inflated, gave the appearance of large breasts—an attribute of the 1930s movie star, Mae West, who was famous for coining the seductive line of "Come up and see me sometime.") We made sure our flashlights had the red lenses in place so our night vision would be protected. We were ready. The truck would take us to the Pagoda for our briefing.

I'm pretty calm. This is what we're trained for and it looks like a nice night. The formation flight to the target will be easy ... good visibility. Quite a send off the guys gave us. Wonder if they wished they were flying the mission? No, don't volunteer; take the luck of the draw. I'm OK ... just do the job. God's on our side. I've got Jean, too. There should be some more mail soon ... love her letters.

The truck stopped in front of the Pagoda. The six of us entered and took seats on the benches in the briefing room. The skipper greeted us and turned the briefing over to Commander Williams of the general's staff. He reviewed the weather forecast for the target area—no problems there. An intelligence report from Navy Headquarters confirmed that the Japanese aircraft were still parked in the coconut groves alongside the airstrip. The major emphasis by the commander, as I remember, was, "Place your bombs in the coconut trees alongside the runways, not on the runways. That's where the Jap planes will be parked." Williams turned the briefing back to our skipper.

"Gentlemen, the weather looks great for this mission. We don't believe the Japanese will be expecting you. They know you've just arrived. We're sure they will not expect a night attack. They will think we're not ready to attack them." He hesitated, then said, "Gentlemen, we're going to give the bastards a real surprise! My thoughts will be with you. Good luck!"

I felt quite calm as the six of us climbed back into the truck that had been waiting for us. We headed for our aircraft—I had practiced everything back in the States that the mission called for, the formation flying at night, the navigation, the bombing run. I had every confidence, too, in my aircraft and in its engine, and in my crew that consisted of a radio operator and a turret gunner. Together, I knew we could do the job. The only unknowns were the attack with live bombs and the possibility of enemy anti-aircraft (AA) fire hitting my aircraft. I certainly didn't know how I would react if I saw enemy AA fire directed towards me.

I sure hope I won't panic! Got to make a good bombing run!

As I started my aircraft and began taxiing out to the take-off position, I found myself concentrating on the present. I had so many things to do, I figured I'd have plenty of time to worry about enemy gunfire later.

After takeoff, we all joined on Shyrock's three-plane section, with my three-plane section flying off to Bill's right. On Bill's radio signal, we all turned off our planes' running lights. The night sky was dark with no moon, but the visibility was good. There were just a few scattered clouds. We had no trouble seeing each other as we flew along in formation.

Bill and I had estimated an hour and 45 minutes to the target. We were approaching the island of New Georgia from the south. The landing field was located next to the village of Munda in the center of the island. I saw that we had flown past the first half of the island. We were flying at 9,500 feet when I heard Bill say, "Airstrip in sight." The Japanese used crushed coral for the one runway there, and the coral made the airstrip highly visible against the dark trees around it. "All planes acknowledge target." One by one, we each responded, "Roger! Runway in sight!"

On the ground, I saw the first flashes of enemy AA fire as the Japanese opened fire on our formation. Son of a bitch! They were not surprised. We knew they could hear us. We could only hope the dark sky would hide us. My problem was that I had no way of knowing how accurate the enemy AA fire was. In daylight, AA fire left a black greasy-looking smudge of smoke as the shell exploded. At night, I couldn't see how close the explosions were to my plane. Then I heard Bill's order, "Echelon to the right. Now!" All five planes moved immediately until we were stacked up on Bill's right. "Diving now! Norm, take the left side of the runway. I'll take the right side."

I remember being told at the preflight briefing that the Japanese planes would be hidden under the trees along side the landing strip. I glanced at my altimeter: 9,000 feet. I made a diving turn to my left and followed the third plane into my dive.

Landing gear down. Bomb bay door open. Arming switch on. Have to be sure those bombs will explode. Steady, in 25-degree dive! Line up with the left side of the runway.

I heard one of my crewmen yell out on the intercom, "Enemy fire! It's coming up from our left, behind us." At 2,000 feet, I pressed the bomb release switch, started my pull out, and felt the four bombs drop away from my plane. I heard one of the crewmen on the plane's intercom radio say, "Bombs looked right off the runway in the trees! All four exploded! Lots of fire visible!"

I turned left, diving even closer to the tops of the trees to avoid enemy fire. Looking back to my left, I could see explosions and bright patches of fire from both sides of the airstrip. I heard my crewman's voice over the intercom, "Goddammit, Sir, we really hit the bastards!"

The first three planes joined on Bill's plane. I remained out to his right as I saw my two wingmen coming up to join on me. Bill had flashed his plane's running lights every 30 seconds now that the AA fire had stopped. The join up was a breeze.

"Anyone hit?" Bill radioed. Number four plane reported some hits on his left wing but had no problems.

Bet it was the AA fire my crewman saw. They hit my number four man.

I checked my compass. Bill was now on the compass heading back to Guadalcanal and Henderson Field.

I can't believe I feel so relaxed, so sleepy. The low drone of the engine; the air so smooth ... better open the cockpit hatch and get some fresh air. Wonder how close the AA fire was? Strange being shot at. I'm sure I saw some tracers from the AA guns; they looked like sky rockets on the Fourth when I was a kid. Nothing hit us though ... I sure as hell gave it to them! I know I got some hits! How much farther to go? God! I feel so tired ... there, Bill's calling.

I heard Bill call the tower at Henderson Field for clearance to land. When the tower demanded, "Approach code of the day." Bill responded with the proper code word. There was no radar at Henderson Field, and this code system was used to prevent an enemy plane from calling the control tower and getting approval to approach the field. We knew that our AA guns were manned. If you didn't give the correct code, you were the enemy.

We landed at Henderson Field after flying a total of three and one-half hours. Our ground crew began refueling the planes as soon as we shut them down. Each pilot signed off on a yellow sheet, indicating any problems with the plane. Chief Williams reviewed those sheets before the aircraft was scheduled for the next flight. Any problems noted on the yellow sheets were corrected. Williams was tough. If it wasn't right, the plane didn't fly. I remember when Williams and I loaded the planes on the carrier way back in Norfolk. He still kidded me about my concerns over getting the planes aboard the carrier.

Finally, the paperwork was done, and all of us, pilots and crewmen, piled into the back of a waiting truck. The next stop was the Pagoda for debriefing on the mission. Everyone was talking at once. The pilot of the last plane to dive was yelling about the fires he'd seen in the target area. Everyone was excited about seeing all the flashes of the AA fire. I heard Bill ask if other planes had been hit. None had, except my wingman's plane. He was yelling that I owed him big time. "Norm, those bullets that hit my plane were sure as hell aimed at you."

We arrived at the Pagoda and scrambled into the briefing room. The first person to greet us was our skipper. He took his time, speaking to each of us—expressing his confidence in our ability as Navy pilots and crew members. He then turned us over the staff air intelligence officer for the debriefing. We were seated by crews, one pilot and his two crewmen together. Each crew was to be debriefed separately. We were asked questions like: "Where did the bombs hit? Point out the map where they hit. Was the AA fire heavy or light? Were any Japanese aircraft visible? How many fires did you see? How many explosions?

How many bombs did you see hit the target? Did you see any Japanese aircraft airborne during the attack?"

In addition to the air intelligence officer, our skipper was helping with the debriefing too. It still took over an hour. There was a reward, though. A medic came into the room and gave each of us a small bottle, about two ounces, of Lejohn brandy.

"The doc thought you guys might need some liquid support."

After the debriefing, we got into the back of the truck once again and went to our tent area. It was after midnight, but the guys were all still up, slapping us on the back, asking questions. "How much AA fire? Did you get some bomb hits?"

After things calmed down, each of us who had flown the mission met with our crewmen to ensure everyone was all right. We'd been warned by our squadron flight surgeon to be aware of signs of fatigue or tension after a combat mission. My crew seemed fine—very excited, talkative, but no signs of excessive fatigue. They headed off to their tent still talking about the attack.

Looking at my pilot's log book today, I remember that night so vividly. I stripped to my skivvies and climbed inside the mosquito netting over my cot. I lay there, sipping on that little brandy bottle, thinking—an easy flight, no sweat. But then, I remembered those flashes of the AA guns, the bright tracer bullets searching for me. I felt some tears on my face. Suddenly, my body was trembling, legs quivering. I gulped down the rest of the brandy. Nothing helped as I buried my face in the blanket. I didn't want anyone to hear my sobs or know how afraid I was.

Self-doubt

I had no flights during the next few days. As a result, all I had do was worry about my future flights. That night attack against the airfields at Munda on New Georgia Island was still fresh in my mind.

> *Damn! I've got to come to grips with my fear. I've been avoiding my squadron mates. I'm so confused. Am I afraid of death? No! It won't happen to me! I'll survive ... I just know it! No, it's fear of failure! I'll chicken out! Damn, why has it always been like this? Always on the verge of failing ... school ... Navy flight training ... now this, combat.*

My thoughts were interrupted by George Hartman as he came into our tent. He asked me if I'd like to go find a party. A bunch of Army Air Corp pilots were living next to us, and George suggested we pay them a visit. We'd have a chance to tell them a few sea stories about real aviators. I made sure that my Navy wings were pinned on my shirt. As we walked down the muddy dirt road to the Army area, we saw a group of guys standing around a make-shift table. Everyone had a coffee cup in his hand. One of them saw George and me.

"Hey, you swabbies. Come on over. Help yourself to a drink. We're drinking it with water—sure kills the chlorine!" There were a couple of quart bottles of Schenley's black label whiskey on the table. I grabbed a cup, poured in some whiskey and water, and George and I joined the party.

I woke up the next morning with the worst hangover I'd ever had. I lay there trying to remember. I was sure that I'd won a bottle of whiskey in a card game with the Army guys. I pushed one arm out from under the netting, feeling under my cot. There it was. I felt the smooth surface of the whiskey bottle. I lay there, my head throbbing. It was a damn good party. Those Army pilots were lots of laughs. They were impressed when we told them about the bombing attack. It felt good to brag about myself. It must have been the booze. I needed some food to absorb some of that booze.

On March 16, I was back on the flight schedule.

Can't believe it. Two local flights. I need to become familiar with the Guadalcanal area. So, I'll fly around the island and make one night flight, though Jesus, wasn't the Munda bombing mission enough night familiarization?

Upon our arrival on Guadalcanal, the skipper initiated meetings with all pilots each morning. We received an update on our aircraft availability and a general briefing on the military action overnight in the area.

Night Mine-laying Mission

At our meeting on March 19, nine days after our arrival, the skipper reminded us that we'd only had two visits from Washing Machine Charlie, and those attacks had been before midnight. We hadn't lost much sleep, but we did use the bomb shelter. It wasn't so much the danger of Charlie's bombs as it was the pieces of metal falling from the exploding AA shells the Army was firing at him. We already had a couple of slashes in our tent from the AA fallout. The skipper closed the meeting, announcing an all pilot and crewman meeting at the Pagoda at 1300.

For the rest of the morning and in the mess tent for chow, the only talk was of the meeting. It had to be some kind of mission. Maybe the Japanese were moving troops into New Georgia after our attack there, or could it be another attack on the airstrip? If they were moving troops, maybe a strike against the troop ships was in the planning. We all knew the speculation would end soon. All hands were in the briefing room at 1300.

Map of the Solomon Islands area

As we settled into benches, we noticed a large map of the Solomon Islands on the wall. The skipper took over and again introduced the same Navy commander from the general's staff who had briefed us on the earlier mission.

"Afternoon, everyone. The general sends his congratulations on the very successful mission this squadron flew the night of the 12th. You guys really did a job!" There were a few raucous comments about a bunch of so-called "hot pilots" who had flown the mission.

He waited for the group to settle down. "Now, let's proceed. You're aware of the current strategy for defeating the Japanese in the South Pacific, but let me review it with you. We now have control of the Canal. Our ultimate goal is to destroy the major Japanese base at Rabaul by using land-based air power. To accomplish this, we will invade New Georgia and take control of the airstrip located there. That attack will occur in July. The next invasion will take place in the fall, when the Japanese base at Bougainville will be invaded. Once we have that airstrip, the Japanese base at Rabaul will be in easy flight range of our aircraft. The Japanese will have to fight off our attacks over their own base. Any questions?"

There was a low sound of voices as 30 of us tried to absorb this latest information. Then a loud voice came from the back of the room. "Jesus, are we going to be here that long?"

The commander continued, "Sorry, I don't have that information. I'm sure your skipper will keep you informed. Now let's continue."

He turned to the map on the wall and pointed to the island of Bougainville. "Bougainville is the main supply base for the defense of New Georgia. The Japanese have developed an excellent harbor there. Most of the supplies, including troops, come in by boat." He paused, looking at us. "Gentlemen, we've got to close that harbor to Japanese shipping, and we have the means to do it."

There wasn't a sound in the room, just the harsh breathing of men who were afraid to ask the next question.

He continued, "Two days ago, a supply of aircraft mines were flown in from Australia. They're designed to be carried by aircraft and dropped in harbor areas. Once these mines are placed in the water, they will lay on the bottom and explode whenever a ship passes over them. One mine will sink a transport-size ship. They're very deadly."

Sweet Jesus! I bet a TBF will hold one. That damn map. It must be 300 miles from here to Bougainville and all the islands along the flight have some Japs on them. I've never dropped a mine! Bet we'll have to be flying low and slow. The Jap airstrip is damn close to the harbor. We're going to be dead ducks to AA fire! Torpedo Eight all over again. Goddammit to hell . . . I don't like this at all!

Our skipper now stood. "Thanks, commander, I'll take it now." He turned to us, his pilots and crewmen. "Gentlemen, working with the general's staff, I concurred with the need to mine the harbor at Bougainville. Consequently, the staff recommends that three mine-laying missions will be required to close the harbor to shipping, The dates for the missions are the 20th, 24th, and 29th of March. We will supply nine TBF crews and one of our sister squadrons will supply nine crews for a total of 18 aircraft.

"Because of the obvious hazards of a daylight attack, all three missions will be flown at night. Because none of you pilots have recent experience in night formation flying, we will fly the mission individually."

He stopped. The only noise was the sound of bodies shifting on the hard benches and of feet scraping heavy shoes across the floor. I could sense the fear in the room.

"Gentlemen, that's all for today. There will be nine crews flying the mission. Check the flight schedule for your time of takeoff tomorrow night. The final briefing will be at 2000 on the 20th. First plane off—2100. Try and get some rest. It's going to be a long flight. That's all."

We tried to fill the rest of the afternoon with any kind of a routine to keep us from thinking about the coming flights. Some of us took our dirty shorts, socks, and skivvies to the river and rinsed them out. All of us stripped down and bathed in the brownish, sluggish water of the Tenaru River. Anything to feel a little cleaner.

That night, we sat on our cots talking about the mine-laying mission. We all knew what we had to do. We would do the navigation planning together, helping one another before the final briefing. We also planned to go to the aircraft parking area and watch as the mines were loaded in the bomb bays of our aircraft. We also wanted to see the flame dampeners that had been installed on each plane's engine exhaust outlets. These would suppress the exhaust flare from the engine. Anything to reduce the chance of the Japanese seeing our planes during the attack.

Finally, we turned off the kerosene lanterns we used for light, hoping that Charlie would not make a run that night. I lay there, maybe for 20 minutes. I slowly reached under my cot and quietly pulled the bottle of whiskey out from under my cot and into my bed. I was not about to stay awake filled with my fears that night. I took a long pull from on the bottle. I knew sleep would come. My fears would disappear.

By 2000 hours on the 20th, the briefing room was jammed with flight crews. Skipper Butts took over the final briefing.

"Gentlemen, your attention please. As you each know, we will make the trip individually. I want a five-minute, take-off interval for each plane. I also want an indicated air speed for all planes of 150 knots for the entire route. This is most important. This will give us a five-minute spacing between each plane at the target area. The mileage from Henderson Field to the harbor at Bougainville is approximately 300 miles. We're looking at a five-hour round trip flight." He stopped and picked up a stack of papers. "These are critical to the success of this mission. When I call your name, hold up your hand, and I'll see that you get one."

I heard my name and was handed a mimeographed map. It was of the harbor at Bougainville. There was a line drawn starting at a small island at the eastern entrance to the harbor with a compass heading and a time marked on the line. The line ended at the western entrance to the harbor.

"These charts are for you to use to determine where you'll release your mine. Berg, read what's on your chart."

I stood and looked at the chart. "I see a course line with a compass heading and a time marked on the chart," I said. "The line starts at an island at the east entrance to the harbor."

"OK, Norm," he said. "Now here's how each of you will use the chart. Norm, as you approach the harbor, locate that small island. I want you over that island at 200 feet and 120 knots, bomb bay door open. You will be five minutes behind the plane that left Henderson Field ahead of you. Take up the compass heading that's on the chart and note the time you pass over the island. Let's say your chart has a time of two minutes, 30 seconds. That's how far you fly past the island until you drop your mine. Also take note of your take-off time here at Henderson Field. It's listed on your chart. This attack plan will disperse the mines throughout the harbor. Gentlemen, by the time we fly the last mission on the 29th, no Japanese ship will be able to enter that harbor. That's our mission. My take-off time is 2100. I'm first off. Good luck to each of you and God be with you."

The briefing room became very quiet. Every one of the pilots seemed to take one last look at the predicted weather report for Bougainville, as we began to leave to man our aircraft: Scattered clouds, wind westerly at five to ten knots, moon set at 2130.

I checked my watch—time to go to my plane.

This is going to be a son of a bitch ... flying into that harbor. Five hours round trip. Alone ... how long do I have to fly after that island, before I can dump the damn mine? Flying at 200 feet and 120 knots ... suicide! Hope it's real dark with some low clouds in the harbor. Need some low visibility so Jap AA gunners won't see me. What altitude going there? Stay low ... watch the water for wind changes. Less chance of strong winds. Don't go over any land! Stay between the islands ... stay over water.

We manned our planes, a pilot and two crew members per planes. A few minutes later, we were flying into a very dark sky. I leveled off at 1,500 feet, air speed 150 knots, compass heading 310 degrees, navigation lights off. It was going to be a long night.

Not much of a horizon. Pretty black. Watch those instruments. Remember Corpus. Don't get vertigo. Damn, it's black out here. How much time to go? Jesus, two hours more.

First Mission to Bougainville

I settled down into the cockpit, adjusting the parachute harness and safety belt across my thighs. It was going to be a long flight. The red instrument lights had a soft glow as I continually checked my air speed, altitude, and compass heading. The air was smooth with just a few wispy, scattered clouds above me. The moon had set, but the stars were visible. I was surprised by the amount of light the stars produced. I could see the Russell Islands just off to my left. This would be the last friendly group of islands we would see. The Russells were about 50 miles northwest of Guadalcanal. Our forces had occupied one of the islands and had built an airstrip. Our fighter squadrons were based there. By operating our fighters from there, we could intercept any enemy air attack well before it reached Henderson Field. As I flew past the island, I wondered how my friends in our fighter group were doing. Theirs was an entirely different operation, protecting Henderson Field from Japanese air attack.

Later, off to my left, I saw the dark bulk of the island of New Georgia. I altered my course a few degrees to the right. No sense in getting too close to the island. I did not want to be spotted by the Japanese even though they might hear my engine. Hopefully, they wouldn't even know I was there. The memory of the night attack the week before at New Georgia was still vivid.

That AA fire was tough. God, I hope it won't be bad at Bougainville. If I can get in the harbor and out ... I'm number ten flying in ... got a long way to fly from the little island. Watch the compass heading!

Off to my right, I could see the outline of another island. I spread out my map on the navigation board and turned on my flashlight. It had a red lens and in its glow, I identified the island, Santa Ysabel. I was right on course and on time. Folding up the map, I checked my navigation board and figured I had at least another hour and a half before reaching Bougainville.

Santa Ysabel had only a few Japanese ground force troops on the island. We'd been briefed that the Japanese were there to monitor our ship and aircraft movements out of Guadalcanal. There was a coast watcher there also, so there would be some help in case I had to make a forced landing. I checked my engine instruments; engine sounded good. Our guys worked real hard to keep those birds flying.

I remember calling my crewmen every five or ten minutes to let them know what was going on. It gave me something to do. I knew that fatigue would be my major problem. Talking with them helped me stay alert. Opening my cockpit hatch also helped me maintain my concentration. The fresh air blowing through my cockpit was refreshing. Between the poor food in the mess hall and sleeping problems, my general health was deteriorating. I found that a few drinks helped keep me going. I had found an Air Force supply sergeant who was willing to sell me some whiskey. I felt comfortable with a few extra bottles under my cot. I stowed them in my parachute bag.

Suddenly I realized I was well past the island of New Georgia. I could see another island on my right.

Where the hell am I? Check the map! It must be Choiseul. Jesus! Don't drift off like that! Getting close now ... maybe another 45 minutes. Watch the compass heading and don't drift too far left. There's open sea between New Georgia and the Shortlands. Keep Choiseul in sight, but not too close though. Glad the air is so smooth; it's easy to maintain altitude. Good horizon out there. Bet some of the guys are already in the Bougainville Harbor by now. God! I hope we surprise them. If we don't, I can't think about it. How much more time? Need to spot that small island at the eastern entrance to the harbor.

Soon after, I saw Bougainville with its high mountains rising up from the sea. I estimated I was about 15 minutes from the harbor area. I was trying to match what I was seeing with the map of the harbor. When I matched it, there was the small island at the entrance to the harbor—my check point.

I called my crewmen, alerting them we were about to begin our approach to drop the mine we were carrying. I told them to keep a sharp lookout for enemy aircraft. There was always the chance that the Japs might have an airborne night fighter. I reminded them, too, that if we began to receive AA fire from the beach, we should not use our guns to return the fire. I didn't want to reveal our position to the enemy gunners.

Flying at about 500 feet, we flew over the flat little island that was our check point. I cut the throttle back and let the plane drop down to 200 feet. I quickly checked the chart giving me my heading and flying time to my drop point. My air speed was 120 knots. A little left rudder, and I was on the assigned compass heading.

Bomb bay doors! Damn! Get them open! Arming switches on. Get with it ... can't see any other planes ... what time did I go over the check point? Damn it! I didn't check it! Can't be more than 30 seconds ago. Another minute and a half to go. There are some gun flashes on the beach. Looks like heavy AA fire. Maybe the Japs think we're at altitude instead of here in the harbor. We must have surprised them. No AA fire here in the harbor. Funny, I can't see another plane anywhere. Wonder if I am alone here? No! The guys ahead of me must have made it ... 30 seconds to go! There! Drop the son of a bitch and let's get out of here!

I decided to stay low over the water until I got clear of the harbor. I closed the bomb bay doors and advanced the throttle to full power. My air speed quickly built to 180 knots as I flew low between two islands that ringed the harbor. Then I saw what looked like a string of bright beads arching up from my left toward our plane. They were a reddish-yellow color, glowing in the dark. Twenty millimeter AA fire. I remember diving for the surface of the water as the bright, shiny beads passed over my cockpit. I leveled off at under 100 feet, made a violent skidding turn to my right, and got behind the island. I was out of the harbor now. My heart was pounding. My fear was real. We'd almost been killed. I'll never forget that string of bright reddish-yellow beads heading for the plane's cockpit. I climbed back up to 1,500 feet and took up the compass heading which would take me back to Henderson Field. After setting up a cruising speed of 160 knots, I estimated we'd be home in a little over two hours. Again I passed the same unfriendly island as my plane droned along, the dull throbbing of the engine forcing me to fight my desire for sleep.

> *That was close. Thank you, God. I'm so tired; talk to the guys in back. Talk about the Dodgers, the break up of the Yanks. Give someone else a chance; can't stop my legs from trembling. Man! That first drink will help. Jesus! This is just the first mission . . . two more to go! Need some sleep. It's after one o'clock, but there's Russell Island. I can see the fighter strip . . . almost home.*

I landed, taxied to the parking area, and I shut down the engine. I just sat there in the cockpit for a few moments. One of my crewmen climbed up on the wing and helped me out of the cockpit. There was a Jeep waiting to take us to the debriefing at the Pagoda. I felt OK by the time the debriefing was over. The skipper had debriefed my crew. He was a surprised when I told him about the 20-millimeter AA fire. He had seen no AA fire at all. There was no question; we had surprised the Japanese with our mining attack. So far, the first ten of us were all back. I wanted to wait until everyone had returned, but that's when the flight surgeon saw me. I guess he must have seen how tired I looked. He gave me the usual bottle of brandy and sent me to my tent.

The tent was empty. My tentmates had not yet returned from the flight. I sat on the edge of my cot and gulped down the brandy. Then I got a tin cup and reached into my parachute bag—I felt the cool smoothness of a whiskey bottle. I filled my cup, crawled into my cot, rearranged the netting, and lay there sipping my booze. I hadn't failed. I dropped the damn mine, and the AA fire didn't get me. Now, only two more missions to go.

Second Mission to Bougainville

On March 24, I saw I was scheduled for another mission to Bougainville. Well, here I go again, I thought. I saw the flight listed on the flight schedule "Nite Attack on Bougainville." What the hell was this? A night attack, not mine-laying?

Again there were 18 of us. Our skipper was the briefing officer.

"Gentlemen, as all of you are very aware, this will be our second mine-laying mission. We have had some reports back from a coast watcher in the Bougainville area. The Japanese were caught completely by surprise by our first mission. However, they now know their harbor has been mined. According to our coast watcher, two cargo ships have already been sunk by our mines." He paused, looking at us. We all knew the element of surprise was now gone.

He continued. "While it's obvious that the surprise element is gone, we must continue with the mining operation. We must close that harbor to Japanese shipping before the invasion of New Georgia, scheduled for July, can commence. I believe we can accomplish this by using a diversion tactic. We will have two planes making bombing attacks on the airfield at Bougainville while the remaining sixteen aircraft carry out the mine-laying."

The skipper turned to Commander Johnson. "Commander, will you continue the briefing of the pilots scheduled for the mine-laying mission?"

"Berg and Johnson, I see you two are scheduled for the bombing mission. Please follow me. We'll use the staff office for the briefing." Walking to the staff office, the skipper introduced me to Lieutenant Johnson, explaining that he was attached to one of our sister torpedo squadrons based at Henderson Field with us. The briefing didn't take long. Both TBFs were to carry ten 100-pound bombs. We would depart individually. Our take-off times were staggered to insure that one of us would be over the airfield at Bougainville until the entire mining operation was completed.

The skipper closed the briefing by saying, "I want you two to operate between 8,000 and 12,000 feet. Use oxygen for the entire flight. As you orbit over the airstrip at Bougainville, drop one bomb every two to three minutes. Your bombing will split the Japanese defenses so the mine-laying mission can be carried out with less risk. Be sure to vary your altitude. Remember, the Japanese have no radar. They can't see you. Let's make this work. Good luck and a safe trip."

A Grumman TBF-1 Avenger being brought up to the flight deck
(Courtesy of the U.S. Navy)

I was scheduled to leave ahead of the first mine-laying plane. I had some time before the first plane launched, so I sat down on a bench outside the Pagoda and lit a cigarette. I still remember my thoughts.

Could I do this? I knew why the skipper had picked me. It was that bombing attack against the Japs at New Georgia. Now I've got to bomb Bougainville! New Georgia was easy—I dove and was out of there. Jesus. This time I've got to fly around in the dark for at least 30 minutes. God. I wish I had a drink. What if they have search lights? Ah, to hell with it. It's time to leave.

I met my crew; briefed them; taxied out for takeoff; got a green light from the tower; and we were rolling down the runway.

Gear up; flaps up; reduce power; set up rate of climb at 500 feet per minute. Damn! It's black out here over the water. Hardly any horizon and lots of clouds. Get on the oxygen mask. Damn it! I'm in the clouds ... I'm in a turn! Instruments! Get on them! What's my heading? Three hundred degrees. Goddamn, I feel like I'm turning, losing altitude! Fly those gauges; needle in the center; compass steady; just like Corpus ... needle, ball, air speed! I've got vertigo; stay on those gauges. There. I'm out of the clouds. Steady now ... I can fly this bird.

I got back on the correct compass heading and continued to climb. I was clear of the initial group of clouds, but I could see more build-ups ahead. I checked the time—I'd been airborne about 45 minutes. The island of New Georgia was visible off to my left. Then I heard a slight change in the sound of the plane's engine. I glanced quickly at the engine instruments. The oil pressure gauge appeared to be fluctuating.

Engine problems! What's the cylinder head temp? It's high, I think. The fuel pressure gauge is jumping around too. There, oil pressure looks normal; fuel pressure looks OK. There's that change in the sound of the engine again ... something's wrong! Now the engine sounds fine, but the damn oil pressure gauge is moving again. Should I go back? What about the mission? There's that sound again. Goddammit! I'm back in the clouds again. Get on the gauges; I'm losing altitude; level the wings. To hell with it ... get out of the clouds and go back to the field. Get back before the damn engine quits.

I came out of the bottom of the clouds in a shallow dive. At about 2,000 feet, I leveled the wings and got the air speed under control. I could feel the sweat running down my face from under my oxygen mask. I remember my struggle trying to control the plane, fighting vertigo, and the bouncing instrument indicators, as the plane came out of the bottom of the clouds.

I could see Guadalcanal ahead of us as I called the tower for landing clearance. I gave the proper code word and was cleared for landing. As we taxied to the parking area the engine sounded fine, gauges all normal.

God! What if there's nothing wrong with the engine? The skipper could ground me! I could even lose my wings! Failure to carry out an order! There has to be something wrong. I know it. I wasn't afraid of the mission. I wasn't ... it was the engine. I didn't want to land in the water with an engine failure.

I shut down the engine as we arrived at the parking area. Chief Williams greeted me with the yellow sheet, which I filled out listing the problems I'd observed with the engine. All the chief said was that he'd check it out. Nothing was mentioned that I'd not completed the mission—that I'd returned early. A jeep picked me up and drove me to the Pagoda. I knew I had to complete a debriefing. The debriefing was short and very low key. I answered all the commander's questions.

Yes, I understood the mission. No, the weather was not a factor. I was assigned to fly between at 8,000 to 10,000 feet. I was climbing through the clouds when the engine problems developed. Yes, I believed that I made the correct decision to abort the mission. I believed that the engine would fail before I could complete the mission. I left the briefing room still struggling with the commander's closing comment. "Glad you made it back, Mr. Berg. Let's hope the one plane that did make it caused enough confusion with its bombs to protect the pilots flying the mining operation. We'll know if we suffered any losses when the planes return." The jeep took me to my tent. I was alone. My three tentmates were all flying the mining mission.

One little drink ... I've got to stay up. Got to wait until everyone is back. God, help them all get back ... please. The damn engine; I know something was wrong. I had to turn back ... had too! I'm so tired. Just one more little one ... there! I hear a plane; they're coming back. Please, God, I tried. The engine was bad ... I tried. I can't lose my wings! Please ... help me.

I awakened early, sat up abruptly, and looked through the netting above my cot. All three of the cots were filled with sleeping guys. I hadn't managed to stay awake until all the planes returned. I still didn't know if everyone had made it back. I decided to go over to the mess tent. I had to get some news. At least my tentmates were here. They made it back.

I arrived at the mess tent and, as I got a cup of coffee, I saw the skipper and Bill Shyrock alone at a table. Bill saw me and called, "Hey, Norm. Come on over here. Join us." I sat opposite the two of them. These two men whom I respected—men I would follow anywhere—said nothing.

Finally, I had to ask, "Skipper, Bill, did everyone make it back last night? Did we lose anyone?"

Bill responded. "Norm, everyone returned. A couple planes were shot up, but they made it back."

"Man, that's great news!" Then the skipper asked, "Norm, the briefing officer told me that you aborted the flight and returned with engine trouble. Tell me what happened."

So I told my story to these two men I admired so much. I felt I had to convince them that I wasn't a coward. My engine was failing. I'd experienced vertigo. Finally, I stopped talking.

The skipper broke the silence between us. "Norm, Chief Williams saw me privately late last night. Your plane checked out perfectly. He found no problems with the engine." His voice softened. "Norm, just three things. I believe you thought you had engine trouble. Consequently, you made the correct decision; you aborted the mission. There will be no disciplinary action. I'm not going to ground you. Second, you will be assigned to the next mine-laying mission. This squadron needs your leadership. You're the senior JG in the squadron." Then his voice changed, and with a very firm tone, he said, "Mr. Berg. You will turn over your supply of booze to the flight surgeon. When the time comes, we'll use it for a squadron party." I left the mess tent.

Another chance! He doesn't believe I'm yellow ... too scared to do my job. I won't fail him!

Night Mine-laying for the Third Time

The third mine-laying mission to Bougainville was scheduled for March 29, 1943. As expected, I was on the flight schedule. That morning, a truck picked up all of the pilots at our living area and dropped us at the Pagoda for the briefing. As we all settled down, the tension in the briefing room became obvious. There was no joking or outlandish remarks about being the best torpecker pilots in the Navy. Every pilot and crew member there knew the Japs would be ready for us. Our mines had done a job on their merchant ships. We were still getting reports of ships being destroyed. Everyone in that room knew this mission would be tough, and every pilot in that room believed he would make it back. We were ready.

The briefing was routine. The procedures were the same as the earlier missions. The weather was excellent with some low clouds and no moon. We would have some Army Air Corps guys bombing the Japs while we were flying into the harbor with our mines. There were some remarks about whether or not those "Army pogues" could find Bougainville at night.

My crew and I manned our plane and rolled down the runway a little after 2100. Our total flight time was estimated at six hours. I set up air speed at 150 knots, altitude 1,500 feet. The air was smooth with excellent visibility. The dull roar of the engine and an occasional comment from crew members were the only activities we experienced. I'd made this trip before, so navigation was a snap.

A lot different from the last flight when I had to abort. I feel different. Resigned, I guess. I must fly the mission. Wonder how my crewmen feel riding in the .50-caliber gun turret and in the belly of the plane. Funny, I've never asked them. They would probably say it's their job. We're all volunteers in this business of getting shot at. There's Bougainville. Better get set up for my run. Only two minutes before the drop.

I came across the flat, little island (my check point) at 200 feet and 120 knots air speed, bomb bay doors open, mine armed. Then, I saw the AA fire.

Goddammit! The entire area around the airstrip is nothing but gun flashes. There are some of those reddish-yellow lines ... again those beads arching out from the beach. I'm taking hits! I can feel the hits! My rudder pedals are vibrating! "We're taking hits, Sir! In the tail, Sir!" "Turret gunner, open up on that firing coming from our starboard." Oh, Jesus! A plane ahead of me just exploded! They got him! Now, drop that mine. Get down just above the water ... left turn, full throttle ... get out of here! Who got hit?

I cleared the harbor and took up a compass heading for Henderson Field. I could feel some vibration in my rudder pedals. I guessed it was from those AA hits we took. I called my gunner. "Smitty, can you see any damage on the tail surfaces from that AA fire?"

"Yes, Sir, the vertical stabilizer is full of holes!"

"How about the fuselage? Any damage under the tail surfaces?"

"Sir, this is Mac in the radio compartment. I took some hits down here. The bullet holes are in the back of the compartment and just where the tail of the plane joins the fuselage."

"OK guys, I'm going to make a few shallow turns. Mac, you check if there is any movement of the fuselage just below the tail assembly."

Very gently, I pushed the left rudder pedal and then the right rudder pedal. The plane responded with left and right shallow turns. "Mac, see anything?"

"No, Sir, no sign that the bullets did any damage other than put holes in the fuselage."

I turned back to my original compass heading. "OK, I guess this bird will get us home. Let's go!"

We made it back to Henderson Field. Once again, my crewmen helped me out of the plane's cockpit after we parked and shut down the engine. I felt numb, exhausted, as we got into a jeep and headed to the Pagoda for the debriefing.

Who got it? God! Hope it's not one of our pilots! Poor bastards didn't have a chance. How did I make it?

The debriefing was short and quick. All the returning pilots reported heavy AA fire. Two of us had seen one of our planes explode. We were both briefed carefully as we made our statements on what we saw. I was the tenth plane back. We would not know who had been shot down until all the planes returned. We waited at the Pagoda— all of us on the benches outside. The medic had given each of us the usual small bottle of brandy. No one felt like talking. We sat, looking at the dark sky and the stars, smoking and sipping slowly on the brandy. It was after three o'clock in the morning when we got the news—it wasn't one of our pilots and crew. We all climbed in to the back of a truck and returned to our tents. The guys from the TBF squadron who had lost their friends that night accepted our quiet words. "Sorry, guys." "I remember him, great guy." "Good pilot. I knew him at Corpus. We were in the same class." "Good crewmen. So sorry."

The last mine-laying mission was over, and all of the guys in our squadron had made it. There was a great sense of relief. None of us had ever expected to face such a challenge—such fear, flying those long, dangerous missions. We had done it, but were we ever glad it was over.

The next day, March 30, the skipper scheduled a meeting of the TBF squadron in the mess tent after lunch. All the pilots from the squadron and our crewmen were present. We were one quiet bunch. We really didn't know what to expect. The skipper entered with Bill Shyrock. We all stood as Bill called, "Attention!"

Dive-bombing and torpedo plane pilots of composite Squadron 28 at Henderson Field, Guadalcanal, April 1943. Commanding Officer, Lieutenant (jg.) Spencer Butts in front row, fifth from left. Lieutenant (jg.) Norman Berg in third row, sixth from right

The skipper slowly removed the stub of that ever-present cigar from his mouth. "Seats, gentlemen. I have a couple of announcements to make." His eyes roved around the room. He took his time, looking at each pilot and crewman. "Each of you has done a magnificent job these past two weeks. The demands have been almost overwhelming, and this squadron has meet every challenge." He paused. "I met with the commanding general this morning. He sends a 'well done' to each of you. He also agreed with me on one other item." Again a pause. "Gentlemen, as of today, there will be no flight operations for Torpedo Squadron 28 for the next two weeks."

There was a moment of silence, then from the back of the room came the words, "Sweet Jesus! Thank you!" The entire group began to yell at once, pounding each other's backs, shaking hands, everyone grinning like kids at a surprise party. The skipper just stood in front of us, also grinning.

That evening we had a party with my confiscated whiskey.

The next two weeks were not the leisure time I'd expected. I woke up following the party with much more than just a hangover. I ached all over, my skin felt hot to the touch, and I felt very warm as if I had a fever. I was terribly thirsty. I blamed my condition on the party, but by late afternoon, I finally asked one of my tentmates to get a doctor from the Army field hospital to see me.

For the next ten days, I was hospitalized with an attack of malaria. I was released on April 10 and cleared for flight operations by the squadron flight surgeon. I felt well-rested, and in fact, I think I ate better than in the mess tent. I took the usual kidding about the nurses and taking life easy while my squadron mates were sweating out tent living and the mess tent.

Three days later, I was on the flight schedule for a night familiarization (or fam) flight. Before the flight, Bill Shyrock asked me to meet with him. We met at the Pagoda where Bill told me that the skipper was being detached as the CO of our squadron after we completed this tour at Henderson Field. I wasn't surprised. We were all sure the skipper would make admiral before the war was over. "Who's the new skipper?" I asked.

Bill's reply took me completely by surprise. "Norm, I'll be Butt's replacement. I'll begin flying with the dive-bombing squadron, the job that the skipper has done."

He stopped. Looking at me, he said, "Norm, you're the senior pilot in the torpedo squadron. The skipper wants you to take over the leadership of the TBF squadron."

Hot damn! I'll be leading the guys. Just like the bull ensign back in Norfolk. I can do it; the skipper believes in me. Remember how the skipper leads, nice and easy. Be an example.

He continued. "I've scheduled you for this night fam flight tonight, then a practice bombing flight on the 18th." He stopped. "Norm, the general wants a night bombing mission against Bougainville on the 19th. He wants to keep those Jap bastards awake. The skipper and I believe you should take the flight. I'm sure you understand the skipper's thinking. Any problem with your making the flight?"

I flew the night fam flight and the practice bombing flight.

My crew and I took off on the 19th for the attack on Bougainville. We were airborne at 2100 hours.

This isn't going to be an aborted flight. Get on those gauges. Set the throttle for a 500-feet per minute climb. The hell with the clouds. Level off when clear of the clouds. There ... 6,500 feet; air speed 160; in the clear and passing New Georgia. Another hour. Add some power; start to climb. Go over the harbor at Bougainville at 12,000 feet. Oxygen mask on. There's the airstrip. The coral runway really shows up. Set up an easy circle. Bomb bay doors open. Bombs armed. One 100-pounder at a time....

I heard my radioman call, "Sir, lots of AA flashes on the ground."

"Roger, Mac. I'm going to dive to 9,000 feet—now!"

I heard Smitty, my gunner. "Gunner here! Jap searchlight just came on!"

I saw the searchlight begin to probe for our plane. "Gunner, if the lights finds us, start firing at it. Open up on it with the your turret gun!"

Level off. Reverse course. Drop another bomb. Add power; climb back to 11,000 feet. Drop another bomb. That goddamn searchlight is still moving around ... searching. Son of a bitch! White light! Can't see outside the cockpit ... it's got us! Dive for the ground; there goes Smitty's gun. He's firing. Release the rest of the bombs. Maybe one will hit the bastard. Get on the gauges. There, we're out of the light. Altitude ... stay low. Right turn out over the harbor. Don't go between those two islands; go over one of them. Let's go home!

The next few days were hectic, but no one minded. The squadron was packing. The skipper had received orders for the entire squadron to fly out of Henderson Field with our aircraft on April 25, 1943. Our fighter group took off first, then the dive-bombers, and finally the TBFs. Again, a Navy transport plane arrived for the maintenance crew. This part of the Cactus Air Force was going back to Efate.

My log book has two entries for April 25. A four-hour flight to Espiritu Santo, code name "Button," and a one-hour flight to Efate, code name "Roses."

When our TBFs arrived at Roses, we made a low pass over *Chenango*. She was anchored in the harbor at Efate. We were home.

Return to Efate

We were back on our island of Efate living in metal Quonset huts—four of us to a hut. We had hot showers and a Navy-run mess hall with food supplies brought ashore from *Chenango*. In addition to the officers' club and an enlisted mens' club, there were volleyball courts and a white, sandy beach alongside the warm, blue South Seas. After our experience at Guadalcanal, all this felt as if we were at an expensive beach resort.

Upon our arrival, the squadron flight surgeon, a medical doctor with specialized training in aviation, met with us. He warned each of us that we should gradually increase our activities, but warned, "Don't try to do everything at once." His flight physicals of the pilots and the crewmen indicated and average weight loss of 15 to 20 pounds as a result of our tour at Guadalcanal. I went from 150 pounds to 135. We were a bunch of skinny guys.

The flight surgeon cleared me physically for flight operations on May 1. By then, our aircraft maintenance crews had checked out the aircraft, patched up the bullet holes, and serviced each plane's engine. My first flight was that day—a test flight on a TBF. These flights were to ensure a reported discrepancy on any particular aircraft had been corrected. What a pleasure it was. I flew around the island at about 500 feet. There were white beaches, small fishing villages, and coconut trees—thousands of them—so peaceful, so beautiful. With a few scattered clouds and the dark, blue ocean; it was flying at it's best!

On May 6, the skipper called a meeting of all hands, pilots, crewmen, and maintenance personnel. We met in the mess hall and, as the skipper entered, we all stood at the command for attention.

"Seats, gentlemen. I'm sure all of us have enjoyed this vacation on our South Sea island. Any complaints?" Almost in unison came the sound of "No Sir, Skipper!"

"I want to bring you up-to-date on our planning for the next month. I've had a conference with Captain Wyatt, the captain of our carrier. We're a carrier air group, and pilots and the carrier personnel need to be both retrained on carrier operations." He turned to Bill Shyrock. "Bill, please schedule all pilots for field carrier landing practice (FCLP). I want everyone ready to fly aboard *Chenango* on the 11th. We'll be spending the next two weeks flying off the carrier. I want refresher flights for formation flying, tactics, and bombing for all dive-bombing and TBF pilots. The fighter squadron will schedule its flight programs. Any questions?"

What's going on? What about the invasion of New Georgia in July? We were told about it while we were at Henderson Field. Maybe we're not going back to the Canal. That would be a relief. Good to get back on board the ship, though. No one shooting at us; just good flying.

We all did well with the FCLP refresher. The landing signal officer (LSO) suggested that we must have wanted to get back to shipboard life—we were actually answering his signals properly.

It was delightful to be back aboard. I was no longer sleeping in a bunk room with three other guys. I now shared a stateroom with Bill Shyrock. It was good to meet and talk with the ship's officers again, and to take our meals with them in the ward room. They were our hosts. The ship was their home—we pilots were just visitors. Most of all, though, were the sounds of the ship as she steamed through the waters of the South Pacific—the wind over the flight deck and the sound of the water sliding past her hull. A ship at sea takes on a life of her own, like the sound of announcements of "The smoking lamp is out" or "Third watch report for duty." Then there was the creak of metal as the ship rolled in the ocean swells and the soft sounds of men moving through the narrow passageways, up and down ladders between decks, carrying out their duties, making the ship a living thing. It was good to be aboard.

Between May 11 to 20, I made seven carrier landings, practicing bombing and tactical flight as well as formation flights. The tactical flights involved flying with the dive-bombing and the fighter squadrons on coordinated bombing attacks. We were getting to be very efficient as a carrier group. This refresher training was important, not only for the pilots, but for the carrier crew as well. Carrier operations require a real team effort to launch and recover aircraft in a safe and rapid manner. By the time we left the ship and returned to Efate on May 20, the ship's crew was operating with newly honed skills. Captain Wyatt gave us a "well done" as we left the ship, thanking us for the excellent training experience we'd given the ship's flight deck crew.

It was a short stay on Efate. We did have some time to do some final maintenance on our planes, get some additional training in glide-bombing, and do some partying. The skipper had announced earlier that he was being transferred, so on May 30, we had a farewell party for him. Actually, there were two parties, one organized by Chief Williams with enlisted men of the three squadrons, and the other organized by Bill Shyrock and me.

It was a very proud moment for me when the skipper announced that Bill would take over as commanding officer, and I would lead the TBF squadron. Lieutenant Anson, our air intelligence officer, was assigned the job of executive officer. That was fine with me; I would do the flying and Anson would do the paperwork.

For the first time ever, I left the party early. I did buy a round of drinks for the torpecker pilots, as I was reminded that I was still the bull ensign. Now, I was the Bull JG.

That night, laying in my cot, I contemplated the future.

Bet we'll go back to the Canal ... back into combat. This time I've got to lead. It will be different. Got to watch the booze. Have to make tough decisions. They are my friends. Don't want to hurt anyone. Pray we all make it back.

Back on *Chenango*

Our squadron left Efate for *Chenango* on June 16, 1943. She'd left the harbor the previous day and was about 50 miles west of Efate. *Chenango* was assigned to escort a convoy of supply ships to Guadalcanal. As I flew out to the ship, I had a very special letter in my pocket. I was a brand new father. Jean had just given birth to our son, Donald Edward Berg.

What's it going to be like? A baby to care for. It's Jean's job, I guess. I've got my job ... flying ... what about our love making? Wonder if the baby ... no ... Jean will still be passionate. Should be going home soon. We've been away since December. Bet we get one more trip to Henderson. Damn! Back to getting shot at ... hope there won't be any more night stuff. There's the ship. My first time leading the TBF squadron. Let's make it a good one. The guys are flying a real tight formation ... let's get aboard!

Between June 16 and 23, I flew seven antisub patrols as *Chenango*'s planes protected the convoy en route to the Canal. Most of the flights meant flying an out-bound leg of about 100 miles after leaving the ship; flying a second leg of about 30 miles that paralleled the ship's course; and finally turning to the inbound leg for the return to the ship. All the flights were routine, except for one.

On June 22, my log book records one four-hour flight, launching at 1500 hours. Based on the direction and speed of the wind and my plane's speed, I estimated 3.4 hours of flight time. I would be back at the ship at approximately 1830, a full hour before sunset. The weather prediction was partly cloudy with scattered showers. I flew the outbound leg and turned at my estimated time onto the second leg. We were flying at 1,000 feet as my crew and I watched for any possible submarine activity—that feather of white water made by a sub's periscope. I checked the time and made my turn to the inbound leg, heading back to the carrier. The rain showers were getting heavier and more frequent and the cloud cover above me was about 80 percent. I eased the plane down to 500 feet, flying through the rain showers and checking the time. I was about 30 minutes from my ETA (estimated time of arrival) at the carrier. I flipped on the switch for the YE, the ship's radio homing transmitter.

What the hell? No signal. Maybe I'm too low to receive the signal. Better not climb above the clouds ... might miss seeing the ship. Stay on course and get closer to the ship's position. I'll probably pick it up.

I called my radioman in the lower compartment. "Mac, check the YE receiver. I'm not getting a signal."

I heard his reply. "Sir, the receiver's power light is not on. Is your YE switch on?"

"Affirmative. Guess our receiver is out. OK, guys, I estimate we're about 20 minutes from the ship's position. We'll find her."

Damn! Weather's not too good and visibility stinks. No sense in calling the ship; they can't help. It's not an emergency yet; don't want to risk the ship. Get the navigation board out and lay out a square-search pattern. Better hurry ... if you don't see the ship in just ten minutes, that's the ETA, start the square search.

A square-search pattern was a navigational plan a carrier pilot could use at sea to locate his ship. I had first learned about it at Corpus Christi while in flight training and we reviewed the procedure in our squadron training at Norfolk.

When I reached my estimated time of arrival at the ship's position, I didn't see the carrier. I knew the ship's compass course was 030 degrees, speed 12 knots. I had been airborne about three hours and 20 minutes. I quickly calculated the ship's speed times the three hours and 20 minutes I'd been flying. The ship could only have moved about 40 miles. I completed the navigation plan for the square search and started the search.

OK. Turn to a heading 210 degrees. That heading was the reciprocal of the ship's heading of 030 degrees. Fly for one minute. No ship. Turn right 90 degrees to a heading of 300 degrees. One minute. Turn right to a heading of 030 degrees for two minutes. Nothing. Turn right heading 120 degrees. Two minutes. Still no ship. Turn right. Heading 210 degrees. Three minutes. Damn! Nothing. It's getting late ... when's sunset? How's my fuel? Where the hell is she? Turn heading 300. Three minutes. There, she's just getting clear of that rain squall. Made it!

Those twelve minutes seemed like forever. I orbited the carrier until I saw the red Charlie flag stream from the signal bridge. That was my signal to prepare to land aboard. *Chenango* turned into the wind, getting ready to take me aboard. We got aboard on the first pass between two severe rain showers. I was damn glad to be home, and I hadn't had to call for help.

That evening, our new skipper, Bill Shyrock, called a pilots' meeting in the ready room. I was the one who called "Attention" as Bill entered the ready room. He grinned at me and said, "Thanks, Norm, it does take a some getting use to, this 'Attention' stuff." He continued, "Guys, today I received orders for the squadron. The message came from Navy Headquarters in Noumea. We'll fly off *Chenango* on June 26th for the airfield at Espiritu Santo. There, we will refuel and fly on to Henderson Field. Again, we'll be part of the Cactus Air Force. Our job will be to support Army landings at New Georgia." The ready room was quiet as we all absorbed the news.

> *God! Another tour at Henderson. Hope the living is better. Those damn tents were pretty bad and the malaria too. I've got to lead the TBF guys. Hope we all make it. Wonder when we'll get home. More combat ... I'll make it. Got to ... Jean and Donnie are back in Bremerton.*

Bill continued. "Our maintenance people will remain on the ship. Only our crewmen will accompany us to Guadalcanal. A Navy combat aircraft service unit (CASU) is now based on the Canal, and they will maintain our aircraft. One more thing. Living conditions have improved. There are now Quonset huts and a new mess hall. You'll even have hot water, just like Efate." He looked around. "Guys, we're ready for this. The extra training we've had this past six weeks has sharpened our skills. I'll be leading the dive-bombers, and Norm will lead the torpedo squadron. I know we'll do the job were trained for."

We stood as Bill left the ready room. A couple of the guys asked me if I knew when we might leave for the States. Another asked if I knew whether or not we would be flying night attacks again. I told them I just didn't know. As I left the ready room, it was obvious the guys were affected by the skipper's news. There was only the quiet murmur of conversation. There was certainly no excitement nor any sign of eagerness to go back into combat. We'd survived this far. I wasn't sure that everyone was capable of flying more combat missions. Maybe we'd been shot at too many times.

That evening, Bill and I and the squadron flight surgeon met in Bill's and my room. I expressed my thoughts about some of the comments by the pilots and about the overall morale of the group. Our flight surgeon agreed. He had also noticed some of the pilots' concerns. Bill's solution was clear. First, he and I would lead every mission. The other pilots would rotate. Only the two of us would fly every mission. He also asked the flight surgeon to spend time with the pilots, observing and talking with them.

I lay in my upper bunk that night thinking about Shyrock's plan.

> *God! Every flight! Got to do it. No choice. None. Quit? Can't quit. God, please help me make it. Please ... I've so much to live for. Help me do my job ... help me get all the guys home.*

Return to Henderson Field

The torpedo squadron arrived at Henderson Field on June 27. The old Pagoda was gone, replaced by a bunch of Quonset huts that served as the operations area. We all met there on the 28th for our briefing. Navy Commander Johnson welcomed us back to the Cactus Air Force. There were no surprises in the briefing. We would be in support of the Army landing on New Georgia Island. Our combat mission would include bombing attacks on the airfield, ship searches to prevent the Japanese from bringing additional troops to the island, and bombing attacks to support the Army landings on Japanese troop positions. Someone in the back of the room asked about enemy anti-aircraft fire. "Light to moderate" was Johnson's reply.

We settled into our living area: Quonset huts, a shower house with hot water, and a new mess hall. There was also a great improvement in the food. I thought these new living conditions would certainly help the squadron's morale. As I talked with my fellow pilots, a change in attitude was apparent. There was more joking and a greater sense of comradeship between the men.

I led my first flight with six aircraft on June 30, 1943. It was an attack on the airfield at New Georgia. This time, we cratered the runway with 500-pound bombs. The AA fire was light, and none of our planes were hit. After that, we waited for the invasion to begin. I was the leader on just two flights between July 1 and 8. The one on the first was another bombing mission on the airfield at New Georgia. The general's staff there at Henderson Field was determined to keep the Japanese airfield unusable for enemy aircraft. The flight on the eighth was an antishipping search. The staff was aware that the Japanese were using small boats to move troops to New Georgia from Bougainville. I led four planes to search an area northwest of New Georgia. We split up into two-plane sections, and my wingman and I searched the area around the island of Kolombangara. The other two aircraft searched the area around the island of Vella Lavella. My wingman and I were flying at about 500 feet and paying special attention to any small coves or harbors that might conceal small Japanese boats. We were not finding any targets when suddenly my gunner called me on the intercom. "Sir, I think there's a boat under those trees in that little cove right at our three o'clock position."

I called my wingman. "Orbit your position. Possible target three o'clock. I'm taking a look. Out."

I rolled into a left turn and headed toward the suspected target.

Jesus. I hope there's nothing there. Too many men are dying. Damn war.

Just like before, I saw those red and yellow flashes arching toward our plane. AA fire!

"Target sighted! I'm receiving fire!"

I called my wingman and ordered him to start firing at the area with his .50-caliber turret gun as I dove low over the trees. My gunner began firing our turret gun as I turned back and began circling the target.

I called my wingman. "Maintain 700 feet." I could see the outline of a small vessel hidden under the trees. I could see our tracer bullets hitting the boat.

Suddenly, there was an explosion, and I saw fire and a column of smoke rising from the target area. We circled the area, watching the fire and the continuing small explosions. We didn't see any Japanese soldiers escaping from the burning target.

I called my wingman and gunner. "Good shooting, guys. We got him! Join on me. We'll keep looking. Maybe there are others. Out."

Goddammit! That Jap almost got us! That was close. Jesus, I wish this would end. It's just too much. I'm so scared. I must believe I'll make it home.

New Georgia Invasion

Beginning July 12, up through the 25th, I led eleven flights against the enemy. The invasion of New Georgia was underway. One flight, in particular, remains very vivid in my memory.

On July 14, 1943, I led a six-plane flight on a bombing mission against New Georgia. U.S. Army troops were advancing against the Japanese defenders. Again, our target was the airfield. We were at 9,000 feet, in a loose formation of two three-plane sections. Suddenly, my radio crackled. I heard my wingman's voice, saying, "Four bogies! Nine o'clock high!" I looked up and to my left. There they were, four Japanese fighters—Zeros—in formation.

Goddammit! Where are our fighters? Looks like they're turning towards us ... got to get ready for possible Jap fighter attacks on us!

I went on the radio. "Cactus flight, this is the Bull. Bogies sighted. Close on me now! Close up!" The five other planes quickly closed on me, forming a very tight formation. Another radio call. "Turret gunners commence tracking those Japs!" I could see all six gun turrets moving as they swung the .50-caliber machine guns toward the enemy fighters.

I called, "Gunners, on my signal, all guns fire a burst. Set your aiming point well below the enemy fighters. I want them to see our fire power. I don't want them to attack!"

I ordered, "Fire now!" A stream of bullets from the six turrets arched out from our formation.

What are those bastards going to do? They're still circling. Maybe I should take the flight down. Get low over the water. Can't let them get below us. Still got the bombing mission. Wait a minute. They're getting out of here; they're turning away! Damn! We were lucky. At this altitude, they would have massacred us ... we would have had to dive and get low over the water to have a chance against those fighters.

I called the flight, "Nice work, guys. Great formation flying, and gunners—you scared the bastards off. Let's head for the airstrip. Got to drop these bombs."

We made the return trip to Henderson Field with no problems.

I led another six-plane flight on July 25, another bombing attack against targets on New Georgia in direct support of advancing American troops. Each of our planes was carrying one 2,000-pound bomb with a fuse designed to explode just before hitting the ground. By exploding before hitting the ground, they were very effective in killing personnel. There was no AA fire. We all made it back to Henderson Field.

That evening, the skipper called a meeting at the mess hall. All pilots and crewmen were present and wondering—why a meeting? As usual, we all stood as the skipper entered the room.

"OK, guys. Please sit down." There was a shifting of benches as everyone took seats. Shyrock looked around. "Gentlemen, please note that I'm using the word *gentlemen*. A word always used by Commander Butts when he was our skipper. I do wish he were here to make this announcement. Gentlemen, today was our last mission. We've all survived, and I suspect many of you thank God that we all made it."

The cheers started all over the room, guys hugging one another, shaking hands, pounding each others' backs.

Shyrock continued, as we quieted down, "On the 27th, a Navy transport plane will fly us back to Efate. We will leave our aircraft here at Henderson. At Efate, we will board *Chenango* and depart for San Francisco. Gentlemen, we're going home!"

It's over! I'm going home to Jean ... to our baby too. We've been so blessed; we're all safe. Not a single person wounded or killed. Some of it was tough, like that flight I aborted. God! I was so scared. Those night flights, so lonely. It's over; I made it and I get some leave. Wonder what's next? Don't think about it; just get home to Jean. Get home.

Chapter 7

Squadron Training in California

The Navy transport aircraft was waiting for us at the Henderson Field operations building. It was August 5, 1943. We were on our way home. The pilots from the fighter squadron, the dive-bombing pilots and their crews, and our TBF pilots along with our crewmen climbed aboard the transport plane with no regrets. We left our aircraft parked at Henderson Field. We were going home in style aboard *Chenango*. There would be no flight operations during the ten-day trip back to the States.

The same day, we flew from Henderson Field to Efate—the small island in the central New Hebrides where we had been based before. Trucks were waiting to take us to the harbor where we boarded small boats for the ten-minute trip out to the anchored ship. By the time we got settled and ate dinner, the carrier was underway.

The trip back to the States was just what we needed. Good food, plenty of rest and, most importantly, a chance for exercise. With the ship's hangar deck empty, there was room for volleyball and basketball. We had a series of tournaments in both sports among the ship's officers, among the squadron officers, and between the officers and the enlisted personnel.

In addition, all squadron members were inducted into the "Shellback Club" when we crossed the equator. A senior member of the ship's crew served as King Neptune, who controlled the ceremony. Each candidate had to crawl through a canvas gunnery target filled with the ship's garbage, then "kiss the baby's belly." The "baby" was the fattest sailor aboard, and his belly was smeared with black grease! Candidates were all equal in the eyes of King Neptune. After this rite of passage, we each received a Shellback membership card from *Chenango*'s commander, Captain Ben Wyatt.

We first saw the Golden Gate Bridge on August 15. What a sight! The fog was lifting and the tops of the steel pillars supporting the bridge were visible. The morning sun was breaking through the fog, bathing the bridge in hazy sunlight. It was truly golden. *Chenango* moved slowly across San Francisco Bay until she reached her mooring alongside the dock at the Alameda Naval Air Station. We could see the skyline of San Francisco from the flight deck of the ship.

That day, all the squadron officers and enlisted personnel were transferred to the Commander Fleet Air (COMFAIR) Alameda for temporary duty awaiting assignment. Following dinner at the officers' club, I spent the early evening in a BOQ room at the air station wondering when my leave would start. As soon as I disembarked from the ship, I was able to find a pay phone on the dock and call Jean, collect. When the call went through, she told me she was staying with my folks in the small basement apartment in their house. "We have a place of our own, darling," she said. She sounded so happy. She continued, telling me that Donnie was fine, and that she could hardly wait until I got home to her and the baby.

A baby … he's about three months old. Wonder if he sleeps all night. Bet we have to be quiet so we don't wake him. What about us? Our love making? Maybe Mom will take the baby for a few days … Jean and I could go away … just for a few days….

A knock at my door—it swung open. "Hey, Norm!" Three of my squadron buddies were standing there. "Come on, Norm! We're heading for Frisco and "The Mark." We've reserved two double rooms for the next week. Come on, it's time for a party."

We took a cab to the ferry landing, caught the ferry to Frisco, hailed a cab to the Mark Hopkins Hotel, checked into our rooms, ordered a couple bottles of whiskey, rum and mixers from room service, and started the party. Ours was just one of three or four other groups from the fighter and dive-bombing squadrons that had rooms at The Mark.

Our three squadrons received some publicity in the San Francisco papers because of our experiences flying out of Guadalcanal. A couple of the local pilots had even been interviewed. The Top of The Mark—top floor of the hotel—had a panoramic view of all San Francisco. It was the most popular nightclub in the city. It was filled every evening with attractive young women who wanted to dance and drink with naval aviators back from the war. We certainly gave them the chance. For me, the booze and the dancing were enough. Just holding a woman—her perfume, her soft hair alongside my face, her slim body pressed against me as we danced—that was all I allowed myself. The memories of my fear, of the flashing AA fire all faded away in the arms of those beautiful women at the Top of The Mark.

The party ended when we received a phone call at the hotel from our air station's duty officer. An awards ceremony was scheduled with the admiral. Following that, we were free to commence our 30-day leave. Even though I had a bad hangover on August 29, I appeared in my dress blue uniform and was decorated with my first air medal for "Meritorious Service Under Combat Conditions."

Home to Bremerton

Using a Navy travel voucher, I caught a commercial flight and headed for Seattle. I was going to be a husband again and a father for the first time. I was going home. Everything was going to be just fine.

My parents and Jean met me at the Seattle airport. I left the plane and hurried to the wire fence in front of the airport waiting room. Jean was standing by the gate, wearing a red dress under a soft-looking white coat. I remembered that this was the dress she had worn when I came home from Corpus Christi. She was radiant as she stood waiting for me with Donnie in her arms. My parents and Jean surrounded me as we held one another in our arms. Jean pulled free. "Norm, here's your son, Don." She handed me a little bundle, wrapped in a fuzzy white blanket. Gingerly, I took my son into my arms, looking down at him. He was sleeping. "He's asleep," I said. "Here, Jean, you'd better take him. I don't want to wake him up." Jean took him as my mother said, "Oh, Norman, there's white fuzz from the baby's blanket all over your uniform." I brushed my uniform off as we retrieved my luggage and walked to my dad's car.

"Sorry about the lint from the blanket, Norm." I grinned at my lovely wife and replied, "It's all right, Jean—just part of being a new father. If that's the worst I'll get when I hold him, I'll be lucky."

The first night with my folks was a short evening. We had dinner together as I tried to answer the questions Dad was asking. "How many bombing attacks did you make? Were you ever hit by enemy fire?" My mother finally hushed him up. I watched as Jean fed the baby his bottle, and we excused ourselves early. Jean had the baby, so I followed her to the basement apartment. It was perfect: a small livingroom, a tiny kitchen, one bedroom, and bath. I watched as she got Donnie ready for bed. The crib was in our bedroom. "Jean, can't we have the crib in the livingroom?" I asked. Jean smiled at me. "Honey, I can't have the baby that far away from where we sleep. I'd be afraid I wouldn't hear him if he woke up." She covered the baby with a light blanket and led

Jean and baby Donnie, summer 1943

me into the living room. She turned and pushed her slim body up against me. I could feel her breasts pressing against my chest. Her warm mouth whispered, "Darling, don't worry. I'm sure you remember how to make love on a couch," then her tongue darted into my mouth.

The first week of my leave flew by. Mother had a "welcome home" party for me with all of my parents' friends. Dad insisted on taking me to the American Legion meeting and to the Elks' Club. Jean and I visited with her parents, Anne and Phil Devaney, but that visit didn't go so well. Jean's mother was upset that we were staying with my parents. I think she expected us to stay with them. The only space they had was one bedroom. She didn't seem to understand our desire to have a place of our own while I was on leave.

We saw very little of our old high school friends. Many of them were in the military and had left Bremerton. A few of them were working in the Navy Yard. We had dinner with one couple, but it was miserable. The conversation during the entire evening was about the terrible shortages of gasoline, meat, and liquor. Even the old high school dance pavilion, Pearl Maures, was a disappointment.

My mother agreed to babysit Donnie while Jean and I went dancing. I was in dress blues with my ribbons and my gold wings. Navy regulations required personnel to be in uniform while in public in wartime. We were greeted by a scruffy-looking group of young men with yells of, "Hey, swabbey, kill any Japs yet? Who's the hot-looking broad with you?"

As we started to enter the dance pavilion, I noticed they were passing around a bottle. Jean said, "Norm, don't pay any attention. They are defense workers who have come here from all over the country to work in the Navy Yard. Bremerton is a much different place, today, than when you left."

We stepped inside the hall and looked around. There was not a single person in uniform to be seen; they were all civilians. I was especially aware of the looks some of the men were giving Jean and me. It was obvious that men in uniform were not welcome. We, who were in the military, saw these young men as "draft dodgers." According to Jean's father, who worked in the Navy Yard, most of these guys were unskilled labor. They were using the defense industry to avoid serving their country. Jean and I left. It was just too uncomfortable.

War Bond Duty

The following Monday morning, my mother called down to us, "Norm, you have a phone call." It was early—only a little after eight o'clock. I went upstairs and took the call, wondering what kind of a phone call it could be. It was the Navy commandant's office in Seattle. The person on the phone was a commander, the admiral's public information officer. He told me that the admiral was issuing me orders to participate in a War Bond drive scheduled for a ten-day period in various cities in the Northwest. I was to report to the admiral's office within 24 hours.

When I asked "Why me?" I was informed that my name had been submitted by the Navy Department to the admiral's office as a decorated Navy pilot just returning from the South Pacific.

"Commander, I'm home on leave. I'm married with a new son. Can my wife come with me? I'll pay her expenses." He agreed that, under the circumstances, it would be appropriate. In fact, it might even sell more bonds. I bounded down the stairs. What a great vacation, a Navy car with a driver, hotel rooms, and meals out. As I explained the plan to Jean, she just stood looking at me. She seemed both surprised and stunned.

"Norm, can the Navy do this to you? You're on leave! You're just home from the Pacific!" I explained to her that yes, the Navy could do it, and what a great time we would have.

"Norm, what about the baby? What's your plan for Donnie?" When I suggested that my mother would be happy to take care of Donnie, a frown crossed Jean's face.

"No, Norman, I can't do that! Please understand. It's too long a time. I just can't leave him for that long, even with your mother. He's barely three months old. Please, Norm, can't you even try to convince the admiral that you can't go, you can't leave your family!"

I left for Seattle the next day. Jean didn't seem to understand that I had no choice.

The War Bond tour went well, although I did have to eat a lot of chicken at service club lunches. And then there were the obligatory rounds of drinks with members of the American Legion. The older guys were very nice, but we had little in common. I heard plenty of stories about their war—World War I. It was exciting though—a war hero talking to audiences about the need to buy bonds.

I called Jean every couple of days but avoided talking about the bond drive. I was lonely. I had time to consider my new role as a father. It was obvious that I was no longer the only person in Jean's life. That was very clear when she refused to come with me on the bond tour. I couldn't understand or accept her reason. Didn't she trust my mother? I wondered if the baby was more important to Jean than I was. There was also the issue of my next assignment. Jean told me that she didn't expect me to volunteer for another carrier squadron. I reminded her that I went where the Navy sent me. I knew she wanted me stay with her and the baby. "Ask for duty as a flight instructor, maybe back at Corpus Christi or even N.A.S. Seattle," was her suggestion.

Hell! I didn't know what I wanted. I only felt that my life was changing, and I didn't like the feeling. I finished the War Bond tour and received a letter from the admiral. It would be entered in my service record commending me for a job, "Well done."

Gone Fishing

Two days later, I received a call from a friend of my folks inviting Jean and me to their fishing lodge on Hoods Canal. It would be a short drive for us. The lodge was only about 100 miles north of Bremerton. I wondered if Jean would consider going. I had only about ten days of leave left. I could do some trout fishing—hike into the Olympics—great trout fishing in some of the lakes in the mountains. I knew just the place. I used to fish there when I was in high school. It would be great. Jean and the baby could stay at the lodge. She used to love going there while we were dating in high school. She knew the people who ran the lodge. I bet Dad would loan me his car for the trip. I could get the extra ration gas coupons because I'm on leave from the military. I sure hoped she would do it.

Later that day after a wonderful dinner, I talked with Jean about the invitation. I tried not to be insistent, but I reminded her that my leave was almost over, and I really wanted to go trout fishing. Her smile told me she would go. "All right Norm, we'll go. After all, you fished up there before you and I were married, and I do like the lodge."

Packing for the four-day trip was some chore—crib, bassinet, diapers, baby food, bottles, baby clothes, stroller, and play pen. This didn't count my fishing gear or our clothes. God, I thought, it was sure different before the baby.

The four days were wonderful. I spent some time learning to hold Donnie, to feed him and even to change his diapers. I was trying and so was Jean. Nothing more was said about the Navy and my next assignment. On the first day, our hosts took Donnie on a shopping trip into the little village. Jean and I made love that afternoon. It was almost like high school again, when we first made love there at the lodge and promised that we would always love one another.

Our host and I left on the third day of our vacation for the trout fishing trip. We had to walk about four miles to the lake where we wanted to fish. The fishing was extremely good. We each had our limit of rainbow trout when we started the walk out to the car. I didn't realize how much walking we'd do. I had only my fishing boots to make the eight-mile walk in and out. As I got into the car and removed my rubber boots, I saw the blisters on my feet. Those boots weren't made for hiking.

We arrived at the lodge at dinner time. Jean met me at the door to the lodge. "Honey, I've a surprise for you. We have reservations at that lovely country club you like for dinner and dancing. I've made arrangements for a babysitter for

Donnie. Why don't you shower, and we'll get going?" I didn't dare mention the blisters on my feet. Besides, I loved dancing with Jean.

I had to report to COMFAIR Alameda on October 4, 1943. I assured Jean that I wouldn't volunteer for another tour of combat duty. I did remind her, though, that I must accept my orders no matter where they sent me. She kissed me good-bye at the airport. The night before, we agreed she and Donnie would join me as soon as I had orders. Jean told me she was not going to stay in Bremerton with her parents or mine.

Promoted!

I reported to the personnel office at COMFAIR Alameda as ordered and was sent to the office of a Navy lieutenant commander. I walked in and saluted, "Lieutenant Berg, reporting as ordered, Sir." He invited me to take a chair in front of his desk.

"Lieutenant Berg, I have some good news for you." He handed me a copy of an ALLNAV, a teletype message from the Navy Personnel Command in Washington, D.C. used to announce promotions. "Mr. Berg, your name is on the promotion list. You are no longer a Lt. (jg.). Your date of rank as a full lieutenant is October 1, 1943. Congratulations."

As he looked through some papers, I scanned the ALLNAV. I found my name on the promotion list.

A full lieutenant ... not bad for a kid from Bremerton. Jean will be so proud. She'll be happy for me. Nice pay raise too. Now comes the rest. He's still shuffling papers. Where are my damn orders? Come on, commander, let's get to it. Jean hopes for shore duty I know; I won't volunteer.

Finally, he said, "Here they are, your orders. Let me fill you in, lieutenant. Your old squadron, VGS-28, with its fighter, dive-bombing, and torpedo squadrons has been decommissioned by the Navy Department. Replacing it will be Air Group 28 with a fighter squadron and a torpedo squadron. I will read you your orders."

LIEUTENANT NORMAN BERG, 112307 USNR. WHEN DETACHED FROM COMFAIR ALAMEDA YOU WILL REPORT TO THE COMMANDING OFFICER OF AIRGROUP 28 FOR FURTHER ASSIGNMENT TO TORPEDO SQUADRON 28. REPORT NO LATER THAN 5 OCTOBER 1943.

Jesus, back to combat. Back to the old fears. I've got to live through this ... again!

Reporting for Squadron Training Duty

I reported the next morning to Torpedo Squadron 28 at N.A.S. Alameda, hangar three and presented my orders to the squadron duty officer. The orders were dated October 5, 1943, my reporting date. The squadron duty officer directed me to the office of the executive officer of the squadron, Lieutenant Ronald Gift. I stood at the open entrance to his office until he saw me.

The lieutenant stood. "Come in. We've been expecting you. Norm Berg, isn't it? Just back from leave and a carrier cruise in the Pacific, right? Come on in. I'll fill you in on what's happening. By the way, call me Rip. We're pretty informal around here. We're all naval reserve officers, including the skipper, Art McHolland, so there's not much Navy protocol among the officers."

Sure different, I thought, than the days with Commander Butts and the "Attention" call when he walked in.

I spent a good hour with Rip. He was in the Guadalcanal area at the same time I was. He was assigned to a heavy cruiser flying SOC aircraft. (The *S* stood for scout; the *O* for observation; and the *C* for the aircraft company that built the plane.) The SOC was designated by the Navy as a scouting and observation plane. The plane would be catapulted off the cruiser then, after completing the mission, would land in the ocean alongside the cruiser to be hoisted aboard by the ship's crane.

When Rip and I compared our dates in the Guadalcanal area, we discovered that in March 1943, he was with a Navy task force of battleships and cruisers off Guadalcanal. The task force was protecting the cruiser *Chicago* after she had been damaged by Japanese planes. At the same time, I was flying off *Chenango*. I told Rip about our skipper's offer to support the task force with aircraft and the refusal by the task force admiral. He didn't want *Chenango*, "that 18-knot carrier," in his task force.

After learning about each other's flight experiences, Rip filled me in on VT-28. "Norm, the skipper here is Lieutenant Art McHolland. For nearly three years, Art's been assigned to the training command teaching cadets to fly, so he's ready for a fleet assignment. We currently have 14 officers assigned, including two nonflying officers. Our complement of torpedo planes is nine. The squadron has a complement of 35 enlisted personnel to serve as air crewmen."

He stopped. "Norm, this squadron has been organized with a new concept. When we are based at a Naval Air Station, the maintenance of our aircraft will be performed by personnel attached to it. When we go aboard the carrier, personnel assigned to the ship will perform all maintenance on our planes. All we have to do is fly the birds."

He paused for a moment. "I guess that about covers it, Norm. Now, any questions?"

"Three questions, Rip. What's my job going to be? Do we know which carrier we will be assigned? Do we have a deployment date? I'm married and my family wants to join me as soon as possible."

He laughed. "You're certainly direct. I like that. You sound like you're ready to go to work, Norm. You'll be the squadron's operations officer since you have the most experience in carrier operations. I want you to set up a training program for the pilots based on the syllabus set by the Commander Air Pacific (COMAIRPAC.) We don't yet have a firm deployment date, but it will probably be no earlier than April 1944. We are assigned to USS *Monterey*. She's been designated as a CVL (aircraft carrier, light), just commissioned this past year. She's not like your old 18-knot carrier, *Chenango*. This one is built on a cruiser hull and will do over 30 knots."

He looked directly at me. "Norm, I'm glad you're aboard. This outfit needs your combat experience as well as your carrier experience. Your office is just down the hall. As soon as the skipper comes in, I'll bring him down to meet you. Let's get together for dinner tonight at the club, OK?"

I left Gift's office and walked down the hall to my office, which had a sign on the door that read, "Operations." It wasn't much—no window, a scratched old wooden desk, and a gray metal file cabinet. There were two wooden "in" and "out" baskets. The "in" basket was already full.

I sat in my new office after that meeting with Rip wondering if I understood the reason for my assignment. The squadron leadership had no carrier experience nor direct combat experience. The junior pilots had just completed their advanced training and this is would be their first squadron assignment. I was the only one in the squadron who had both carrier and combat experience. The highest rank in the squadron was lieutenant. As pilots getting ready to fight a war, we were all equal. My job was to get us ready for combat.

I pulled a bound binder out of my "in" basket. It was the flight training syllabus from COMAIRPAC. It was almost identical with the training I did back in Norfolk: glide-bombing, gunnery, tactics, navigation, FCLP, torpedo tactics, and night familiarization (fam). Nothing was new here about our training. Then I remembered what Rip had said: this aircraft complement would be nine TBMs, not TBFs.

The TBM versus TBF Aircraft

The TBM was identical to the TBF in performance, but they were built by General Motors rather than Grumman Aviation that built the TBFs. The Navy made the decision in 1942–43 to have Grumman Aircraft build only fighter aircraft because there was a need to increase production of fighter aircraft. Grumman was building both fighter planes and torpedo planes; consequently, some Grumman engineers were transferred to one of the General Motors plants, and the plant was redesigned to manufacture torpedo planes rather than automobiles.

There were some improvements in the TBM over the TBF. The TBM had two forward firing .50-caliber machine guns, one in each wing. Also, it had an autopilot, a shoulder harness rather than the old lap belt, and high frequency radios in the radioman's compartment.

With tailhooks down, TBF/TBMs ready for landing on USS *Hornet*
(Courtesy of The Tailhook Association and The Hook*)*

I sat there at my desk knowing that this cruise was going to be different than *Chenango* and Guadalcanal. Flying the TBM, a plane with better armament and better radios on board, gave the pilot an extra safety factor. No more radio silence with the high frequency radios. Operating off a new, faster 30-knot carrier was going to be much safer too. We would always have at least 30 knots of wind over the deck for takeoffs and landings.

Still though, at the strangest moments, perhaps over a drink or thinking of Jean, that nagging memory returned. The sound of those bullets hitting my plane, those red and yellow lines arching for my cockpit, the plane exploding that night at Bougainville. I was still going to fly missions attacking the enemy. Some of the flying would be routine, such as antisub patrols and search missions for enemy shipping. I had no choice; I was going to fly against the enemy again, and I was going to lead others.

Jean and Donnie Move to California

I shook off the thoughts, put the binder with the training syllabus into a drawer in my desk and turned again to check my "in" basket. There was a letter from Jean! It had been hidden under other papers. I tore it open. It was only one page, but the message was clear.

"Norm, I've had to move back with my folks. After you left, my mother insisted that I couldn't stay in the apartment. I think she wanted me home with her and Daddy so I could take care of the house while they both worked in the

Navy Yard. It's terrible here. Both Mom and Dad come home from work, start to drink, then the fighting starts. Please, when can we join you?"

I called Jean that night, and we set a date for her to join me. I told her I would find some place to live. She reminded me of the time she arrived in Norfolk with no place to live, but this time she was laughing.

The next weekend, I found one room with a bath and a small kitchen in a private home in nearby Oakland. I felt very lucky to find even a room. Housing was very critical in the Oakland area. The room was close to the bus line, so I could get to work. Jean and Donnie arrived by train on October 12, and we moved in. We had no crib or bassinet for the baby. Jean didn't bring them with her on the train. Donnie slept in a bottom dresser drawer, and Jean bathed him in the kitchen sink.

I was happy to have Jean with me, but I found that the close living in one room with a baby was trying. It had been different when I was home on leave. We had the use of Dad's car. We could get out, go shopping, visit friends. All we had here in Oakland for entertainment was a radio in the room and the baby. We had no car. We couldn't go out except to take a walk with the baby. Our dinners in the room were difficult too.

Jean was not the best cook, especially when trying to prepare a meal in a very small kitchen. I began stopping at the officers' club after work. My excuse to Jean was that it was part of squadron life—we had to socialize—to relax from the stress of flying. I would get back to our room about 1900. Donnie would usually be fed and ready for bed. Jean and I would then eat a simple supper as soon as Donnie was asleep, and then I would want Jean to go to bed.

This is tough living. The club helps ... a few drinks ... being with the guys ... flying again. Responsible for the training; all those new pilots. They don't know about combat; getting shot at. I want sex with Jean to forget those nights at the Canal. The baby is always here ... I love her and him. It's so damn complicated. Wish Jean would come to bed; I get aroused just looking at her.

Training in Crows Landing

Almost a month had gone by since I'd reported to the squadron. We were getting organized. Flight training had commenced with familiarization flights in the new plane, the TBM. I was in my office at the squadron one afternoon when a dispatch arrived from COMFAIR Alameda.

The squadron was moving to an outlying field at Crows Landing, California, on October 30. Crows Landing was a small farming community about 100 miles south of San Francisco. The airfield was still under construction, but offices and ready rooms had already been completed, as well as barracks for the enlisted men and a BOQ for single officers. Torpedo Squadron 28 would spend the next four months at Crows Landing, training for our combat mission and, when finished, joining the Pacific Fleet aboard the carrier USS *Monterey*. With just 48 hours to prepare for moving the squadron, the action was hectic. Arranging for transportation for our personnel and getting the squadron records and files packed all had to be done in just a couple of days.

Jean and Donnie in Crows Landing, CA

Personally, I had a major problem too. How would I get Jean and the baby to Crows Landing? We had no car, and I was scheduled to fly a TBM to the new base. Jean and I talked about her and the baby taking a bus because there were no train connections. Jean didn't think a bus trip was feasible. I looked at the transportation schedule for the move and saw that Lieutenant (jg.) Harry Bridgmen, our personnel officer, would be driving a Navy truck to Crows Landing, which would carry our personnel and operation records. I asked Harry if he would pick up Jean and the baby at our room in Oakland, then drive them to the hotel in Crows Landing where I'd made reservations. He agreed, and Jean told me the trip went very smoothly. Donnie slept the entire trip.

That night, Jean, Donnie, and I moved into the local hotel in Crows Landing. We had two rooms, a bedroom with a bath and a living area with a small kitchen. The rooms were nondescriptive with inexpensive furniture. The living room had a couch, one overstuffed chair, and a table with a lamp. A slightly worn rug laid on the floor, and the bed sagged in the middle. The kitchen had a two-burner gas stove and a refrigerator. Previously that afternoon, I'd bought a crib and bassinet, and that evening, we unpacked and got settled. Jean seemed pleased with the arrangement. The skipper and his wife had the other two-room suite on the same floor as ours. They had a young child, too, so Jean had some company. The hotel was clean and pleasant with a small dining room and a bar. There was no officers' club at the field. I figured the bar at the hotel would served as my "O" club.

The flight training was rigorous. During the time at Crows Landing, I pushed the pilots hard to complete the training quickly. Each pilot was scheduled for at least two flights per day. I flew as an observer, watching individual pilots as they carried out the assigned training missions. After each flight, I would debrief the flight, pointing out problem areas I'd observed. I watched, especially, for problems like a slow join-up of a formation or poor glide-bombing technique by an individual pilot. Good formation join-up meant better fuel consumption for each aircraft. Time wasn't wasted waiting for planes to join the formation. Poor bombing technique meant missed targets. The idea was to hit the target with the bomb. My goal was for each pilot to complete 155 hours of training. Flight time spent on each phase of training was: 60 hours glide-bombing; 20 hours practice torpedo runs; 35 hours tactics with fighter and dive-bombers; 15 hours gunnery; and 25 hours night flying. These totals would meet the requirements of the COMAIRPAC training syllabus.

Life for Jean and I was filled with surprising contradictions. There were times when we were very happy. We had a surprise at Thanksgiving when my folks came down for a visit. We all had dinner together in the hotel restaurant with the owner and his wife. My father was still operating a restaurant in Bremerton, so he and the hotel owner had a good deal in common. My mother had a wonderful time with her first grandson. It was a great visit, especially for Jean. My mother stayed with Donnie while Jean and I took a bus to San Francisco for Christmas shopping. We had dinner and went dancing at the Top of the Mark. The last bus got us back to Crows Landing at two o'clock in the morning.

Christmas that year was a new experience. It was the first Christmas for our six-month old son. He loved the small Christmas tree we put up in the living room. A local family invited the three of us to their home for Christmas dinner. It was delightful—a bottle of wine with a wonderful dinner and some little presents for Donnie.

We had to stay at the hotel for New Year's Eve. We couldn't find a babysitter for Donnie. The skipper and his wife went to her parents' home in San Diego, so we were alone. I wanted Jean to go down to the bar with me, but she wouldn't leave Donnie alone in the room. So I went alone. I wanted to celebrate. I remember coming up to our room around three o'clock in the morning. I barely remember Jean coming down to the bar asking me to come up. I didn't go with her, and Jean locked me out that night. I woke up the next morning in the hallway, realizing that I'd passed out. That's how I ushered in 1944.

The damn bar is so handy and I'm trying so hard. I want our pilots to be the best; they have to be to survive. I know; I've been there. Those red and yellow streaks of light arching toward my cockpit ... that plane exploding in front of me. Got to go out there again. The booze helps.

Afterwards, I tried my best to stay out of the bar. Later in January, I came home from a day of flying just as Jean was coming in with the baby.

"Everything all right?" I asked. "Where have you and Donnie been?"

Jean got Donnie settled in his playpen. "Norm, I've been to see the doctor." She paused, looking at me. " I'm pregnant. The doctor just verified it."

That's the last thing I want right now! Another baby. I thought Jean was taking care of it. It must have happened when she joined me in Oakland.

I reached out to her as she came into my arms. She was crying. "Norm, when I left Bremerton, our family doctor fitted me with a diaphragm. I thought it would be fine. I wanted to wait until you came back from this cruise. I'm sorry."

I held her until her crying stopped. "Darling," I said, "it's all right. We both wanted another child. It's just that this one is coming earlier than we planned. Just be sure that you take care of yourself and the baby. I'll be fine. I'll make it home to you and our two babies, Jean. Don't worry."

Early in February, the squadron received advanced orders to plan a move to the Auxiliary Naval Air Station at Watsonville, California, on March 1, 1944. It was the usual procedure to base us closer to the torpedo training area in Monterey Bay. We would complete our live torpedo training there.

With gas rationing and travel limitations, the owners were renting their summer homes in the Monterey area to military people. Through a real estate agent, Jean and I rented a lovely completely furnished two-bedroom cottage. We were anticipating the transfer of the squadron on 1 March. For once, I felt as though I was preparing for Jean's and my future.

On February 17, 1944, my 24th birthday, Jean had a birthday cake for me. Donnie helped blow out the candles. We were still at Crows Landing. After Donnie went to bed, I wanted Jean to come to the bar with me. I wanted to continue celebrating. She looked at me and said, "Norm, why don't you go on down? You've been working hard, and it is your birthday. Go ahead. I'll stay here with Donnie." I went to the bar.

It must have been about ten o'clock when a woman, I guessed her in her thirties, entered the bar. I knew her. She was married to the commander of the air station at Crows Landing. I asked her where the commander was. She told me he was away at a conference. So I bought her a drink, and we sat at the bar talking. We'd had a couple more drinks when I felt her foot rubbing against my leg. I lit a cigarette for her. Her hand touched mine as we looked into each other's eyes.

Suddenly, she made her move. "It's getting late, Lieutenant. I'm staying here tonight. My husband is picking me up tomorrow. We're going on a little vacation. I'd better go up to my room."

I followed her up the stairs. Her room was on the same floor as mine. I blocked the entrance to her room with my arm. "Do I get a good-night kiss?" I asked. She smiled at me. "Lieutenant, I think that's your wife standing in the doorway to your room there at the end of the hall." She slipped under my arm and opened the door to her room as I turned and saw Jean.

I slept on the couch in the livingroom that night.

The next morning, Jean gave me an ultimatum. "Norm, I'm ready to call my father for the money to get Donnie and me a train ticket to Seattle. Is that what you want? I can't live with you this way. I'll go to Watsonville with you only on one condition. No drinking!" I agreed. I had no choice. I wanted her to stay. I couldn't let my marriage fail.

What in the hell is wrong with me? I don't need another woman. Jean is a beautiful lover; it's just the baby. We can't find time alone and it's the pressure of getting ready to leave. Wonder if I'll run out of luck this time? Maybe Watsonville will be better. No booze though. Got to do it. Jean's talking about staying in Watsonville after I leave. She should go home to have the baby. Get a place of her own until I get back. I don't want her here alone. Damn! Sometimes, it's just too much.

Training in Watsonville

As scheduled, the squadron moved to the air station at Watsonville, California on March 1, 1944. Again, Jean and Donnie rode with Harry Bridgmen in a Navy truck for the trip to our new home. Harry took Jean right to our rented house. I joined my family late that afternoon after flying one of squadron planes to our new base. Jean and I were looking forward to a pleasant couple of months in our rented cottage. It had two bedrooms, a bath, a living and dining area, and a kitchen. It was completely furnished, including bedding, linens, dishes, and cookware. Donnie had his own room too. The furniture was Mission California, light in color and bulky in appearance. It was perfect for the Monterey area with all its sunshine and warm weather. There was a lovely fenced in yard loaded with flowers and thick green grass. Donnie loved it.

The town of Watsonville was a small farming community, as well as a vacation spot for the Bay Area population, but it was more than that. It was a very supportive community for service people. The local Army National Guard unit had been mobilized in 1940 and sent to the Philippines for duty. We learned that nearly every family had suffered a loss of a loved one when the Japanese invaded the Philippines. The local people were friendly and helpful to all of us. We were looking forward to our assignment at the air station there.

That evening, Jean and I were out on the front porch. Donnie was in a swing chair bouncing up and down. We'd finished dinner, and I was sober. I was not stopping at the officers' club, but was coming home in a car pool with other married officers who lived in the area. I was telling Jean that our departure date must be getting close. We had been notified by COMFAIR Alameda that the squadron was scheduled for carrier qualifications on March 5, aboard the carrier USS *Copahee*. She was a Jeep carrier about the size of *Chenango*. I heard our phone ringing in the house. I went in and answered the phone. "Lieutenant Berg, this is the Naval Air Station duty officer. A confidential message for VT-28 just came off the teletype. I can't read the entire message because of its classification." I asked him if there was a date in the body of the message. When he replied, "Yes," I told him to read me the date. All he said was, "15." I put down the phone. I knew Jean and I weren't going to have a couple of months. I knew that date was our deployment date for the Pacific. I joined Jean on the porch.

"Who was it?" she asked. I told her what I thought. The squadron would be leaving about March 15. She lifted Donnie out of the swing and they both sat next to me on the porch settee. We sat silently, then Jean spoke.

"Oh Norm, I wish I could stay here until you come back! We've talked about it before, but it's so perfect for Donnie and for me. I know you believe I should go back to Bremerton to have the baby but, honey, I could have the baby here just as easy."

I looked at her. "Jean, please. Bremerton has the Navy Hospital where Donnie was born. Both our folks are in Bremerton. You have no one here in Watsonville. Darling, I would worry so much—you would be alone. Please understand my feelings."

"OK, I know you're right. I'll go home, but I'll have a place for us when you get home. We'll be waiting for you, darling. I know God will bring you home to me."

We put Donnie to bed and we held each other for a long time, unable to sleep as we thought of the future that we faced apart.

The next week was busy with planning for Jean's trip back to Bremerton. I found a 1940 Chevie two-door coupe with good tires. I wanted Jean to have a car while she was waiting for the baby. I called Dad, and he wired $1,500 for the car via Western Union. Jean's mother agreed to come down by train, to drive back with Jean and Donnie. Jean's mother was only with us for one night. I had to tell her that Jean was expecting. On March 10, she and Jean left. Jean's mother didn't say good-bye.

The squadron took delivery of nine new TBM aircraft, and on March 14, we flew to N.A.S. Alameda from Watsonville. There, the planes were loaded aboard USS *Barnes*, a Jeep carrier used for transporting our aircraft and personnel to Hawaii. That evening, the squadron officers went to Frisco. We had dinner at a French restaurant, then went to the Top of The Mark for a final dance with the lovely girls of San Francisco. We had an early evening. We had to be back aboard the ship by midnight. We were on our way. Rip and I had a stateroom—two bunks, one desk and a wash basin. I lay in the upper bunk. Sleep didn't come easily.

God, help me make it home!

Hawaii and Death

The smells of San Francisco Bay and the smoke of the cities around the bay faded as the smell of the sea touched my senses. I was on the flight deck of USS *Barnes* as it moved under the Golden Gate Bridge. We had loaded all our aircraft aboard back at N.A.S. Alameda and were now on our way to Hawaii. I could feel the swells of the Pacific Ocean against the hull of the ship as we headed out of San Francisco Bay. It was a familiar sensation—it was hard to realize it had only been seven months since my last trip on a carrier. The last time I passed under that bridge, I was on my way home. I certainly didn't know then, when *Chenango* moved under the Golden Gate last August, that I'd have to face my old fears again. I hoped it might be different this time.

I believed, however, that we were better trained for combat this time. In our four months of training at N.A.S. Norfolk, before our first deployment to the Pacific, we felt we were barely trained. Our aircraft for this second tour were better equipped for the cruise. These planes had high frequency radios that certainly would have eased the hazards of the long navigational flights we flew from *Chenango*. No longer would we worry about radio silence or having to use a square search to find our carrier, we could rely on the carrier's radar for help.

In addition, we would be operating off the carrier USS *Monterey*. She was a new carrier and had been operating with the Pacific Fleet since being commissioned early in 1943. Because of the need for additional carriers, the Navy elected to convert some cruiser hulls into light carriers, classified as CVLs. Her hull was initially designed for a light cruiser with a power plant that produced 32 knots of speed. The aircraft complement on USS *Monterey* would be 24 fighter aircraft and 9 torpedo planes. The carrier's faster speed would be a great advantage. Aircraft would come aboard much slower than was possible on *Chenango,* and the landings would be much safer.

I took a final walk back to the flight deck and watched the Golden Gate Bridge disappear from sight. I didn't feel like walking forward to watch the bow of the ship slide through the Pacific. Somehow, I felt that I was going the wrong way, away from Jean and Donnie. I went below to the ready room. I didn't want to think about the future—I was afraid it might hold too much pain, too many threats to my future.

That evening, the skipper, Art McHolland, called a meeting of all pilots. He'd scheduled Joe Anson, our air intelligence officer, to give us a briefing on the coming operations. Joe stood and began the briefing.

"Guys, in August of 1943, a conference was held in Quebec, Canada. Attending the conference were President Roosevelt, Prime Minister Churchill, and representatives from both China and Russia. The purpose of the meeting was to set priorities for conducting the war against Germany and Japan.

"At that meeting, the decision was made for our naval forces to launch a series of attacks against key Pacific islands held by the Japanese. The key Japanese islands were defined as those where the Japanese had constructed airfields from which their aircraft could control our sea routes as we moved across the Pacific. The first of those attacks was in November of last year when we invaded the island of Tarawa. Our Marines took terrible losses in that battle. In fact, the American public was shocked. They were asking why we wasted so many lives on such a small, seemingly unimportant island. The public soon understood as our aircraft began operating from the captured airfield on Tarawa, protecting our sea routes and our carriers from what would have been land-based Japanese aircraft. The plan was intended to eventually defeat the Japanese." He stopped, looking at us. "Any questions so far?"

A question came from the back of the room. "Joe, are you saying that we'll take every airfield that the Japs have built in the Pacific?"

"No, some we'll just bypass. If the airfield is no threat to our advance in the central Pacific, we will not invade the island. The Navy planners use the term 'island hopping.' We will, though, keep those airfields we bypass under attack by aircraft based on the fields we have captured. The constant attacks will cut off all supplies to the enemy. We won't need to invade them since they will no longer be a threat to our forces."

He stopped, poured a cup of coffee, took a sip and continued. "Let me bring you all up-to-date on our forces. Believe me, we have enough to do the job. When we launched the invasion of Tarawa, we had 17 carriers involved in the attack." He looked at me. "Norm, it's a hell of a lot different than when you and I were on old *Chenango*. Remember operating around Guadalcanal in early 1943? We had the carrier USS *Enterprise* and three *Chenango* class carriers. Those were converted oil tankers with a top speed of 18 knots."

We were all surprised at the numbers Joe was using.

I had no idea the United States was building carriers at such a rate. I quickly estimated that we must have built at least twelve carriers between late 1942 and March 1944.

Damn, maybe this cruise won't be so bad. All those planes on all those carriers. All that fire power. Wonder what airfield we'll be attacking. Still … the Japs are tough. At Tarawa, they fought to the end. They won't stop shooting. Damn! I still see that arch of bullets just over my cockpit.

I heard Joe again. "Fellas, our carriers are currently organized into Task Force 58 under the command of Admiral Mark Mitchner. The force has eight Essex-class carriers (CVs). The aircraft complement for the CVs total 82 aircraft, including fighters, dive-bombers, and torpedo planes. Also part of the task force

Essex-class carriers (CVs) were designed with the ability to recover aircraft on either the forward or after flight decks, having sufficient astern speed and a dual set of arresting gear   *(Courtesy of the U.S. Navy)*

are eight Cabot-class carriers (CVLs) like *Monterey.* These carriers have a complement of 33 aircraft, including fighters and torpedo planes. Guys, that's a total of 899 planes! There's no doubt that we have the carrier power to win this war."

I remember asking the question. "Joe, where does *Monterey* fit into this task force? Also, where are the next Japanese airfields we're going after?"

With that question, the skipper took over. "Thanks, Joe. Good briefing. Norm, as to your question, *Monterey* will be part of Task Force 58. When we arrive in Hawaii, the squadron will have a short training period before going aboard the carrier. I expect that will be in early June." Art paused, looking around the ready room. "Guys, this next information is classified confidential. We will be part of the invasion of the Marianas. Three of the islands, Saipan, Guam, and Tinian will be invaded. We will be part of the air support for that invasion force. I will keep you informed as our training program in Hawaii proceeds. That's it. We're due in Pearl Harbor on March 30th."

I left the ready room.

Jesus! We're going in to combat. It's sure different than the Canal. What a job our country is doing! Sixteen carriers, all operating together. So damn many planes; this isn't going to be so tough. We'll just overwhelm the Japs. Hit them so hard they won't be able to fight back. I'll be home. Bet earlier than I thought. Bring on those Japs. We'll blow them out of the sky.

Barnes anchored at Pearl on schedule, and our torpedo squadron was bussed to N.A.S. Kaneohe for training in antisubmarine warfare. We flew planes attached to the training school, learning to use a new listening device that would help us locate a submerged sub. They would be dropped into the water over a suspected sub's location. I flew 14 flights between April 1 and 11, and dropped a lot of the listening devices. They actually worked. We pilots knew though, having flown a lot of antisub patrols, you had to find the sub first.

The weather was great, and we did get into Honolulu twice for dinner and for some sight-seeing. There was still evidence of the Japanese attack on Pearl Harbor. The battleship, *Arizona*, a monument to those killed in the Japanese attack, was visible in the harbor. It was a somber visit for our group remembering that surprise attack on our Navy.

On April 12, 1944, we picked up our planes at N.A.S. Ford Island, a base in Pearl Harbor and flew to our new base, the Naval Air Facility, Barking Sands, on the island of Kauai. Kauai was north of the island of Oahu where Pearl Harbor was located. The island had a very small population, but it had several large coconut plantations, one small village, and some wonderful beaches. The base was very primitive. Officers lived in barracks, as did the enlisted men. The barracks were a large room with cots and a mess hall that was not too clean. There were absolutely no recreational facilities, except for the beach. It reminded me a little of the Canal, except that we had barracks instead of tents.

Funny, this place is kind of nice, no officers' club. Don't seem to miss the booze. Tough back in Crows Landing; almost lost Jean. She would have left me. Feel pretty good now. OK about flying against the Japs ... the combat. Got to be all that air power we have. It's not like the Canal, but I feel all alone. I can handle this.

In spite of the facilities, we were able to obtain excellent additional training. I flew 25 training flights between April 13 and 30. We practiced glide-bombing, gunnery, navigation, FCLP and joint training with our fighter squadron. One of the joint missions with the fighters was a simulated attack on Oahu. Unlike the Japanese attack, we were intercepted this time by Army fighters based at the Army Air Base at Hickham Field on the island of Oahu.

One of my duties as operations officer was to review the teletype messages each morning. On May 1, ComHawSea Frontier directed us to conduct a search for a missing aircraft. The search was to be centered in an area 20 miles west of our base. I notified the skipper, Art McHolland, then I contacted

LSO directs pilot of F4F-3 Wildcat during an FCLP practice
(Courtesy of the U.S. Navy)

two of our pilots telling them I was scheduling them to conduct the search. I was briefing them on the details and search procedures when the skipper came into the room. He listened for a moment, then said, "Norm, put me on the schedule too. An extra plane won't hurt—just another pair of eyes."

I told him I didn't recommend an extra plane out there. A traffic problem could develop if debris or a life raft was located. When something was spotted in the water, pilots tended to fly low over the water in an attempt to identify the object. There was a real danger of a mid-air collision. The skipper assured me he would control the search by maintaining radio contact with the other two planes.

The flight launched and the three planes headed out to the search area. I had a radio in the operations office, so I could monitor the radio traffic between our planes. I wasn't really listening that morning, until I heard a garbled message. The pilot sounded almost frantic, rushing to make his report.

"Barking Sands control tower. This is Able Two conducting a search mission for a downed aircraft. There's been a mid-air collision with two of the search planes. One aircraft exploded on contact with the water. I'm escorting the second aircraft back to the base. The crash site is marked with a smoke flare. Out."

That evening, our squadron and the fighter squadron held a memorial service for our skipper, Lieutenant Art McHolland, and the two crewmen who died with him in the crash. The service was held in a small church in the village.

An accident investigation was carried out by the squadron as required by Navy regulations. The cause of the accident was determined to be pilot error. The two pilots who witnessed the accident testified that some debris had been spotted on the surface. The three aircraft were in a loose column formation circling at about 500 feet. Suddenly, the skipper pulled up in a tight turn and his right wing was struck by the propeller of the following plane. His plane went out of control, hit the water in a steep dive and exploded. The report closed with the statement. "Nothing remained visible on the surface except for an oil slick."

Goddammit. Our first loss ... a stupid accident. Art was a good skipper. Fair and interested in all of us. He and his wife lived in the same hotel with Jean and me in Crows Landing. He was so glad to get out of the training command. He wanted to face the challenge of combat. He did not have a lot of time in the TBM; he came right to the squadron from teaching cadets to fly. That may have contributed to the accident. He got excited and wanted to help the search. Such a waste. Rip's been assigned as our commanding officer. I take the job as the squadron's executive officer. More responsibility. Glad I'm off the liquor. Sorry about Art. I wrote Jean. She'll want to contact Art's wife. God, ... this damn war.

The squadron flew aboard *Monterey* on May 15 for three days of flight operations. My log book shows eight carrier landings, three catapult shots, and five deck launches during the period. This was a refresher period for the ship's crew as well as for the pilots. We were operating very smoothly at the end of the shake-down period. The training program we had carried out was paying dividends. We were ready for the fleet.

On May 20, we moved to N.A.S. Barbers Point on Oahu where we took delivery of nine new TBMs. We had a chance to tour the island, see Diamond Head, go to Waikiki beach, and do some heavy partying at the Royal Hawaiian Hotel. The women were as lovely as those at the Top of The Mark.

On the morning of 29 May 1944 we departed Pearl Harbor aboard USS *Monterey*. My second combat cruise had begun. The training was over. I felt ready and relaxed.

In fact, my squadron mates gave me a new nickname—I was now "Doc." The guys told

USS *Monterey* CVL-26 with her flight deck elevator open

me that it was appropriate—I was always willing to listen to their concerns about facing the dangers of combat flying. I'd been there.

Chapter 8

Marianas Islands Invasion

The first few days aboard *Monterey* were devoted to getting settled and being brought up to speed on the up-coming mission against the Marianas Islands. As usual, our air intelligence officer (AIO), Joe Anson, gave us a briefing.

He started by reminding us of the overall plan for the war against the Japanese.

"Guys, over the past nine months, our carrier task forces have carried out antishipping strikes at the Japanese bases of Rabaul in November 1943 and at the Truk Atoll in February 1944. The task forces also covered the invasion of the islands of Kwajalien and Tarawa. This policy is part of the overall strategy of isolating Japanese bases and taking over those islands where the Japanese have built air bases. Our next targets are the Marianas in the western Pacific. Our objectives are the Japanese airfields on the islands of Guam, Saipan, and Tinian." He paused, "Guys, the Japanese are going to defend these islands to the bitter end. They know that if our forces control these airfields, we can reach the home islands of Japan with land-based bombers. Japan will then suffer the same destruction that the cities in Germany have suffered. Guys, this mission is going to shorten the war." He turned to the skipper, "Anything else, Sir?"

Rip stood. "OK. I'll take it from here. The actual invasion is scheduled for the 15th of June (1944). Captain Ingersall, *Monterey*'s captain, tells me we're due to begin our strikes against Japanese targets on the 13th. We have some time, so we'll do some training en route to the Marianas operating area. Starting tomorrow, check the flight schedule. The first flight is scheduled to launch at 0800. That's it, guys. Get some rest. It's going to be a tough battle."

Between May 23 and 31, I flew two torpedo training flights and two glide-bombing flights.

Damn! Practice torpedo runs. Didn't Torpedo Eight teach us anything? Bombing is safer, and we'd do more damage. Do they think the Jap Fleet will challenge us? God! I hope not. Why don't they listen to us? Torpedo attacks are suicide. I'll talk to Rip. I really thought this cruise would be different. All this power. All these carriers. Torpedo attacks. Stupid.

I flew three antisub patrols as *Monterey* approached the rendezvous area with Navy Task Force 58. We joined the fleet on the morning of June 12. The task force was divided into four attack groups spread out over a 50-mile area. Our group, 58.2, was assigned an operating area off the island of Tinian. When I launched that morning on an antisub patrol flight, I could see the entire task force as I proceeded to my assigned search area—16 carriers with their destroyer escorts, plus cruisers and battleships. We had an overwhelming force.

The Philippines

Attack on Tinian

The following day, I flew my first mission against Japanese targets on the island of Tinian. I was leading three other planes, and our target was a railroad bridge. I quickly discovered that all that carrier power didn't have any effect on the Jap gunners protecting that bridge. I rolled into my dive at 8,000 feet, bomb bay doors open, ready with four 500-pound bombs. Halfway down in my dive, the black, greasy-looking blotches of heavy AA fire appeared.

I felt my plane jerk as the concussion from the explosions of the AA fire affected my dive. I was having trouble keeping my plane lined up on the target. I could see holes suddenly appearing in the wing of my plane. I dropped the four bombs and pulled out of my dive. I heard my gunner yell, "Right on the bridge!"

Then I heard my wingman over the radio. "Pull out! Pull out! Oh shit! Number four plane has crashed! He never pulled out of the dive."

It was a quiet trip back to the carrier.

Jesus. Who was it? Number four man ... Joe. I hardly knew him. He joined us just before we left Hawaii. He was one of our replacement pilots, and he was lost on my flight. What the hell happened? I gave him a careful briefing; the air intelligence officer said this was lightly defended. Bullshit! God, that AA fire was heavy! How many more times? A goddamn bridge! Probably wasn't even used by the Japs. A life lost, and for what?

After our debriefing, I sat down with the skipper in our room. We'd received four replacement pilots just before we left Hawaii for the Marianas operation. This was standard procedure. These pilots had finished operational training in TBM aircraft back in the States. They were well-trained on tactics, bombing, and navigation. They were assigned to squadrons as extra pilots to help carry the load of combat missions. We didn't like to use the term, "replacement pilots"—much too negative—replacement for whom? These pilots had not trained with the rest of us. There was not the trust level among the squadron as to their ability as pilots since they were so new to the squadron. Consequently, Rip and I had restricted them to antisub patrols and to attack missions against lightly defended targets. Unfortunately, the intelligence on the anti-aircraft defenses at the railroad bridge had been incorrect. Joe was one of those pilots. We not only lost a pilot, but we also lost two crew members, the turret gunner and the radio operator. It was a sad day.

LT Norman "Doc" Berg aboard the USS *Monterey*, June 1944, beside a TBM-1 in which he flew combat missions. The patch on the tail, a repaired bullet hole

Since I was the lead pilot when we lost Joe, I told Rip I would write the ensign's parents and arrange for a shipboard memorial service. I wondered if maybe I should not have scheduled him for the mission. I thought it would be an easy flight for him. He wanted to fly it. He came to me asking to be on the flight.

What to say? Sorry about your son? He was a fine pilot; well thought of by all of us? He will be missed? Goddammit! I hardly knew him. He was just another ensign, a new kid in the squadron. He wanted to serve his country ... did I fail him? I had talked to him about the mission; it was his first combat; his first time facing the enemy. Luck? God's will? Chance? Jesus! It could have been me. Write the letter. Get on with the damn war.

Attacks on Guam

Between June 14 and 19, 1944, I flew two bombing missions against the Japanese airfield on the island of Guam. Our mission: place our bombs on the runway to prevent the Japanese from using the airfield. Again, we attacked against heavy AA fire, but all planes made it back to the carrier. Although, my plane and one other had a few holes from the AA fire. During this time, I was also assigned to antisub missions protecting the task force from enemy submarine attack. We wondered if the Japanese knew about our invasion of the Marianas by that time.

The Japs Are Coming

One evening, we had an all pilots' meeting in the ready room. Our AIO, Joe Anson, was ready with a briefing on the current situation.

"Fellas, the admiral's staff has passed the following info on our current situation." Joe opened his briefing book and proceeded. "Ships of the Japanese Fleet have left their bases in Japan and are proceeding to the Marianas area. Our staff has no doubt that they will attack our invasion force. The estimate is that they will deploy at least six carriers, plus support ships. We know that the Japanese communication capability has been severely damaged by our attacks on their command facilities. As a consequence, our staff thinks that the Japanese admiral knows of our invasion, but may be unaware that the airfields on Guam, Tinian, and Saipan are under attack by our aircraft."

Joe stopped, "Guys, the Japanese commander knows that we outnumber his carrier force by three to one. He won't risk getting his carriers in range of our carrier aircraft. Our staff believes he will launch his carrier aircraft, attack us, and then proceed to land his aircraft on the airfields here in the Marianas."

Joe turned his attention to the pilots of our fighter squadron. "You fighter pilots may just have a damn busy day if our staff is correct in its analysis. The sky may well be filled with Jap planes. That's it, guys. We'll just wait to see what develops. One thing we do know, the Japanese will attack."

That evening, in the ward room and the ready room, all the talk was about the Japanese attack. We were convinced that the Japanese would fight. The guys were one bunch of excited fighter pilots. Each pilot seemed to want the chance to dog fight against a Japanese fighter pilot. We torpedo pilots were relieved. The Japanese Fleet would not get within range of our torpedo planes.

On June 19, I flew a four-hour search flight northwest of the part of Task Force 58 that was still operating in the area of the Marianas. Admiral Mitchner, Task Force 58's commander, wanted information on the location of the Japanese force. My search, however, over 150 miles out from our task force, didn't yield a visual contact with the Japanese Fleet.

The next morning, I was launched on an antisub patrol. Upon my return to the task force, I was ordered by *Monterey* to orbit well clear of the carrier. The ship informed me that the task force was under attack by Japanese aircraft.

After a delay of about 30 minutes, I was cleared to land aboard. After landing, I went to the ready room and learned some of the details of the Japanese attack on our fleet. The attacks had started about 10 o'clock in the morning. It was now nearly two o'clock in the afternoon. So far, there were no reports of any damage to our ships, and there was information that our fighter pilots had successfully fought off the attacks by the Japanese. One of our fighter pilots, Lieutenant "Buck" Baily, had returned from his flight and was in the ready room. He had shot down six enemy planes that morning. He'd already seen his gun camera film confirming his kills. When he saw me, he grabbed me, and said, "Goddammit, Doc, I'm an ace!"

The ship's combat information center (CIC) was piping aircraft radio transmissions to the ready room, as we tried to follow the action of the air battle. Most of the action seemed to be around the Japanese airfields where their planes were trying to land.

Attack on the Japanese Fleet

The ward room sent sandwiches and coffee to the ready room. We were helping ourselves to the food when the skipper came into the room. I called, "Attention," as Rip said, "OK, guys. We've been assigned a mission. The Japanese Fleet has been located." He stopped, looking at a deadly quiet ready room. "The Japanese carrier group has been located about 300 miles to the northeast of our position. We will launch four TBMs armed with four 500-pound bombs. Our launch time will be 1630." Rip paused, looking at us. He knew we were mentally calculating the total flight time. We all realized that it would be dark when we returned. Rip confirmed our fears. "Guys, it will be dark when we return. I know none of us has ever landed aboard at night. The weather is predicted to be clear, and there is a moon. And, guys, there's always a first time for everything. We can do it." He looked at me. "Norm, you will remain aboard. As the XO, I want you here since I will be leading the flight. Now I want volunteers. I need three pilots to join me." Everyone raised their hand except me. I had been ordered to stay on the ship. I wasn't going.

The skipper, with three of our mates and their crews, launched at 1630, heading off to the northwest. They weren't alone. I could see each carrier in our task group was launching both torpedo planes and dive-bombers, all heading for the Japanese Fleet. We remaining pilots stood on the flight deck until the last planes disappeared over the horizon. I remained alone on the flight deck as the rest of the pilots went back to the ready room.

I wish I was on that flight. Bombing those carriers; doing the job I was trained for. Sure hope the guys make it back. The TBM has enough fuel to make the flight. I made those long flights out of Henderson Field.

Rip's a great leader. He'll get them home. God, Rip's got to make it back. I want to stay his XO. He's the skipper. I don't want it like it was with Art McHolland back at Barking Sands. I know they'll all make it.

It was about 2000 hours when the ship's CIC began feeding aircraft radio transmissions into the ready room. We could hear pilots reporting fuel shortages or requesting radar headings to their carriers. I went up on the flight deck, hoping to see our planes. Suddenly, I saw all the ships within my sight turn on their searchlights.

Hot damn! The admiral must have ordered the lights turned on. Now the guys will make it back—they'll see the search lights.

Within the next 30 minutes, three carriers in our task force began to take aircraft aboard. When I heard "Flight Quarters" sound over *Monterey*'s P.A. system, I headed for the signal bridge above the flight deck where I could observe the planes as they landed. I heard the sound of planes over our carrier. I could see their dark outline, the red navigation lights on the wings of three aircraft now on the downwind leg of their approach, getting ready to land aboard. I waited until three planes were aboard before I headed for the ready room.

Damn! Just three planes. Did we lose one?

Rip was already there. I grabbed him by the arms.

"Is everyone back, Rip? I only saw three land aboard. How was it?"

Rip grinned at me. "We got a carrier, Doc. I saw at least four hits. I know three of us got aboard. I think that Smiley, the number four guy, landed alongside a destroyer. I saw him and his crew get out of this plane. We all made it, Doc!"

What a relief! Everyone made it back! Smiley and his crew was picked up by a destroyer. God, Rip was lucky. Still wish it had been me. Admit it, I'm a little jealous. Bet all of them get decorated. Forget it. You're still here. Still alive ... just be glad the guys made it back.

A few days later, we learned that we lost over 200 planes on that mission. The pilots either ran out of fuel, got lost trying to return to the task force, or were lost during the attack on the Japanese Fleet. I flew a search mission the next day and spotted two life rafts with pilots and crewmen. I radioed the nearest destroyer that was also searching for downed pilots. The crews I spotted were picked up. Between searches with both aircraft and destroyers, we were able to recover almost 80 percent of the downed pilots and crewmen over the next three days. Sadly, the remaining pilots and crewmen were listed as missing in action. It was a high price to pay to damage the enemy.

We talked about the overall mission in the ready room. The decision of the admiral to launch so late in the day was a tremendous risk, although his decision to turn on the searchlights did save a great many pilots and crews. We all thought, though, that the greatest gain for the United States was taking out the best of the Japanese Navy pilots when they tried to attack our carriers. That day became known as the "Marianas' Turkey Shoot." The name was an invention of the news media back in the States. The Japanese had over 300 planes shot down by our fighters that day. We all believed that with those losses, the Japanese carrier forces would no longer be a threat to our Navy.

July 1944 Losses

July was a tough period for me, dealing with combat missions and the morale of the squadron. The difficulty started with a bombing strike on the small island of Pagan located between Guam and Tinian. Except for Rip's flight against the Japanese Fleet, it was our first bombing mission since we lost Joe back in June. It was a four-plane flight, all with regular pilots. The strike went very smoothly with just light AA fire. Then came the rest of July.

Even today, I dread looking at the July 1944 entries in my log book. The squadron was assigned a total of ten bombing missions during July. The majority were against the smaller islands in the Marianas, Pagan and Rota. Our briefings by the intelligence officer on the ship indicated that we would face little resistance from the Japanese on these islands. The information was inaccurate. Nearly every flight faced heavy AA fire. The result was that we lost two more pilots and four crew members, shot down by AA fire, in attacks against these two islands. One pilot and crew was lost on July 5 and the other on the 15th.

Following the loss of the second pilot, Rip and I met with the torpedo plane pilots. We both understood the concerns of our pilots. When there was a death of a pilot and his crew members, the experience readily transferred to every pilot, radio operator, and gunner in the squadron. Each man was conscious of the possibility—it could have been him. Although never expressed, the thought of who might be next was always present. The joking between pilots stopped. Conversations were limited, mostly to routine subjects, and pilots tended to spend time alone. The possibility of death became very real.

Rip closed the meeting announcing that, on July 25, *Monterey* would depart for Hawaii for some vital repair work on the ship's power plant.

Guys are pretty subdued, not much excitement. We still have more missions to fly. Hawaii is what we need. Away from our fears. Rest. Mail from home. Bet Donnie is getting big. Hope there are some pictures. I know I have another mission. God, help me do it. Help me get my guys back safe.

On July 22, I was scheduled for a bombing mission against the island of Guam. I asked for volunteers to fly the mission with me. I didn't feel I could order my friends to go on the flight. We were going to Hawaii soon. A rest from combat. Just one more mission to fly. Four of us flew the mission. I prayed that we would make it back. I had too.

R and R in Hawaii

Monterey, escorted by two destroyers, was detached from Task Group 58 on July 25 and departed for Hawaii. There were no flight operations during the period while the ship was en route to Pearl Harbor. When *Monterey* arrived at Pearl Harbor, she docked at Ford Island and all the squadron's enlisted personnel were bussed to the Royal Hawaiian Hotel. The hotel had been taken over by the Navy as an "R and R" (rest and recreation) hotel. The officers were taken to the home of a wealthy pineapple plantation owner, Mr. Cris Holmes. He offered his home to the Navy as R and R for small groups of officers. It was located on the beach just beyond the famous Waikaki.

All of us, our crewmen at the Royal Hawaiian and the officers at Cris Holmes', enjoyed fresh fruit, breakfasts cooked to order, huge buffet lunches and dinners, and all the fresh milk we could drink. There was no morning reveille for us. The officers and enlisted men could step right from their rooms to the warm sand of the beach and the sparkling blue water of the Pacific. The war was forgotten for a few days.

Our mail caught up with us, and I had a chance to read all the news from Jean. She was under the care of a doctor at the naval hospital in Bremerton. She told me we were expecting our second child in October. One line in that letter remains with me still today. "Darling, Donnie and I hope you will be with us when our baby arrives. We pray for your safety."

I know she means when the cruise will be over. I will be home. I'm glad for her prayers. It's not over yet. We go back aboard on August 31. Back again. Damn, I wish it would end. We all want to go home. Write her back. Tell her you love her. That's about all I can say. Keep your fear and don't tell her.

The squadron began flight operations on August 14, 1944, flying from N.A.S. Kaneohe located on the east coast of Oahu. We had gone by bus from the ship to Kaneohe and were flying TBMs assigned to the antisub school. We were back learning new tactics to combat the Japanese submarines. There were new weapons too: rockets that would be carried under the wings of our TBMs. Each TBM would carry six rockets. The rockets would be propelled just like the rockets we played with on the Fourth of July when we were kids. The idea was to fire the rockets at the sub while it was on the surface. Again, as with the listening devices, first, we had to find the submarine.

Honored before Departure

On August 28, we boarded *Monterey* at Ford Island in Pearl Harbor. Nine new TBMs were hoisted aboard using the carrier's crane. At 10 o'clock in the morning, the ship's company and the air group were in formation on the flight deck. Our skipper, Lieutenant Ronald (Rip) Gift, three other squadron pilots, and eight crewmen were recognized for "outstanding performance of duty on June 20, 1944 during an attack on a Japanese strike force."

The three pilots and our skipper, Rip Gift, were awarded the Navy Cross and each of the eight crewmen were awarded the Distinguished Flying Cross. The awards were presented by an admiral attached to the headquarters of the Pacific Fleet in Hawaii. It was a very proud day for Torpedo Squadron 28.

Chapter 9

Attacks on the Philippines

We departed Hawaii on 30 August 1944, and the next day Rip scheduled a briefing meeting for all pilots and crewmen with our AIO, Joe Anson.

"Well, guys we're at it again. Now that the Marianas are secure, a major decision has been made in our war against the Japanese. The planners in Washington have agreed with General MacArthur that our next objective will be the Philippines. Once we invade and defeat the Japanese in the Philippines, our force will move against the island of Okinawa. Guys, this island is part of the Japanese homeland." He paused, looking at us. "I'm sure you can all guess where our strategy is leading—ultimately, the invasion of Japan." Joe waited as we absorbed this information. "We're going to see a lot of new targets, guys, but we have the advantage. The Japanese carriers are no longer a threat to our carrier task forces. They lost too many carrier pilots in the Marianas. Any questions?"

"Joe, what about the Jap land-base defenses, the AA guns and the land-based aircraft? Won't that be a problem for us?"

"Yeah, you're right, but plans call for fighters to escort the TBMs on assigned attack missions. The admiral's planning staff hasn't been able to give you guys much fighter support because of the threat of enemy attacks on our carriers. Now our fighters will go after the land-based Japanese planes and AA positions while you TBM drivers carry out the bombing attacks."

Rip took over. "OK, Joe. Thanks. Fellas, our first bombing attacks will be on September 3rd against Wake Island. You remember the fight the Marines had against the Japanese invasion of Wake Island back in December of 1943. The Japs took the island, but they've been helpless ever since. The only supplies they've received have been by submarine and those visits have been few and far between. Our targets will be the heavy gun emplacements that can threaten the three cruiser class ships that will be bombarding the facilities on Wake Island with their big guns. That's it, guys."

I was scheduled to fly two missions against targets on Wake Island. The briefing for the mission was typical of many of the Torpedo Squadron 28 missions.

The following description comes from unpublished material researched and written by Lieutenant (jg.) Harry Bridgmen, the squadron's personnel officer:

A History of Torpedo Squadron 28 from 4 May 1942–January 1945

No typical or normal strike existed, but the following is roughly representative of what occurred when strikes were being conducted. Previous to the first day of operations, the air intelligence officer (AIO) gave lectures on the area; summarized the operation plan; discussed survival intelligence; analyzed targets; and gave refreshed recognition on the types of planes thought to be in the area. Briefings on assigned targets and tactics to be employed were conducted the evening before the strike by the AIO, commanding officer and strike leaders. Any late information of interest was disseminated at this time.

On the strike day, the squadron duty officer—usually a pilot not assigned to the strike—was awakened early and he turned out all pilots involved, the AIO, the gunnery officer and the air crewmen. Early breakfast was provided and on some days, it included steak. Following breakfast, the pilots reported to the ready room in flight gear and checked their plotting boards getting any late information from the AIO. Radiomen were also provided with all possible information and especially with that relating to codes, frequencies, channels, identification signals etc. Meanwhile, the squadron gunnery officer inspected every plane's bomb loading and fusing and assisted the ship's ordnance officer in any final checks. Although the ship's ordnance officers supervised most of the planes arming, the torpedo pilots felt more secure in the knowledge that their own gunnery officer had checked and approved each plane.

On gathering all necessary flight and strike data, the pilots donned life jackets, back packs etc. and stood by for the order from Air Plot, "Pilots and crews, man your planes." At this, pilots and crews groped their way into the pre-dawn darkness and along the flight deck to their planes.

Succeeding strike flights were rebriefed in advance of take-off time and followed the same procedure, taking off before the first flight landed. Upon landing, the first and following divisions of pilots and crews were interrogated individually by the AIO, who gave preliminary summaries to the ship's AIO for transmission to the admiral's staff. Following this, he began the preparation of his action report.

I can vouch for the pilots that we felt secure after these briefings that we had all available information to survive each mission.

Between September 4 and 16, I flew five antisub searches. We had rejoined the carrier task group, only this time it was designated Task Force 38 rather than Task Force 58. Admiral William McCain relieved Admiral Mark Michner who'd commanded Task Force 58 during the Marianas Invasion. The size of the carrier force remained the same: four carrier groups composed of four carriers each. The only change was that the new admiral and his staff commanded the task force.

On September 18, squadron pilots received their first briefing by *Monterey's* AIO on the plans of Admiral "Bull" Halsey's staff for the first strikes on the Philippines, which were scheduled to commence on September 24. A great many details were presented about enemy strengths during the briefing, such as AA defenses and the types of Japanese aircraft we might encounter during the attack. I can only remember the targets we were assigned. I would lead a four-plane division of TBMs armed with torpedoes. Our targets were Japanese merchant ships in the harbor at Manila.

First Torpedo Strike

Our four-plane division was launched from the carrier early on 24 September, 1944. I inspected the deadly looking torpedo nestled in the bomb bay of my plane before getting in. I wanted to check the arming cables.

A goddamn stupid mission! Torpedo Eight again. Jesus, that damn torpedo better work. Risk my life. What if the bastard doesn't explode? Risk for what?

The weather was clear, with only a few scattered clouds. There were white caps on the ocean as a brisk wind was blowing, so there was plenty of wind over the deck for our launch. The other three planes quickly joined on me, and we made an orbit around the carrier as we waited for our four-plane fighter escort. As the fighters took position above our flight, I began a slow climb on a compass heading that would take us to the target area, Manila Harbor.

Map of the Philippines

I pulled my navigation board from under the cockpit instrument panel to check my compass headings and time to the target. Task Force 38 was operating on the Pacific side of Luzon Island, the main island in the northern Philippines. To reach our target, the ships in Manila Harbor, we had to fly across the island of Luzon until we could identify the harbor at Manila. At that point, I would lead my flight past the harbor until we could reverse course and enter into the open end of the harbor. This was the only way we could launch our torpedoes at the ships anchored there. We had to be at an altitude of 150 feet and air speed of 120 knots for the torpedo launch. The enemy ships were anchored close to the city of Manila at the closed end of the harbor. The recovery for our planes after the torpedo drop would have to be over the city of Manila.

Jesus, my time is right on. I'm past the harbor entrance. What's my altitude? Eleven thousand feet. Call the fighters. I want them to go in just ahead. God, hope they hit the AA positions. I'm going to be low and slow ... 150 feet ... 120 knots ... just like the damn mine-laying back at the Canal. That was night; this is daylight. Every damn AA gunner can see me. Got to drop the damn torpedo ... stupid planning by the staff.

"Fighter leader, this is Able One. Reversing course now. Will enter the harbor at 1,000 feet altitude. Starting descent now."

As I reversed course, I pulled back my throttle and began a diving descent at 220 knots, lowering my landing gear to help control the speed. My other three planes spread out abreast in a line. I could see the fighters still above us. I knew that as we entered the harbor, they would go past us strafing the AA positions along the shore with their six .50-caliber machine guns.

I'm in the harbor. Get the speed down to 120 knots, altitude 150 feet. OK, get the bomb bay doors open. Get the damn speed down! Cut the throttle; where's my target? That looks like a tanker. I'll get the bastard. Landing gear up. How far is the tanker? Don't drop too soon. Tracers coming at me. Those damn colored balls.

"Gunner, open up on that gun firing at us!"

Now! Drop the damn torpedo! I'm about 1,000 yards out. Goddamn! Great! Our fighters are coming back again. Open up the throttle. Bomb doors closed. Stay low over the city. Jinx around those buildings. Get out of here!

"Able leader here. Able flight join on me after we clear the city. Report."

Each pilot called in. All reported hits with our torpedoes, as did my gunner. Our fighters joined us, escorting the flight back to the carrier.

Thank God. Our fighters really did a job. We made it. So helpless, so slow and low. How could those guys of Torpedo Eight have done it? Suicide. Can't fight back; can't change altitude; got to be low and slow or torpedo will break up when it hits the water.

The fighters landed first on the carrier. We were right behind them. The debriefing after the flight credited us with three merchant ships sunk and one damaged. We relaxed in the comfort of our ready room. Our flying was over for that day. I silently thanked God that we'd made it. Memory of the courage and dedication of those pilots in Torpedo Eight has always challenged me. Now, after flying a torpedo attack mission, I understood even more, the bravery of those pilots at the Battle of Midway in June 1942.

For the remainder of September and through October, Task Group 38 moved freely through the western Pacific. Our targets were Japanese airfields located on the islands of Negros and Okinawa. The goal was to prevent the Japanese from re-enforcing their Philippine-based air force that was defending against our invasion.

Kamikazes

It was during this period, the Japanese introduced a new element in the battle with our invasion force. They began sending land-based twin-engine aircraft to locate our carriers. Once our forces were located, they became targets of a totally a new weapon, kamikaze pilots. The Japanese no longer had enough trained pilots to attack our carrier force with bombs or torpedoes. We were suddenly faced with unskilled Japanese pilots willing to die for the Japanese emperor. Once our forces were located, these pilots were launched from bases in southern Japan or Okinawa to dive on a ship and die in the crash. Many were shot down by our ships' AA fire and by our fighters, but some always got through.

To combat the threat of the kamikazes, the admiral's staff began adding extra aircraft searches. In addition to the antisub searches, we began flying what were called "antisnooper" searches. The idea was to intercept the land-based Japanese bombers that were searching for our forces and prevent them from finding our ships.

A Deadly Encounter

On 10 October 1944, I was flying an antisnooper mission about 30 miles from the task force at an altitude of about 1,200 feet. There were some scattered showers in the area. Then I saw it—a twin-engine Japanese plane. I could see the red ball of the Japanese insignia on the fuselage. It was below me and crossing in front of my plane.

"Able Base. This is Able One. Sighted one 'Betty' west of the task force. I'm attacking!"

Jesus! A Jap bomber. Arm the wing guns. Now!

"Turret gunner! Jap bomber 11 o'clock, low. Prepare for an attack."

There, he's crossing below me. Dive now. Full throttle ... get on his tail. Gun switch on. What's that? He's firing at me. Tail gun ... see the flashes. Slide outside. Get away from that tail gun. Get alongside him and use the gun turret.

"Turret gunner! Take him under fire! Aim for the wing where it joins the fuselage!"

Good God! I can see the co-pilot looking at us. Oh, shit! He's beginning to burn; his wing's on fire. Oh, Jesus, there goes his wing. Oh, Jesus.

As I watched, the plane rolled over, then exploded as it struck the water. I circled the point where it crashed. The only thing I could see was some burning debris on the surface of the ocean. I heard my radio.

"Able One, this is Able Base. Status of enemy contact? Over."

"Able Base, this is Able One. Splash one 'Betty.' No survivors at the site. Continuing the search mission. Out."

Damn, we got a Jap plane. The fighter guys will be pissed. A torpecker getting a kill. Wish I hadn't seen ... wonder ... was he the co-pilot? He was looking right at me. I had to do it. If they had found the task force, kamikaze pilots would attack. I had to kill him ... no. No! I had to shoot down the plane. It wasn't the man; it was the plane ... the enemy's plane. Goddamn this war, I killed a man.

Following that October 10th flight, I flew seven more antisnooper flights. As I was launched on each flight, I hoped I would not make contact with another enemy plane. The image of that pilot looking at me as my gunner shot him down disturbed me. The memory of that face staring at me was locked in my mind forever. The attack I made on the Japanese plane had become personal. I wanted go forget it. I took myself off the flight schedule on October 26. I did not fly another antisnooper flight. I think Rip understood. The war had become very personal to me.

Bombing Manila Harbor

By 5 November, I was back flying again, an antisub search. On the 13th, I led a six-plane bombing flight against a merchant ship in Manila Harbor. I was the first plane off the carrier, and the other five planes quickly joined on me as we headed for the target area. I remember how relieved I was that this was a bombing mission. I did not have to worry about launching torpedoes. I was concerned, though, that we had no fighter escort. The pre-flight briefing indicated that AA fire in the area of Manila Harbor had been reported as very light. As we crossed the island of Luzon and Manila Harbor came into view, I hoped the briefing was accurate.

We were now at about 9,000 feet. At the briefing, we agreed to make the bombing attack so our recovery would be over the city of Manila. We knew that most of the Jap AA positions were around the edges of the harbor, not in the city. This was different than the torpedo attack. I didn't have to come into the harbor low and slow. I led the formation out over the harbor until the ships were to our left. "Able Flight, Able One. Prepare to attack!" The flight moved to form an echelon to the right as I opened my bomb bay doors, lowered my landing gear, closed my throttle, and made a diving turn to the left.

OK, there are at least six ships. We'll get them all. Go after the big one ... a little left rudder ... slide to the left. AA fire. Steady ... it's close! Goddammit, we're catching shit! I'm taking hits! I feel it in the tail. Those red and yellow balls again. Stay on the target. Now! Drop the damn bombs! Get out of here!

I headed out over the city clear of the AA fire.

"Able Flight, join on me. Report." I received four "Rogers." Then my number five pilot came on the radio. "Doc, this is Benny. Saw number six get hit. He went straight in. No chance of surviving. Out."

Oh God! That was Billy ... a replacement pilot. What's wrong? Rip and I have tried ... joined in Hawaii, but they had to fly on combat missions ... only fair. A new kid. The second pilot I've lost. Please let this thing be over. Let us go home. Please, God, it's too much.

Time Off at Ulithi Island

Task Group 38.2, with *Monterey* and three other carriers, departed the combat area on 21 November for the harbor at Ulithi Island. This small island was located between the Marianas and the Philippines and had been developed as a harbor and supply base for carrier Task Group 38. Surrounding the island was a coral reef that formed a lagoon. Within a week, the entire Task Force 38, 18 carriers with their support ships, battleships, cruisers, and destroyers, were all at anchor in the lagoon. Also present was a hospital ship, as well as tanker ships

Carriers at anchor in the lagoon at Ulithi, 2 December 1944   *(Courtesy of The Tailhook Association and* The Hook*)*

with aircraft fuel and oil for the ships, supply ships with food and supplies, ships designed to carry ammunition and, most important a CVE, which was a light carrier assigned to deliver replacement aircraft to the carriers. It was an overwhelming force.

Our mail caught up with us at Ulithi. It was then I learned our second child, Normajean Berg, had been born a month earlier, October 13, at the naval hospital in Bremerton, Washington. Jean's letters were exciting as she told me of moving into an apartment, located near the waters of Puget Sound just outside Bremerton. She closed every letter with "Darling, we can't wait for you to get home. I love you, so much."

Standing on the flight deck of our carrier with those letters, looking across the lagoon, seeing this tremendous display of naval power, I reflected that none of this had prevented the deaths of four of our pilots and their crews. Standing there with Jean's letters, I suddenly felt emotionally drained, that I had no control over my life. I knew I could not prevent my death if it was to be.

I placed Jean's letters in my pocket and looked again at the ships in the harbor. It was obvious that the fleet was preparing for more action. All one had to do was watch the barges moving from ship to ship with supplies, tanker ships refueling destroyers, and replacement aircraft coming aboard the carriers, including *Monterey*. We knew, without a briefing, that the next objective was going to be the Japanese island of Okinawa. The plan to ultimately invade Japan was still the goal of the staff planners.

On 5 December 1944, *Monterey* departed Ulithi assigned to carrier Task Group 38.2. On the 11th, I led a practice tactics flight with our fighter squadron.

Typhoon!

By the 15th, Task Force 38.2 had ceased flight operations. The weather deteriorated to overcast skies, rain squalls, and winds in excess of 35 knots. The ship was moving through waves over twelve feet high. The ship was rolling too, so breakfast was difficult—plates would slide across the table unless they were held in place. The talk that morning in the ward room was that a possible typhoon was moving towards our position. Two days later, a dangerous typhoon overtook the task force.

I was on the hangar deck at about eight-thirty that morning checking on our aircraft. We had both fighters and TBMs parked there undergoing routine maintenance work. I remember standing by an open area on the side of the hangar deck watching huge waves roll past our ship. They were over 20 feet high and as they rolled by, their white tops were being blown off as spray. Our ship was rolling heavily as she struggled to move through the high waves.

The possibility of danger suddenly crossed my mind. Could *Monterey* survive this vicious storm? I'd never experienced a storm at sea, feeling the carrier pitching and rolling against the wind and waves. My only experience with the ship was launching and then returning to the carrier for a landing. I knew very little about how the ship operated. As I continued to watch the huge waves roll past me, I realized that I was probably perfectly safe aboard *Monterey*. I knew Captain Ingersall, and I trusted him. He had over 25 years of experience at sea, serving in many positions as a ship's officer before assuming command of *Monterey*. I knew, too, that the ship's crew was well-trained. I'd observed the many drills aboard the ship, as the crew practiced the various procedures, such as testing all valves that control the water sprinkling system on the hangar deck and the tests would insure the systems functioning in case of fire. I knew that if an emergency occurred due to the storm, the ship's crew would know what to do. It was a comfortable feeling knowing that I was safe on *Monterey*.

I left the hangar deck, thinking I'd better check the planes on the flight deck. By the time I arrived on the flight deck, I saw some of our pilots and crewmen checking the metal cables used to tie down the planes. When they finished, we all gathered in the shelter of the ship's bridge. With the roar of wind and the blowing spray hitting our faces, it was difficult to talk.

Suddenly, I saw a steel tie-down cable snap free of one of the fighters. "There goes a cable! The tie downs won't hold them!" I yelled over the sound of the storm. We stood there helpless, as we saw a TBM break loose from the tie downs and disappear over the side of the flight deck. Then one by one, as we watched, all remaining planes slipped over the side of the flight deck and disappeared into the ocean. By now I estimated the wind at over 70 miles per hour. Holding each other's hands against the force of the wind, we carefully made our way off the flight deck to the ready room. Then we heard on the ship's P.A. system the harsh sound of the emergency bells and the announcement: "General quarters! General quarters! Damage control teams report! Fire on the hangar deck."

The order, "general quarters," was one drill everyone on the ship, including the pilots, was required to respond to. It was an order immediately requiring mobilization of the ship's personnel to protect the ship in an emergency due to enemy attack or, in this case, a raging typhoon in the South Pacific. Every individual on the ship was assigned a function and a location aboard the ship. For the pilots, we were assigned to our ready room. We had no assigned function, except to stay out of the way of the ship's crew and officers.

If there was an immediate danger to the safety of the ship, such an emergency would be dealt with by the ship's damage control teams. These were selected ship's officers, and men trained to contain damage to the ship caused by explosions, fires or flooding due to enemy action, or in our case, the typhoon. When we heard, "Fire on the hangar deck," we all knew that he had a serious emergency, but we also knew that the ship's damage control team was trained to deal with it.

The intercom squawked, "Ready room! Hangar deck fire is threatening ammunition storage on port side. Request personnel to remove the ammunition and jettison it over the side of the ship. Acknowledge." One of the pilots responded as a group of us headed for the catwalk outside the ready room just below the flight deck. Two enlisted men from the ship's company were already at the ammunition locker and had it open. We quickly formed a line and began passing the 40-millimeter shells over the side of the ship. The waves seemed almost ready to break over the ship as we braced ourselves against the wind and got those shells into the ocean.

A messenger met me as I returned to the ready room.

"Mr. Berg, the ship's executive officer, Commander Allen, requests that you assist in the evacuation of personnel from below decks to the flight deck. Please follow me to your station."

The young man led me to a passageway in the forward part of the ship. It was just below the flight deck with an exit to the flight deck. He stationed me at a point in the passageway where there was a sharp turn before leading to the flight deck. We were both aware of the smoke in the passageway from the hangar deck fire.

"Sir, the men will come up from below decks to this passageway, move past you and onto the flight deck. I will report your compliance to Commander Allen's request."

I remember standing there waiting. Then, through the smoke, came the first of the sailors moving through the passageway to the fresh air of the flight deck. Some had wet clothes over their mouths and noses. Then the line stopped. The smoke seemed to get thicker and warmer. I could hear a murmur of voices. Suddenly, a young sailor standing in front of me began yelling, "Get me out! I'm choking!" He began pushing the man ahead of him. I reached out and put my hand on his shoulder.

"Son. Take it easy." He turned, looking at me. "You know me, son. You pulled the chocks on my plane." He stuttered, "Yes Sir, you're Mr. Berg—a pilot." He paused, "Sir, are we going to be all right?"

I patted his shoulder, "Sure, son, the ship's captain knows what he's doing. We'll be OK."

As the line began to move again, he quieted down. Within ten minutes, the evacuation was complete. By mid-afternoon, the fire was out and the ship was underway, still fighting the remainder of the typhoon. The wind had diminished in force, but the ship was still rolling as she plowed through the steep waves.

Monterey lost eight men that day with over thirty others injured fighting the fire. The injured were being cared for in the ship's sick bay. A memorial service was held for those men who died in the fire. The eight men who died were buried at sea. The ship's company and the squadron were all in formation on the flight deck as an honor guard of their shipmates consigned their remains to the sea. It was a very moving ceremony.

We rejoined the task force the next day and received orders to proceed to Ulithi. As we departed for Ulithi, Captain Ingersall, the commanding officer of *Monterey*, announced over the P.A. system that we had received a "well done" from the task force admiral for saving our ship. The admiral also expressed his personal condolences on the loss of our shipmates.

Two days after our arrival at Ulithi, a team of inspectors boarded our ship to assess the damage done by the fire. Rumors were flying that they were going to recommend that the ship return to the States for repair. There was a feeling of tenseness, of anticipation throughout the ship. Everywhere, groups of men were talking—hoping. We were just as anxious.

Then on Thanksgiving Day, November 24, 1944, just before dinner was to be served throughout the ship, the ship's P.A. system came on. "Attention." Then, "This is the captain speaking. You have all been aware that an inspection team has evaluated the damage done to your ship during the typhoon. The inspection has been completed. The recommendation, as a result of the inspection, is that on December 1, *Monterey* will depart Ulithi and proceed to the naval shipyard in Bremerton, Washington, for repairs. Happy Thanksgiving from your captain!"

There was an explosion of sound—cheers, yells of joy throughout the ship, and from some of us, silent prayers. I was going back to Bremerton—to Jean and my children. I was going home.

Back home in Bremerton, WA. The author, Jean, Donnie, and baby Normajean, late January 1945

Aircraft Specifications

To help you better understand the code letters of all the aircraft mentioned throughout *My Carrier War*, this appendix features a brief description of each. In general, the aircraft code letters can be read as follows:

- The first letter represents the type of mission the airplanes were built for.
- The second number or letter represents the model or particular use.
- The third number or letter represents the company that built the aircraft.

The specific codes vary in the amount of letters and numbers from aircraft type to aircraft type. These codes were important in communicating aircraft types, especially during battles and training, and as pilots, we had to memorize the codes and the manufacturers. To help us recognize aircraft and learn their codes, we had regular sessions on aircraft recognition. In these sessions, we used small aircraft models of Navy, Army, and Japanese planes. Upon sight, we had to be able to recognize the type of aircraft (fighter, bomber); its capability (how fast it could go and how high could it fly); and what kind of armament it had when we saw it attacking us. The aircraft manufacturer was really incidental, but usually, we knew what aircraft company built which aircraft.

BT-1   B is for bomber; T is for training; and 1 is for first version. Built by Northrop Aircraft Corp. in the early 1930s, the BT-1 was carrier-based.

F2A   F is for fighter; 2 is for second version; and A is for Brewster Aircraft Corp., who built the fighter in the early 1930s. This fighter plane was carrier-based.

F4F   (a.k.a. "Wildcat") F is for fighter; 4 is for fourth version; and F is for Grumman Aircraft Corp., who built the plane in the early 1940s. The

Wildcat was carrier-based and used in WWII until replaced by the F6F (a.k.a. "Hellcat") in 1943–44.

N2S   N is the code for trainer; 2 is for second version; and S is for Stearman Aircraft Corp., who built the plane in the late 1930s (a.k.a. "Yellow Peril").

OS-2U   O is for observation; S is for scouting; 2 is for second model; and U is for the U.S. Navy, who built the planes in the late 1930s. These planes were based on battleships and cruisers. They could land on the open sea and be recovered by the mother ship.

PBY   P is for patrol; B is for bomber; and Y is for Consolidated Aircraft Corp., who built the planes in the early 1930s. These amphibious planes could land on the open sea as well as on airfields.

SBC-4   S is for scouting; B is for bombing; C is for Curtis Aircraft Corp.; and 4 is for fourth version. These carrier-based planes (a.k.a. "Helldivers") were built in the late 1930s and designed for dive-bombing.

SBD   S is for scouting; B is for bombing; and D is for Douglas Aircraft Corp., which built the plane in the late 1930s. These planes were carrier-based and designed for dive-bombing. They were used in the Pacific Fleet until 1945.

SNC   S is for scouting; N is for training; and C is for Curtis Aircraft Corp., who built the SNCs in the late 1930s.

SNJ   S is for scouting; N is for training; and J is for North American Aircraft Corp., who built these planes in the late 1930s.

SNV   S is for scouting; N is for training; and V is for Vultee Aircraft Corp., who built the planes in the late 1930s.

TBD   T is for torpedo; B is for bomber; and D is for Douglas Aircraft Corp., who built the planes in the early 1930s. These carrier-based TBDs were used in the Battle of Midway in 1942.

TBF   T is for torpedo; B is for bomber; and F is for Grumman Aircraft Corp., who built the planes in the early 1940s. These aircraft (a.k.a. "Avenger") were carrier-based and used in the Pacific Fleet from late 1942 to the end of the war.

TBM   T is for torpedo; B is for bomber; and M is for General Motors that built the planes. The TBM was basically the same aircraft as the TBF, but with some improvements. The TBMs replaced the TBFs in 1943.

Index

Printed in the United States
1777